Three Years in the Federal Cavalry

With all Original Illustrations

By Willard W. Glazier

Published by Pantianos Classics

ISBN-13: 978-1540499585

First published in 1870

Contents

TO
THE GALLANT AND UNASSUMING SOLDIER,

MAJOR-GENERAL HENRY E. DAVIES, JR.

WHOSE STAR ALWAYS SHONE BRIGHTEST ON
THE FRONT LINE OF BATTLE,
THIS VOLUME IS RESPECTFULLY
dedicated
BY
THE AUTHOR.

Preface

I have for a long time intended the publication of this book, for I thought that such a work would not only be found interesting to the public, but would do justice to the brave men with whom it was my fortune to be associated during the dark hours of the rebellion. To serve them is and ever will be my greatest pleasure.

The remarkable features and events of our late Cavalry movements in Virginia and elsewhere, visible to me during the campaigns of the Army of the Potomac, were noted daily in my journal. From that diary this story of our raids, expeditions, and fights is compiled.

My descriptions of battles and skirmishes, in some cases, may seem too brief and unsatisfactory; to which I can only say that scores of engagements, which to the participants appear to be of vast importance, have very little general interest. On the other hand, however, it is to be regretted that where our gallant horsemen have done the most brilliant things, it has been impossible for me, in many instances, to secure reliable and detailed accounts with which to do them full justice.

Willard Glazier.

New York, October 8th, 1870.

Our Cavalry Leaders

Three Years in the Federal Cavalry

Chapter I - The War for the Union - Contest Begun

1861.—Enthusiasm of the North.—Washington Threatened.—Bull Run, and Its Lessons.—General Scott and the Cavalry.—Enlistment under Captain Buel.—Harris Light Cavalry.—Leaving Troy, New York.— Captain A. N. Duffié.—Drilling and Fencing at Scarsdale, New York.—Bound for the Seat of War.—Philadelphia.— Baltimore.—Washington.—Camp Oregon.

The eleventh of April, 1861, revealed the real intention of the Southern people in their dastardly assault upon Fort Sumter. The thunder of Rebel cannon shook the air not only around Charleston, but sent its thrilling vibrations to the remotest sections of the country, and was the precursor of a storm whose wrath no one anticipated. This shock of arms was like a fire-alarm in our great cities, and the North arose in its might with a grand unanimity which the South did not expect. The spirit and principle of Rebellion were so uncaused and unprovoked, that scarcely could any one be found at home or abroad to justify them.

President Lincoln thereupon issued a call for seventy-five thousand men to uphold and vindicate the authority of the Government, and to prove, if possible, that secession was not only a heresy in doctrine, but an impracticability in the American Republic. The response to this call was much more general than the most sanguine had any reason to look for. The enthusiasm of the people was quite unbounded. Individuals encouraged individuals; families aroused families; communities vied with communities, and States strove with States. Who could be the first and do the most, was the noble contention which everywhere prevailed. All political party lines seemed to be obliterated. Under this renovating and inspiring spirit the work of raising the nucleus of the grandest army that ever swept a continent went bravely on. Regiments were rapidly organized and as rapidly as possible sent forward to the seat of Government; and so vast was the number that presented themselves for their country's defence, that the original call was soon more than filled, and the authorities found themselves unable to accept many organizations which were eager to press into the fray.

Meanwhile the great leaders of the Rebellion were marshalling the hordes of treason, and assembling them on the plains of Manassas, with the undoubted intention of moving upon the national capital. This point determined the principal theatre of the opening contest, and around it on every side, and particularly southward, was to be the aceldama of America,—the dreadful "field of blood."

The first great impulse of the authorities was in the direction of self-defence (and what could be more natural and proper?), and Washington was fortified and garrisoned. This done, it was believed that the accumulating forces of the Union, which had become thoroughly equipped and somewhat disciplined, ought to advance into the revolted territory, scatter the defiant hosts of the enemy, and put a speedy end to the slaveholders' Rebellion. But the hesitation and indecision which prevailed in our military circles were becoming oppressive and unendurable, and hence the cry of "On to Richmond!" was heard from the Border States to the St. Lawrence, precipitating the first general engagement of the war. Our defeat at Bull Run was a totally unexpected disaster, which, for a time, it was feared, would chill the enthusiasm and greatly weaken the energy of the North. But though the South was much strengthened and emboldened by their victory, our defeat had its own curative elements: it taught us that the enemy was determined and powerful, and that to overcome him the ranks of the Union army must be filled with something besides three months' men, or men on any very limited term of enlistment. Other lessons were also gained: our men had formed some acquaintance with the citizens and the country; they had learned the importance of a more thorough discipline and organization; and those who had gone forth as to a picnic or a holiday, sat down "to count the cost" of "enduring hardness as good soldiers." The nation discovered that this struggle for life was desperate and even dubious, and it was thoroughly aroused.

Under the military régime of General Winfield Scott, the cavalry-arm of the service had been almost entirely overlooked. His previous campaigns in Mexico, which consisted mainly of the investments of walled cities, and of assaults on fortresses, had not been favorable to extensive cavalry operations, and he was not disposed at so advanced an age in life materially to change his tactics of war. What few regiments of cavalry we had in the regular army were mostly broken up into small detachments for the purpose of ranging our Western frontiers, while a few squads were patrolling between the outposts of our new army, carrying messages from camp to camp, and pompously escorting the commanding generals in their grand reviews and parades.

But the Black Horse Cavalry of Virginia, at Bull Run, unmatched by any similar force on our side, had demonstrated the efficiency and importance of this branch of the service, and our authorities began to change their views. The sentiment of the people at large seemed to turn in the same channel, and a peculiar enthusiasm in this direction was perceptible everywhere. It was as though the spirit of the old knight-errantry had suddenly fallen upon us.

I was in Troy, New York, when the sad intelligence of the reverse to our arms at Bull Run, was received. This was followed quickly by another call for volunteers, and I decided without hesitation to enter the army. In accordance with my resolve I enlisted as a private soldier at Troy, on the sixth day of August, 1861, in a company raised by Captain Clarence Buel, for the cavalry service. To encounter the chivalrous Black Horse Cavalry, of Bull Run fame, it was proposed to raise a force in the North, and as Senator Ira Harris, of New York, was giving this organization his patronage and influence, a brigade was formed, whose banners should bear his name.

Originally the regiment to which my company was assigned was intended for the regular army, and was for some time known as the Seventh United States Cavalry; but the Government having decided to have but six regiments of regular cavalry, and as New York had contributed the majority of the men to the organization, we were denominated the Second Regiment of New York Cavalry, "Harris Light." This regiment was organized by J. Mansfield Davies, of New York, as colonel, assisted by Judson Kilpatrick, of New Jersey, as lieutenant-colonel. The men were mostly from the States of New York, New Jersey, Connecticut, Vermont, Pennsylvania, and Indiana.

August 13.—To-day Captain Buel's company of Trojans was summoned together for the purpose of leaving for the South. Under a severe, drenching rain we were drawn up in line fronting the residence of General John E. Wool, when the old veteran delivered a most heroic address, which led us quite to forget the pelting rain, and prepared us for our departure. The boys then found a very pleasant shelter on board the Vanderbilt, bound for New York City. The day following all the New York State men rendezvoused at 648 Broadway, and were mustered into the service of the United States by Lieutenant-colonel D. B. Sackett, of the regular army. At four o'clock P. M. we were ordered aboard a train of cars, and told that our destination was Camp Howe, near Scarsdale, twenty-four miles north of the city, between the Harlem and East rivers. We reached the place just in time to pitch our tents for the night—an operation which was not only new and strange, but performed in any thing but a workman-like manner. We had every thing to learn, and this was our first lesson in soldiering.

Captain A. N. Duffié, of Co. A, a Frenchman and graduate of the military school of St. Cyr, France, is in command of the camp, and is to be the superintendent of our discipline and drill. He is undoubtedly well qualified for this position.

August 16.—This morning we commenced the inevitable drill on foot, as we are still without horses. We find this exercise very severe, and yet, in view of its great importance, we accept it with a good degree of relish. Our drill-master is thorough and rigidly strict, after the fashion of the French schools. We cannot avoid learning under his tuition. In the afternoon we were set to policing camp. This comprises the cleaning of one of the roughest farms in the country of stone. And as a remuneration to the owners for the use of this most unsightly of God's forsaken ground, we are compelled to build stone fences—a very unpleasant introduction to military life, and an occupation which by no means accords with our ideas of a soldier's duties. But our hands toil with a protest in our hearts, and with a certain resolve that this kind of fencing must not long continue.

After a week spent in drill and the stone-wall enterprise, we were all surprised one morning with an order to fall into line to receive a Napoleonic harangue from Captain Duffié. So many and even loud had been our protests, and so glaringly manifest our rebellious spirit on the subject of fortifying a farm in the State of New York, that the captain undoubtedly feared that he might not be very zealously supported by us in his future movements, and so, like Napoleon, on assuming command of the army of Italy, he sought to test the devotion of his men. After amusing us awhile in his broken English, and arousing us by his touching appeals to our patriotism and honor, at length he shouted, "Now as many of you as are ready to follow me to the cannon's month, take one step to the front." This dernier resort to pride was perfectly successful, and the whole line took the desired step. We were then ordered to be ready to leave camp at eleven o'clock that morning, which was on the twentieth of August, assured that Washington, D. C., was our destination.

Our ranks were quickly broken, and all due preparation made for our departure. After marching to Scarsdale we took cars and were soon landed in the metropolis, through the principal streets of which our command passed to the Jersey City ferry. Without much delay we reached Philadelphia in the evening, where we were bountifully supplied with rations by her proverbially generous and patriotic people. True to the instinct of "Brotherly Love," the citizens are making arrangements such as would indicate that millions of Union soldiers might be fed at their tables. Here we spent the night. The next morning at 6.30 we were on our way southward. A brief halt was made in Baltimore, whose streets still seem to be speaking of the blood of the brave Massachusetts men. And as we march along, we can but recall the poet's prophesy:

"And the Eagle, never dying, still is trying, still is trying,
With its wings upon the map to hide a city with its gore;
But the name is there forever, and it shall be hidden never,
While the awful brand of murder points the Avenger to its shore;
While the blood of peaceful brothers God's dread vengeance doth implore,

Thou art doomed, O Baltimore!"

At 4 o'clock P. M. we beheld the dome of the nation's capitol, and, after landing, we were marched to the eastern part of the city, and pitched tents near Camp Oregon—named thus in honor of Colonel Edward D. Baker, who represented that Territory in the Senate of the United States, previous to his acceptance of a military commission, and who is now in command of the famous California regiment which occupies this camp.

Chapter II - Camp-Life and its Influences.

1861.—Our unmilitary Appearance.—First Equipage.—My Black Mare.—Good and Evil Influences.—News-Boys.—Mail-Bag.—Letter-Writing.—The Bugle Corps.— Camp Guard.—Guerillas under Turner Ashby.—Mounted Drill.—Laughable Experiences with Horses.—Southern Egotism.—Northern Fancies.

Drill! drill! and camp-police are the order of the day. Indeed we have nothing else to do, and to do nothing at all is the hardest kind of work. We expect soon to have some accoutrements to enable us to drill something besides our feet. Our preparations for war have commenced at the extremities; for thus far nothing but our heads and feet have been instructed. However, as we become better acquainted with this part of our duty we enjoy it better than at first, and we think we are making no very mean progress.

For some time after our arrival here, the Government was unable to supply us with uniforms, or weapons of war, and our appearance was far from being à la militaire, as Captain Duffié would have it. Coming as we did from colleges and schools, from offices and counting-rooms, from shops and farms, and some from no occupation at all, each with the peculiar dress he wore when he enlisted, and already pretty well worn out by our labors at Camp Howe and extensive travelling, we were a most unsightly, heterogeneous mass of humanity, and were a subject of no little sport to our better-clad fellow-soldiers. Especially was this the case when on a certain day General B. F. Butler reviewed the troops of this department, and we were made to appear before him and the multitude with our hats and caps, our coats and jackets, in nearly all colors, and many of them in rags and shags. We certainly had nothing to recommend us to the consideration of military men, except the courageous spirit that throbbed in our generally robust frames. But we were hopeful of better days, when we might have the appearance and equipage as well as the internal qualities of soldiers.

But the Government was so wholly unprepared for war, that our supplies were received very slowly. First came our uniforms, which every man donned gladly, and yet with a feeling that the last link to civil life, for the present, was severed, and that henceforth in a very peculiar sense we belonged to our common country.

A few days after our arrival at Camp Oregon, we were joined by the men who belonged to our regiment from other States. This added fresh enthusiasm, as well as new strength, to our ranks. However, there is as yet nothing in our tout ensemble to distinguish us from infantry or artillery, except the yellow trimming of our blue uniforms, whereas the infantry has the light-blue trimming, and the artillery bright red.

August 23.—To-day I am happy to make the following entry in my diary, namely: the regiment was furnished with sabres, Colt's revolvers and all the necessary appendages, consisting of belts and ammunition-boxes. Every man has now a new care and pride—to keep his sabre bright, and his entire outfit clean, that he may wear them with pleasure to himself and honor to his comrades. The morning and evening of the 24th were spent in sabre exercise, with which we were all delighted. This is the first development in us of the cavalry element as such, and we begin to feel our individuality. We desire to have this growth continue uninterruptedly, and in aid of it, in the early part of September, came quite a large installment of horses and equipments. This occurred while the regiment occupied a camp about three miles from Washington, on the Bladensburg road, which we named Sussex, in honor of Sussex county, New York, our colonel's native county. As the number of horses furnished us at this time was not sufficient to mount the whole command, the number received by each company was proportioned to the maximum roll of its men. After the non-commissioned officers of each company, including all the sergeants and corporals, had drawn their horses according to rank, the privates were made to draw lots for the remainder—a performance which produced no little amount of excitement.

Several of our comrades were of course unfortunately compelled for several days to march on foot, though much against their wishes; for nothing could be more humiliating to a dragoon than to be trudging through the mud and dust, while his companions were gliding past him with their neighing steeds, on their way to the drill-grounds, or to any other post of duty. It was my good fortune to be the recipient of a beautiful black mare, only five years old, full of life and fiery metal, fourteen hands high, and weighing ten hundred pounds. She was a gem for the cavalry service, or any thing else, and a friendship was to grow up between us worthy of historic mention.

We are now fairly out upon the ocean of our new life, and are beginning to feel its influence. It does not take the careful observer long to notice the effects which outward changes and circumstances have upon the characters of most men. Indeed, no man remains unaffected by them; he either advances or retrogrades, and it is very apparent already among us that while soldiering does make some men, it un makes many. The very lowest stratum of life among us, such as represents the loungers in the streets and lanes of our cities,—those who have neither occupation nor culture, is amazingly influenced for the better by military discipline. These men now find themselves with something to do, and with somebody to make them do it. The progress is very slow, it is true, and in some cases exceptional, but this is evidently the general tendency.

But on the other hand, our regiment is made up partly of young men from respectable families, reared under the influences of a pure morality; but they find that the highest standard of morality presented here is much lower than they were wont to have at home, and they soon begin to waver. Thus having lost their first moorings of character, they start downward, and in many instances are precipitated to horrible depths.

"When once a shaking monarchy declines,
Each thing grows bold and to its fall combines."

Only a very few have sufficient force in themselves to effectually resist these evils. It must be remembered that the wholesome and normal restraints of virtuous female society are wholly removed from us. And from what we daily see around us we are convinced that a colony of men only, however virtuous or moral, would in a short time run into utter barbarism. No candid observer can doubt the teaching of the old scripture, that "it is not good for man to be alone."

Moreover, the friends and associates of our childhood's innocence, whose presence always calls forth the purest memories, are not with us; nor do we feel the almost omnipotent influences of the old school-house gatherings, of the church-going bell, and of the home-fireside. When you sever all these ties and helps to a moral life, and throw a man in the immediate association of the vicious, he must be only a little less than an angel not to fall. Here we are all dressed alike, live alike, and are all subject to like laws and discipline. The very man who shares our blanket and tent-cover, who draws rations from the same kettle, who drinks from the same canteen, and with whom we are compelled to come in contact daily, may be the veriest poltroon, whose diploma shows graduation at the Five Points, and whose presence alone is morally miasmatic. Consequently our camp is infested more or less with gambling, drunkenness, and profanity, and all their train of attending evils, and at times we long for campaigning in the field, where it seems to us we may rid ourselves of this demoralization. Hannibal's toilsome marches across the Alps and through Upper Italy only gave hardihood and courage to his legions, who came thundering at the very gates of Rome, and threatening its immediate overthrow; but a winter's camp-life at Capua left them shorn of their strength. But then we have remedial influences even in camp, and we hail them with no little delight. Daily the news-boys make their appearance, calling out: "Washington Chronicle and New York papers!" They enjoy an extensive patronage. With these sheets many moments are pleasantly spent, as their columns are eagerly perused. Then, following hard on the track of the news-boys, comes our adjutant's orderly or courier with a mail-bag full of letters, precious mementos from the loved ones at home. These messages are the best reminders we have of our home-life, especially when they are brim-full, as is usually the case, with patriotic sparkling, and with affection's purest libations. These letters have a double influence; while they keep the memories of home more or less bright within us, and at times so bright that as we read we can almost see our mothers, wives, and sisters in their tender Christian solicitude for us, they also stimulate us to greater improvements in the epistolary art. Men who never wrote a letter in their lives before, are at it now; those who cannot write at all, are either learning, or engage their comrades to write for them, and the command is doing more writing in one day than, I should judge, we used to do in a month, and, perhaps, a year.

No sooner are the contents of the mail-bag distributed, and devoured by the eager newsmongers, than active preparations are made for responding. Some men carry pocket-inkstands and write with pens, but the majority use pencils. Here you see one seated on a stump or fence, addressing his "sweet-heart" or somebody else; another writes standing up against a tree, while a third is lying flat on the ground. Thus either in the tents or in the open air, scribbling is going on, and the return mail will carry many sweet words to those who cannot be wholly forgotten. I suppose in this way we are not only making, but writing history. Camp-life then is not entirely monotonous.

THE BUGLE-CORPS.

Sights and sounds of interest may be seen and heard at almost every hour of the day. The morning is ushered in with the shrill reveille, which means awake and arise. This is well executed by our bugle-corps, which Captain Duffié has organized, and is drilling thoroughly. All our movements are now ordered by the bugle. By its blast we are called to our breakfast, dinner and supper. Roll-call is sounded twice a day, and the companies fall into line, when the first sergeants easily ascertain whether every man is at his post of duty. The bugle calls the sick, and sometimes those who feign to be, to the surgeon's quarters, and their wants and woes are attended to. By the bugle we are summoned to inspections, to camp-guard, to the feeding and watering of our horses and to drill. A peculiarly shrill call is that which brings all the first or orderly sergeants to the adjutant's quarters to receive any special order he may have to communicate.

Thus call after call is sounded at intervals throughout the day, ending with "taps," which is the signal for blowing out the lights, and seeking the rest which night demands.

CAMP GUARD.

Our principal duties now are camp guard and drill, which we perform by turns. Every morning quite a large force is detailed, with a commissioned officer in command, for guard duty. These form a line of dismounted pickets, or vedettes, around the entire camp. They are stationed within sight and hailing distance of each other, enabling them to prevent any one from leaving or entering camp without a written pass in the day-time, or the countersign at night. The rule is to have each man stand post for two hours, when he is relieved. This is the maximum time, and is sometimes made less at the discretion of the commandant.

We are told, as we perform this duty, that it is not very unlike the picketing that will be required of us if we are ever permitted to take the field which confronts the enemy. Indeed, this is picketing on a small scale. And our enthusiasm in this branch of our work increases, as we are almost daily in receipt of accounts of attacks on our pickets along the line of the Baltimore and Ohio Railroad and the Cumberland Canal. It appears that a certain Colonel Turner Ashby, with a force of cavaliers (?) acting as guerillas, singly and in squads, is nightly endeavoring to sever our telegraph wires, to burn our railroad-bridges, and to destroy the canal, or fire at our men on the passing boats; and not unfrequently we read of skirmishes in which several of our pickets have been either captured, wounded, or killed. Of course, we expect before long to face Mr. Ashby and his confederates, and we are preparing ourselves for it.

MOUNTED DRILL.

But this we do specially in the drill. Recently the balance of our men were gladdened with a full supply of horses. Mounted drill is now the general order, and nearly all our time not otherwise occupied is devoted to this exercise. At first we had some exciting times with our young and untrained horses. One of our men received a kick from his horse which proved fatal to his life. Several of our wildest and seemingly incorrigible ones we have been compelled to run up the steepest hills in the vicinity, under the wholesome discipline of sharp spurs, until the evil has been sweated out of them. We find, however, that the trouble is not only with the horses, but frequently with the men, many of whom have never bridled a horse nor touched a saddle. And then, too, these curbed bits in the mouths of animals that had been trained with the common bridle, produced a most rebellious temper, causing many of them to rear up in the air as though they had suddenly been transformed into monstrous kangaroos, while the riders showed signs of having taken lessons in somersets. Some of the scenes are more than ludicrous. Horses and men are acting very awkwardly, also, with the guiding of the animal by the rein against the neck, and not by the bit, as we were accustomed to do at home.

We do not wonder much that the chivalrous Black Horse gentry have expressed their contempt of Northern "mudsills and greasy mechanics," and have made their brags that we could never match them. But then it is said that these Southrons were born in a saddle, and were always trained in horsemanship. They generally perform their pleasure excursions, go on their business journeys, and even to church, on horseback. They were therefore prepared for the cavalry service, before we had so much as thought of it. But let them beware of what they think or say, for we can learn, and it does frequently occur that somewhere in the experience of contending parties, "the first is last, and the last first."

We are improving rapidly. There is so much exhilaration in the shrill bugle-notes which order the movements of the drill, and so much life in its swift evolutions, that the men and horses seem to dance rather than walk on their way to the drill grounds, and both are readily learning the certain sounds of the trumpet, and becoming masters of motions and dispositions required of them. Like all other apprentices, of course, we occasionally indulge in the reveries of imagination, and we think we are laying the foundation of a career which is destined to be important and glorious. Be this as it may, we do not mean to be outstripped by any one in our knowledge and practice of cavalry tactics, and of the general manœuvrings of war.

Cavalry Column On The March

Chapter III - Preparations For Active Service

1861.—First Advance.—"Contrabands," their Hopes and Treatment.—Union Ranks Filling Up.—Promotion.—Foraging and its Obstacles.—Scouting and its Aim.—Senator Harris visits the Command.—Ball's Bluff.—Recruiting Service.—Interesting Incidents.—Camp Palmer.—"Contrabands" at Work.—Drilling near Arlington Heights.—Colonel George D. Bayard.—Fight at Drainesville.

October 15, 1861.—The Harris Light broke camp at eight o'clock, A. M., and marched proudly through Washington, crossed the famous Long Bridge over the Potomac, and moved forward to Munson's Hill, in full view of our infantry outposts, where we established a new camp, calling it "Advance." For the first time our horses remained saddled through the night, and the men slept on their arms. To us this was a new and exciting phase of life.

Since our retreat from Bull Run, the Rebel army has made itself formidable on this line, and though no active movements have been attempted on Washington, we are, nevertheless, apprehensive of such a measure on their part. Hence our picket lines are doubly strong and vigilant, while every means is resorted to to ascertain the position, strength, and intention of our wily foe. Frequently "contrabands" feel their way through the enemy's pickets under cover of the night, and through the tangled brushwood which abounds, and reach our lines safely. From them we gain much valuable information of the state of things in "Dixie." Some of them, we learn, were employed by Rebel leaders in constructing forts and earthworks, and in various ways were made to contribute muscle to the Southern Confederacy. They have strange and exciting stories to tell us, and yet it seems as though they might be of great service to us, if we saw fit to employ them, as guides in our movements. Their heart is with us in this conflict. They hail us as friends, and entertain wild notions about a jubilee of liberty, for which they are ever praying and singing, and look upon us as their deliverers. How they have formed such opinions is somewhat difficult to conjecture, especially when we consider the anomalous treatment they have received from our hands. The authorities have seemed to be puzzled with regard to them; and there are cases where they have even been returned to their former owners. And yet there seems to be an instinctive prophecy in their natures, which leads them to look to Northmen for freedom. Their presence in our camps becomes a sort of inspiration to most of us, and we only wish that their prayers may be answered, and that every chain of servitude may be broken. This sentiment at times breaks out in such as the following poetic strain:

"In the beauty of the lily Christ was born across the sea,
With a glory in His bosom that transfigures you and me
As He died to make men holy, let us die to make them free."

And as slavery was the cause, and not, as some say, the pretext, of the war, if the Union arms succeed, this "irrepressible conflict" and villanous wrong must come to an end.

Our confidence in the ultimate success of our arms is daily increasing. Since the first of August our ranks have been wonderfully swelled; and now regiment after regiment, battery after battery, is pouring in from the North, filling the camps of instruction, and manning the fortifications around Washington. Meanwhile, earthworks are being constructed on all the high hills and commanding positions; strong abatis are made of the forest-trees, and every thing done that can give the city an air of security, and the country round about the appearance of a bristling porcupine. Should this influx of troops continue, we shall be compelled to advance our lines for very room on which to station them. We have some intimations that our advance to this point to-day is preparatory to such a movement.

The day following our advance I was promoted to the rank of corporal, on the recommendation of Captain Buel, my appointment to date from the fifteenth. On the sixteenth our lines were advanced to Vienna, a station on the Leesburg Railroad, and on the seventeenth as far as Fairfax Court House, the Confederates falling back toward Centreville and Manassas without offering the least resistance.

FORAGING AND SCOUTING.

We are spending our time mostly in foraging, scouting, and patrolling. In consequence of imperfect transportation, the cavalry especially is compelled to seek its own forage, with which, however, the country abounds. Corn is found in "right smart heaps," as the natives say, either in the fields or barns, and hayricks dot the country on every side. But there is a certain degree of scrupulousness on the part of some of our commanders with regard to appropriating the produce of the "sacred soil" to our own use, which greatly embarrasses our foraging expeditions, and exasperates not a little those of us who are needy of the things we are at times ordered not to take. It is no uncommon thing to find one of our men stationed as safeguard over the property of a most bitter Rebel—property which, in our judgment, ought to be confiscated to the use of the Union, or utterly destroyed. We do not believe in handling Rebels with kid gloves, and especially when we know that the very men whom we protect are constantly giving information to the enemy of all our movements, and using their property whenever they can to aid and comfort the cause of treason. We are too forcibly reminded of the fable we used to read in our schoolboy days, of the Farmer and the Viper. We are only warming into new life and strength this virus of Rebellion, to have it recoil upon ourselves. We hope our authorities will soon discover their error, and change their tactics.

Our scouting is on a limited scale, though it affords considerable exercise and excitement. Thereby we are learning the topography of the country, and making small maps of the same. We are traversing the forests, through the wood-roads and by-paths which run in every direction; strolling by the streams and ravines, and gaining all the information which can be of use to us in future manœuvrings. We scout in small squads over the entire area occupied by our forces, and often beyond; and, now and then, more frequently in the night, we patrol between our picket posts, to ascertain that all is well at the points most exposed to danger. The principal object of scouting is to learn the strength and position of the enemy, while the object of patrolling is to learn our own.

October 20.—To-day the regiment was honored by a visit from its patron, Senator Ira Harris. After witnessing a mounted drill and parade, which pleased him much, he presented us a beautiful stand of colors, accompanied by an appropriate and eloquent address. He made especial reference to the object of the organization, the hopes of its friends, and their earnest prayers for its future usefulness and success. He dwelt enthusiastically upon the work before us. At the close of the speech the command responded with a rousing round of cheers, expressive of their thankfulness for the banner and of their determination to keep it, to stand by it, and to defend it even with their lives. The occasion was one to be remembered.

BALL'S BLUFF.

Another great pall of sadness has fallen upon our soldiers. The papers bring intelligence of our terrible disaster at Ball's Bluff, and the promising Colonel E. D. Baker has fallen, while gallantly leading his noble Californians. Discussions as to the cause or causes of that fatal advance and bloody retreat are going on throughout our camps. It does seem to many as though gross incompetency or treachery must have influenced the authorities having immediate oversight of the affair, and that our fallen braves have been needlessly immolated upon their country's altar.

"Big Bethel, Bull Run, and Ball's Bluff,
Oh, alliteration of blunders!
Of blunders more than enough,
In a time full of blunders and wonders."

But the boys are enthusiastic over the bravery of our nineteen hundred, who fought against a force more than twice their number, with all the advantage of position and knowledge of the country. All our battles have proven that our men can fight, and, though Providence seems to have been against us thus far, for reasons most inscrutable, we will not waver in our determination to dare or die in the contest. Our chief difficulties are not in the rank and file of the army, but in the general management of the forces, and we trust that ere long right men will be found to take the places of incompetent ones.

RECRUITING SERVICE.

October 28.—To-day I was detailed by Colonel Davies to proceed to New York with Lieutenant Morton, on recruiting service. We went on to Newburgh, near the lieutenant's native home, where we spent a few days together, but on the first of November I was ordered to Troy, to act independently. I spent several weeks in this peculiar work, and with good success.

Though recruiting offices could be found on all the principal streets of our cities and villages, yet a good business was done by them all, such was the enthusiasm which prevailed among the people. War-meetings were frequently held, and addressed by our best orators. The press, with few exceptions, poured forth its eloquent appeals to the strong-bodied men of the country to range themselves on the side of right against wrong. Violence would be done to truth did we not mention, also, that the pulpits of the land were potent helpers in this work, by their religious patriotism and persistent efforts to keep the great issue distinctly before the people. Thus the mind and heart of the North were kept alive to the great problem of the nation's existence, and men were rallying to our standard. It was no uncommon thing to receive applications to enter our lists from young men or boys too young and slender to be admitted, who left our offices in tears of disappointment, unless we could find for them a position as drummers and buglers.

A single instance of enlistment under my observation might be mentioned, as it gives a specimen of the manner in which our work went on. Having taken passage on the cars one day from one point of my labors to another, I fell in with a young man who was on his way to college, where he expected to be matriculated the following day. His valise was full of books and other students' requisites, and his heart full of literary ambition. Attracted to me by my uniform, he soon learned my business, and, after a few moments of pensiveness, to my surprise, he told me to inscribe his name among my recruits. Then turning to a friend on board the car, he said, "Take this trunk to my home, and tell my mother I have enlisted in a cavalry regiment."

December 4.—To-day I returned from recruiting service, bringing with me our enlisted men who had not been sent previously to the regiment. I found the Harris Light occupying Camp Palmer, on Arlington Heights, the confiscated property of the Rebel General Robert E. Lee. On arriving in camp I found that the papers from Washington contained a letter of Secretary Seward, directing General McClellan not to return to their former owners contrabands in our lines. This order, when fully understood by our colored friends, will undoubtedly increase their exit "from Egypt," as many of them style their escape from bondage. The government will probably adopt measures to give these fugitives systematic assistance and labor, that they may be of use to us. Already I find that a goodly number of our officers have adopted them for cooks and hostlers, in which positions they certainly excel; and there is no good reason why we may not employ them as teamsters on our trains and helpers in our trenches. They are generally very powerful, and show signs of great endurance. Nor do we find them unwilling to labor, as we have been so often told they were. However, we do not wonder much that they have acquired the "reputation" of being lazy, for what but a thing or an animal could take pleasure in unrequited toil? Now they have a personal interest, and take a peculiar delight in what they do for us. Their great willingness and ability to work for Uncle Sam or any of his boys, would indicate that they will become eminently useful in the service of their country.

From Camp Palmer the regiment had gone out to drill for some time; and here we continued through the month, generally occupying the large plain which lies between the Arlington House and the Potomac, and in full view of Washington. On this field Kilpatrick, Davies, Duffié, and others, began to develop their soldierly qualities, infusing them into their commands, and imparting that knowledge of cavalry tactics which would prepare us for the stern duties of war. We have recently been greatly encouraged by the movements of Colonel George Dashiel Bayard, of the First Pennsylvania Cavalry, who, on the 27th of November, while on a scout on the road to Leesburg, Loudon county, met a band of the Chivalry near Drainesville, with whom he had a spirited skirmish. The whole affair would indicate that Colonel Bayard is destined to be no mean cavalry leader. Cavalry regiments from most of the loyal States have been organized, and are now in camps of instruction. Occasionally they go out scouting, picketing, etc., and are thus preparing for the coming campaigns.

December 20.—To-day a brigade of Pennsylvanians, including two squadrons of Colonel Bayard's cavalry regiment, the whole force under command of General E. O. C. Ord, while foraging in the vicinity of Drainesville, were attacked by a Rebel force nearly equal in numbers, with General J. E. B. Stuart commanding in person. A lively contest followed, in which the Rebels were thoroughly beaten and driven from the field, losing, according to their own accounts, about two hundred and fifty in killed, wounded, and captured. They left twenty-five dead horses on the field, with the débris of two caissons, disabled and exploded by the well-directed fire of Easton's battery, which accompanied the expedition. The Rebels, who had undoubtedly come out for the purpose of forage as well as ourselves, having a long wagon train, retreated toward Fairfax Court House, with their wagons laden with their wounded. Our loss includes only nine killed and sixty wounded. Unimportant as this victory might seem, it caused an immense rejoicing in the Union ranks. It was a fitting answer to the calumny heaped upon us from both North and South, that our soldiers could not fight, and were no match for their boastful enemy.

Chapter IV - The Advance to the Rappahannock.

1862.—"All quiet along the Potomac."—Preparations.—Army of the Potomac Moves!—Capture of the "Quaker Guns" at Centreville.—Return to Defences.— Guerillas.—Their Attacks and Stratagems.—The Bovine Foe.—Picketing; how it is done.—Sufferings.—McClellan to the Peninsula.—Virginia Weather and the People.—General Augur's Advance to the Rappahannock.—Lieutenant Decker's Bravery and Death.—Night Charge on Falmouth Heights.—Fredericksburg Surrenders.—How Citizens regard us.—Guarding a Train to Thoroughfare Gap.— Fight and Captures at Flipper's Orchard.—Shenandoah Valley.—The Fifth New York Cavalry, First Ira Harris' Guard.—Death of Turner Ashby.—Strange Cavalry Tactics.—Personal Bravery of Captain Hammond.—End of the Peninsular Campaign.

The winter was one of preparation, not of operation. Why we were kept "all quiet along the Potomac," until the announcement, reiterated through the press, elicited only disdainful merriment among our friends, was never satisfactorily explained. The month of December had been beautiful, the roads in excellent condition, the army well supplied and disciplined, so that nothing but hesitancy in our leaders stood in the way of army movements. The North and West, which had supplied myriads of men and millions of money, were becoming very impatient with such a state of things. This feeling was intensified by the fact that it was known that the enemy was tireless in his efforts to increase his army and to fortify his strongholds, while he was also gaining the sympathy of foreign powers, and, by means of blockade-running, was adding not a little to his munitions of war. The army shared largely this general discontent. "Why do we not advance?" was every where the interrogation of eager officers and men.

However, we were not wholly unemployed; for while we waited for reinforcements and cannon, as demanded by the general in command, and for the leaves to fall from the trees to facilitate movements in a country so thickly wooded as is Virginia, we were kept busy with the camp curriculum, namely, the drill, the guard, the inspection, and parade. General Lee's plantation, on Arlington Heights, and the surrounding country, was thoroughly trodden by loyal feet, as men and horses were acquiring the form and power of military life.

THE ARMY OF THE POTOMAC.

But our quiet was to be broken by our grand advance, which commenced on the 3d of March. The Harris Light broke camp at three o'clock in the morning, and, with several regiments of cavalry, under the command of Colonel W. W. Averill, led the advance, the Harris Light having the position of honor as vanguard. We were ordered to move slowly and cautiously, which we did, on the main thoroughfare known as the Little River Turnpike, and, at four o'clock, P. M., we arrived at Fairfax Court House, having marched only about fourteen miles.

What was our surprise to find the place entirely deserted by the enemy, who had left the day previous with the design of retiring beyond the Rappahannock. This change of affairs seemed so sudden as to be full of mystery, and was wholly unknown even to our secret corps. We could not doubt but that this movement was performed in anticipation of some of our contemplated manœuvrings, of which the Rebel leaders are generally informed by their spies in Washington and all through our lines, even before they are known to our army.

Our march was resumed the following day at ten o'clock A. M., and early in the afternoon we captured the "Quaker Guns" at Centreville. The enemy had actually placed in the earthworks or forts which commanded the road, large trunks of trees, resembling cannon of heavy calibre, which frowned down upon us from the heights. Had it not been for the information we had received from contrabands on the march, that the enemy had evacuated, a report confirmed by the curling smoke which rose from various parts of the field, this formidable array of threatening cannon would have terrified us all, and greatly retarded our progress. Indeed, it was not till after the suspicious works had been thoroughly scanned with field-glasses that we were ordered to advance, when the strong position was carried without the snapping of a cap, or a sabre stroke. Chagrin was written upon every face. Not a sign of the enemy was visible, save the deserted remains of their winter-quarters, which fell into our hands.

A very brief halt was here made, and, hurrying our steps, we soon crossed the memorable Bull Run, and came up with the rearguard of the retiring army at Manassas Junction. Here we pitched into them, and kicked up a little dust on the road to Bristoe. This expedition, or wild-goose chase, was continued to Warrenton Junction, where General George D. Stoneman found the enemy in force, but returned without attacking them. Having loitered about these historic fields a few days, our whole force began to fall back towards its old position on the Potomac, establishing our advanced picket-lines, however, as far forward as Centreville, with Fairfax Court House as headquarters. Our line of pickets intercepts the Leesburg turnpike at Drainesville and extends to the Potomac, a distance of about twenty miles.

GUERILLAS AND BUSHWHACKERS.

As guerillas and their brethren, the bushwhackers, infest the country more or less, picketing is dangerous as well as difficult. Between the Rappahannock and the Potomac lies a vast territory which abounds in creeks, marshes, deep, dark forests, with only here and there a village or settlement. A little to the west of this plain extend the Bull Run Mountains, with their ravines and caverns. This is a very fit hiding-place for mischief-makers. The guerillas consist mostly of farmers and mechanics, residents of this region, who, by some means, are exempt from the Rebel conscription. Most of them follow their usual avocations daring the day, and have their rendezvous at night, where they congregate to lay their plans of attack on the pickets.

They resort to every stratagem which a vile and savage spirit could inspire. Sometimes a picket is approached by the stealthiest creeping through the dark thickets, when the unfortunate sentinel is seized and quickly despatched by a bowie-knife, or other like weapon, which a Southron can always use most dexterously. When mere stealth cannot accomplish the task, other methods are used. For instance, on a dark night, a vedette, stationed by a thick underbrush, heard a cow-bell approaching him, and supposing that the accompanying rustle of leaves and crackling of dry limbs was occasioned by a bovine friend, unwittingly suffered himself to be captured by a bushwhacker. But the boys soon learned to be suspicious of every noise they heard; so much so, that one night a picket, hearing footsteps approaching him, cried out, "Halt! Who comes there?" His carbine was instantly brought to a ready, and as no halt occurred nor answer was made, a second challenge was given; but failing to effect any thing, he fired in the direction of the noise, when he distinctly heard a heavy fall, and then groans, as of somebody dying. The sergeant of the post, running up to ascertain the cause of the alarm, found that an unfortunate ox, that had been grazing his way through the forest, lay dying, with his forehead perforated by the faithful sentry's bullet. The incident caused considerable merriment, and the pickets were supplied with poor Confederate beef during the remainder of their term of duty.

But the attacks are frequently of a more disastrous character, resulting in the killing of men and horses, in wounds and in captures. The utmost care and strictest vigilance cannot secure us perfectly from depredations. Our general plan is as follows: The major part of the regiment or picket detail establishes what we denominate the "main reserve" within a mile or two in rear of the centre of the line of vedettes, or at a point where their assistance, in case of an attack, can be secured at any place in the line, at the shortest possible notice. About midway between the main reserve and the picket line are stationed two, three, or four picket reliefs, so situated as to form, with the line of vedettes for a base, a pyramid, with its apex at the main reserve.

PICKET DUTY.

The boys will not soon forget the long, dreary, dangerous hours they spent along this line. Here we find ourselves shivering around a miserable fire among the sighing pines (though in times of special danger we are not permitted to have even this slight comfort, for fear of detection), often compelled to sit or lie down in snow or mud, or to walk about smartly to prevent freezing to death. Sometimes, when much exhausted, we have laid ourselves down on the damp and muddy ground, which was frozen stiffly all around us when we awoke. Frozen fingers and toes are no uncommon things. In this wretched plight we hear the summons to get ready to stand post. We go out upon our shivering horses, to sit in the saddle for two hours or more, facing the biting wind, and peering through the storm of sleet, snow, or rain, which unmercifully pelts us in its fury. But it were well for us if this was our worst enemy, and we consider ourselves happy if the guerilla does not creep through bushes impenetrable to the sight, to inflict his mortal blows. The two hours expire, relief comes, and the vedette returns to spend his four, six, or eight hours off post, as best he may.

Once, at least, during the night, we are visited by the grand guard, which consists of the officer of the day, accompanied by others, whose duty it is to make a thorough, though usually swift, inspection of the picket line. Most of our time is spent in this duty.

March 29.—Considerable excitement prevailed among us to-day, as Colonel Bayard was dispatched with a detachment of his regiment to repulse a dastardly raid made by some of General J. E. B. Stuart's men, on the house of a Mrs. Tenant, a Union lady, residing near Difficult Run, about six miles from Chain Bridge. Colonel Bayard reached the place a few moments too late, and the raiders succeeded in taking Mrs. Tenant as a prisoner, and making off with their prey.

For several weeks the main portion of our grand army has been sent by transports to the Peninsula, with the evident intention of moving upon Richmond by shorter land routes than by way of Manassas. This change in our plans of attack was probably known by the Rebels before they were matured at Washington, and we now understand why they so quietly evacuated their positions on our front.

General McDowell remains in command of the defences of Washington, with a force sufficient, it is believed, to give safety to the Capital, and to harass the Rebels who continue before us. With the departure of General McClellan to the Peninsula, our picket lines were withdrawn to Annandale and Falls Church, within a few miles of the fortifications of Washington.

THE ATMOSPHERE AND THE PEOPLE.

April 4.—The Harris Light and the First Pennsylvania Cavalry were recalled from the picket lines and sent out on a reconnoissance in force, with a division in command of General McDowell. Our march led us through Fairfax Court House and Centreville, near which we bivouacked for the night.

Already, at this early spring time, a luxurious vegetable growth of green is beautifully carpeting the fields through which we pass and in which we halt. Flowers of great beauty and variety of hues and sweetness of perfume greet us on every hand. It would seem as though Nature were struggling to hide the desolations which war has made, and were weaving her chaplets of honor around the graves of our fallen brothers. And it really seems as though Destruction himself had contributed to this lavish growth. Thus,

"Life evermore is fed by death,
In earth, or sea, or sky;
And, that a rose may breathe its breath,
Something must die."

On the fifth we continued on our march to Bristoe Station, on the Orange and Alexandria Railroad, where we encountered one of the most furious snow storms ever known in this region of country. The wind which bore the snow was cold and cutting. It was a season never to be forgotten by those who were quartered in mere shelter tents, or had no tents at all.

So sudden are the changes of the atmosphere here that "no man knoweth what a moment may bring forth." Yesterday we sought shelter from the sun's heat under the budding trees, while grass and flowers and singing birds indicated settled weather. To-day the storm howls music through the bending pines, and snow several inches deep covers the earth.

We are thoroughly convinced that the character of the people here greatly partakes of the nature of these surroundings. Is not this the case everywhere? But we see it here more plainly than we ever did before. The people are fitful, and their spasms are terrible; and yet we find them at times to be as kind and hospitable as any we have ever found elsewhere. After one has witnessed their beautiful days, cooled with a gentle sea-breeze, which generally blows from about nine o'clock in the morning till six at night, and then their cool, calm evenings, he can see why there are so many lovely traits in the nature of the people. But if he experience some of their sudden and terrific snow storms and showers, when the thunder and the lightning are such that a Northerner feels that all the storms he has ever witnessed are only infantile attempts, he is inclined to extenuate, on mere climactic principles, the outbursts of wrath, and "fire-eating" propensities of the people. He who is gendered of fire and brimstone must have some vim in his composition. We believe this study is not unworthy the Christian philosopher and philanthropist.

The day following the storm, the sun came out warmly, and the snow suddenly disappeared, but left us in a bed of mud. The soil, naturally rich and tender, consisting of a reddish loam, trodden by many feet, and cut by the wheels of heavy vehicles, became almost impassable. But it has this advantage, that it soon dries. So the soil, as well as the atmosphere and the people, is suddenly changeable.

April 7.—To-day our expedition continued its march to Catlett's Station, a few miles south of Bristoe. General Augur commands the advance, which consists of a brigade of infantry and two regiments of cavalry.

On the eighth of the month a detachment of the Harris Light was ordered out on picket at six o'clock P. M., and we enjoyed a quiet, pleasant trip on this usually unpleasant duty. Here we spent a few days picketing, scouting and patrolling, and on the seventeenth we advanced from Catlett's in the direction of Falmouth, on the Rappahannock.

DEATH OF LIEUTENANT DECKER.

Our march was rapid and lay through a country altogether new to us, which, however, presented no very interesting features. The Harris Light had the advance, and was followed by the Fourteenth Brooklyn. As our infantry comrades became foot-sore and weary, we exchanged positions with them, for mutual relief, until at last one half of the regiments were bearing one another's burdens. This incident paved the way for a strong friendship to grow up between us.

Seventeen miles were travelled quietly, when a sudden fire on our advance-guard brought every cavalry man to his horse and infantry man to his musket. Every thing assumed the signs of a fight. Kilpatrick, who was in command of the regiment, ordered his band to the rear. This precaution of the commander was no sooner taken than the vanguard, in command of Lieutenant George Decker, was making a furious charge upon Field's Cavalry, which was doing outpost duty ten miles from Falmouth. On the very first assault Lieutenant Decker fell from his horse, pierced through the heart with a fatal bullet. He was a daring young man, well formed, light complexion, blue eyes, and about twenty-three years of age. He was much lamented by his many friends. His fall, shocking as it was to the command, being our first fatal casualty, only seemed to nerve the men for bold revenge. And we had it. Like chaff before the whirlwind the outpost was quickly scattered, and the whole regiment entered upon its first charge with a will, a charge which continued for several miles with wild excitement. Picket reliefs and reserves were swept away like forest trees before the avalanche, and we fell upon their encampment before time had been afforded them for escape. Here we captured several men and horses, with large quantities of stores, and then rested our tired steeds and fed them with confederate forage. The men enjoyed the captured rations. It was near night, and as the sun disappeared the infantry force came up to our newly-possessed territory.

The cavalry was ordered to "stand to horse," and a strong picket was thrown out to prevent any surprise attack or flanking movement of the enemy. In the early part of the evening one of our pickets was surprised by the friendly approach of a citizen of Falmouth, who had come, as he said, "to hail once more the 'old star-spangled banner,' and to greet his loyal brethren of the North."

Such a patriotic and fearless individual among the white population of that section of country was a great rarity, and his protestations of friendship were at first received with some suspicion. He was, however, brought to General Augur's headquarters, where he gave satisfactory proof of his kind intentions, and then gave the General a full description of the position and strength of the enemy.

NIGHT ATTACK ON FALMOUTH HEIGHTS.

A plan for a night attack was thereupon laid and committed to Bayard and Kilpatrick. Our instructions were conveyed to us in a whisper. A beautiful moonlight fell upon the scene, which was as still as death; and with a proud determination the two young cavalry chieftains moved forward to the night's fray. Bayard was to attack on the main road in front, but not until Kilpatrick had commenced operations on their right flank by a detour through a neglected and narrow wood-path. As the Heights were considered well nigh impregnable, it was necessary to resort to some stratagem, for which Kilpatrick showed a becoming aptness.

Having approached to within hearing distance of the Rebel pickets, but before we were challenged, Kilpatrick shouted with his clear voice which sounded like a trumpet on the still night air.

Night Attack on Falmouth Heights.

"Bring up your artillery in the centre, and infantry on the left."
"Well, but, Colonel," replied an honest, though rather obtuse captain, "we haven't got any inf——"
"Silence in the ranks!" commanded the leader. "Artillery in the centre, infantry on the left."
The pickets caught and spread the alarm, and thus greatly facilitated our hazardous enterprise.
"Charge!" was the order which then thrilled the ranks and echoed through the dark, dismal woods, and the column swept up the rugged Heights in the midst of blazing cannon and rattling musketry. So steep was the ascent that not a few saddles slipped off the horses, precipitating their riders into a creek which flowed lazily at the base of the hill; while others fell dead and dying, struck by the missiles of destruction which at times filled the air. But the red field was won; and the enemy, driven at the point of the sabre fled unceremoniously down the Heights, through Falmouth, and over the bridge which spanned the Rappahannock, burning the beautiful structure behind them to prevent pursuit. Quite a number of prisoners and various materials of war fell into our hands. Kilpatrick and Bayard were both highly complimented for their personal bravery on the occasion.
April 18.—This morning, at eight o'clock, General Augur took peaceful possession of Falmouth; and here, with military honors, the remains of Lieutenant Decker and about fifteen others, who fell in the late struggle, were interred. Later in the day, and after considerable hesitation, the mayor of

Fredericksburg formally surrendered the city to the Yankee General, whose guns on Falmouth Heights commanded obedience.

A bridge of canal boats, similar to a pontoon, was constructed across the river, and we took possession of this beautiful, proud city. This was the first appearance of Yankees in this Rebel locality, and we were the subject of no little curiosity. Many of the people, who, by the misrepresentations of their licentious press and flaming orators, had been led to believe that Yankees were a species of one-eyed cyclops, or long-clawed harpies, or horned and hoofed devils; who had been deceived into the notion that President Lincoln was a deformed mulatto, degenerated into a hideous monkey, and that all his followers were of that sort, on seeing us, expressed great surprise and wished to know "if we were specimens of the Lincoln army." They had forgotten that our fathers fought side by side in our common country's early struggles, and that now we, their children, as brothers, ought all to sit unitedly under the tree of liberty which they had planted in tears and nourished with blood.

But it is painful to observe how the spirit of secession has blotted out the memories of past days and deeds, and filled their hearts with bitterness toward us. A few Union families in these parts, whose acquaintance we have made, assure us that their neighbors, who were formerly most hospitable and humane, have become, through this Rebel virus, incarnate fiends. To secede from the Union was evidently to secede from the God of virtue and charity.

April 25.—After spending a few days of tolerable quietness on the banks of the Rappahannock, with our camp near the Phillips House, Falmouth, a most lovely spot, we were to-day ordered out as escort or guard to a train destined for the Shenandoah Valley. Such a job is generally any thing but pleasant to a cavalry force, for the movement is altogether too slow, especially when bad roads are encountered. And in case a team becomes balky or gives out, or a wagon breaks down (incidents which occur frequently), the whole column is in statu quo until the difficulty or disability is removed. And so we are halting, advancing, halting and advancing again, with this monotonous variety repeated ad libitum, while the halts are often longer than the advances. But our slow motion gives us some opportunity to scout the country through which we pass, and to obtain any quantity of rations and forage for man and beast. By this means we are not compelled to consume much, if any, of the contents of our train.

On the twenty-eighth we reached Thoroughfare Gap, through which the Manassas Gap railroad finds its way over the Bull Run mountains. Here we met a force from General Nathaniel P. Banks' army, to whose care we delivered the train. We remained a few days to scout through the country.

On the first of May we started back toward Falmouth, but stopped several days at Bristersburg, a small town, where we spent our time very pleasantly, scouting through the country and living upon its rich products. Here we are very much isolated from the rest of our army. We seldom get a mail or receive any papers, except from rebel sources, and these are so meagre of literary taste and especially of reliable army news, that we dare not put much trust in their representations. However, we are satisfied from what we read, that our grand Peninsular army is making some telling demonstrations toward Richmond, and that the Rebel General Thomas J. Jackson, surnamed "Stonewall," since his famous defeat by General James Shields at Kernstown, near Winchester, is still in the valley.

May 25th.—We reached Falmouth to-day and took possession of our old camping ground in front of the Phillips House. We have but little to do except to graze our horses in the surrounding fields, and to recruit our strength. We also have the usual camp work, namely, policing, drilling, etc. This department is very quiet, though we hear of active movements elsewhere.

On the thirtieth we had a severe rain storm, with thunder and lightning, à la Virginie. The streams were greatly swollen, and mud was abundant, so as to retard movements before Richmond.

June 6.—The Harris Light crossed the Rappahannock and advanced six miles beyond Fredericksburg, where we got only a glimpse of some of Field's cavalry, who had not forgotten us. They kept themselves at a very respectful distance from us, and made themselves "scarce" whenever we made signs of an attack. For several days we bivouacked on that side of the river, and on the twelfth we returned to our old camp at Falmouth Heights. On the sixteenth we were again thrown across the river, and made a reconnoissance several miles south, without finding any force of the enemy.

Nothing of importance occurred until the Fourth of July, when the Troy company of the Harris Light, commanded by Lieutenant Robert Loudon, was sent out to celebrate this national holiday by a reconnoissance on the Telegraph Road, south of Fredericksburg. We left camp at eight o'clock in the morning, and soon came in sight of a detachment of Bath Cavalry, doing patrol duty. After following them for some time, though not rapidly, we halted a few moments, and they lost sight of us, concluding doubtless that we had retired. This was just what we wanted.

ATTACK AT FLIPPER'S ORCHARD.

On the south bank of the Po river, about twenty miles from Fredericksburg, was a beautiful orchard, owned by a Dr. Flipper. This lovely spot had been chosen by our Bath friends for their outpost, their main reserve being a few miles farther south. On arriving at the orchard, with its luscious fruit and inviting shade, the squad we were still pursuing unsuspectingly unsaddled their horses, began to arrange preparations for their dinner, and to make themselves generally comfortable. Of this state of things we were informed by a contraband we chanced to meet. We then resolved either to share or spoil their coffee; so, moving forward at a trot until in sight of them, we swooped down upon the orchard like eagles. The surprised and frightened cavaliers fired but a few shots, and we captured twelve men and nine horses, and escaped with our lawful prey without having received a scratch. It was my good fortune to take prisoner Lieutenant Powell, the officer in command, and to receive as my own a fine silver-mounted revolver, which he reluctantly placed in my hand. It will be a fine souvenir of the war and of this Fourth of July.

SHENANDOAH VALLEY.

Sometime in May Colonel Bayard with his regiment and a large portion of General McDowell's division were sent to the Shenandoah Valley to share in the shifting military panorama which was there displayed. With the removal of the Army of the Potomac to the Peninsula the Confederate authorities despatched General Jackson to the Valley, to threaten the upper Potomac and Maryland, thus making it necessary for a large Federal force to remain in these parts. General Banks was in command of that department.

After the battle of Kernstown, in which Jackson received the sobriquet of "Stonewall" and a sound thrashing, General Banks, who had set out for Warrenton, returned to the Valley, and pursued Jackson, but was unable to bring him to bay. The enemy's cavalry under Colonel Turner Ashby was frequently attacked by the Union Cavalry under General John P. Hatch. On the sixth of May, the Fifth New York Cavalry, First Ira Harris Guard, had a hand to hand encounter with Ashby's men near Harrisonburg, where Yankee sabres and pluck had established a reputation. A portion of the same regiment under Colonel John R. Kenly, at Front Royal, added new lustre to their fame, on the twenty-third of the same month, during "Stonewall's" flank movement on General Banks at Strasburg, and fought bravely during that memorable retreat to Maryland.

At this juncture of affairs, a division of General McDowell's forces, under General Shields, was dispatched to the valley to intercept Jackson, while General John C. Fremont was ordered by telegraph to the same scene from the Mountain Department. But unavoidably detained by almost impassable mountain roads and streams enormously swollen by recent rains, Fremont reached Strasburg just in time to see Jackson's last stragglers retreating through the town. His pursuit was very rapid, though no engagement was brought about until the fifth of June, at Harrisonburg. Here Colonel Percy Wyndham, on our side, and Turner Ashby, now a general, on the Rebel side, distinguished themselves in the cavalry. Ashby was killed. His loss was greatly lamented by his comrades. He always fought at the head of his men, with the most reckless self-exposure, and for outpost duty and the skirmish line he left scarcely an equal behind him in either army. His humaneness to our men who had fallen into his hands caused many of them to shed tears at the intelligence of his death. Men of valor and kindness are always worthy of a better cause than that in which the Rebels are engaged; but their merit is always appreciated.

Upon the heel of this fight followed the battles of Cross Keys, and Port Republic, where Jackson eluded the combined Union forces which had been directed against him.

During this memorable campaign, a curious military modus operandi had been resorted to in the Luray Valley, in which the cavalry had made itself doubly useful. A small force of our infantry and cavalry were surrounded by the enemy on the south bank of the Shenandoah River, which was so high as to be unfordable. As a last resort the cavalrymen plunged into the stream, swimming their horses, and towing across the infantrymen, who clung to the animals' tails!

A striking case of personal daring in this Valley campaign, is worthy of record here. During Banks' retreat from Winchester, on the twenty-fourth of May, four companies of the Fifth New York Cavalry, under command of Captain Wheeler, were moving on the left flank of our retreating columns, to protect them from any attacks by the Rebel cavalry, which infested the wooded hills that lay along our route. Emerging from a thick wood, Captain John Hammond, who had the advance with eight or ten men, suddenly came upon a squad of mounted Rebels, and immediately called on them to surrender. However, they fled, firing as they went, but were closely pursued. Captain Hammond was riding a powerful horse, which he had taken from his home, and as his blood was up, he determined to capture one of the party at least, at all hazard. He soon came up to the hindmost, a strong man, with whom he exchanged several shots at close quarters, but without effect on either side, owing to their fearful gait through the timber and down a hill. Hammond's pistol became fouled by a cap, and the cylinder would not revolve. The Rebel had two charges left. Quick work was now necessary. Another spurring of his horse brought him within arm's length of the flying Rebel, whereupon he seized his coat collar with both his hands, and dragged him backward from his saddle. Holding firmly his grasp, both horses went from under them, and they fell pell-mell to the ground. Luckily Hammond was uppermost, with one hand at the enemy's throat and the other holding the band of the pistol with which the Rebel was trying to shoot him. As the two men were powerful, a fearful struggle ensued for the mastery of the pistol. Meantime up rode one of Hammond's boys, who, by his order, fired at the upturned face of the obstinate foe, the ball grazing his scalp and causing him to relinquish his hold of the revolver, when he was forced to surrender. Thus ended one of the roughest yet amusing contests of the war.

The prisoner proved to be one of Ashby's scouts, and the remainder of the party were all captured. But notwithstanding the personal bravery of our men, disaster and defeat had attended our operations in the Valley. Nor was this the only field of disastrous changes. On the Peninsula sieges had been laid and raised, terrible battles fought, won, and lost, and thousands of our brave comrades had succumbed to the impure water and miasmatic condition of the country. The rebel General J. E. B. Stuart had astounded every body by a raid around our entire army, cutting off communications, destroying stores, and capturing not a few prisoners. On the second of July this jaded army found a resting place at Harrison's Landing on the James River.

Chapter V - Pope's Campaign in Northern Virginia.

1862.—Kilpatrick at Beaver Dam.—Captain John S. Mosby.—Return of the Raiders.—Complimentary Orders.—The Harris Light at Anderson's Turnout.—Rebel Account of the Scare.—General John P. Hatch, his Misfortunes and Justification.— Reconnoissances.—Battle of Cedar Mountain.—Hospital at Culpepper.—General Stuart in Close Quarters.—His Adjutant-General Captured.—Death of Captain Charles Walters.—Pope driven back and waiting for Reinforcements.—Kilpatrick's Fight at Brandy Station.—Waterloo Bridge.—Bristoe Station.—Manassas Junction.—Battle of Groveton.—Second Bull Run.—Chantilly and Death of Kearny.— General Pope resigns.

Our prospects as a nation were any thing but promising about the fourth of July, 1862. Our operations in the Shenandoah Valley had been very expensive and fruitless. The Peninsular campaign, which promised so much at its beginning, which had proceeded at so fearful a cost of treasure and blood, was pronounced a failure at last, and the great armies, depleted and worn, were well nigh discouraged. The celebration of the anniversary of our national birthday was observed throughout the loyal North in the midst of gloomy forebodings, and only the pure patriotism of governors of States, and of the President of the United States, gave the people any ground of hope for success. In the army changes of leaders were occurring, which produced no little amount of jealousy among the "stars," and upon which the opinion of the rank and file was divided.

On the fourteenth of July, General John Pope, having been called from a glorious career in the West, took command of the Army of Virginia, which was a consolidation of the commands of Fremont, Banks, and McDowell.

Before General Pope left Washington, he ordered General Rufus King, who was in command at Fredericksburg, to make a raid on the Virginia Central Railroad, for the purpose of destroying it at as many points as possible, and thus impede communications between Richmond and the Valley. This work was committed to our regiment.

July 19.—About six o'clock this evening the Harris Light was set in rapid motion almost directly south. By means of a forced march of forty miles through the night, at the gray dawn of the morning we descended upon Beaver Dam dépôt, on the Virginia Central, like so many ravenous wolves upon a broken fold. Here we had some lively work. The command was divided in several squads, and each party was assigned its peculiar and definite duty. So while some were destroying culverts and bridges, others were playing mischief with the telegraph wires; others still were burning the dépôt, which was nearly full of stores, and a fourth party was on the lookout. During our affray we captured a young Confederate officer, who gave his name as Captain John S. Mosby. By his sprightly appearance and conversation he attracted considerable attention. He is slight, yet well formed; has a keen blue eye, and florid complexion; and displays no small amount of Southern bravado in his dress and manners. His gray plush hat is surmounted by a waving plume, which he tosses as he speaks in real Prussian style. He had a letter in his possession from General Stuart, recommending him to the kind regards of General Lee.

After making general havoc of railroad stock and Rebel stores, we started in the direction of Gordonsville, but having ascertained that a force of Rebels much larger than our own occupied the place, we turned northward, and reached our old camp at midnight, having marched upward of eighty miles in thirty hours.

Some of us will not soon forget the ludicrous scenes which were acted out, especially in the latter portion of the raid. In consequence of the jaded condition of our horses it was necessary to make frequent halts. To relieve themselves and animals, when a halt was ordered, some men would dismount, and, sinking to the ground through exhaustion, would quickly fall asleep. With the utmost difficulty they were aroused by their comrades when the column advanced. Calling them by their names, though we did it with mouth to ear, and with all our might, made no impression upon them. In many instances we were compelled to take hold of them, roll them over, tumble them about, and pound them, before we could make them realize that the proper time for rest and sleep had not yet come.

Others slept in their saddles, either leaning forward on the pommel of the saddle, or on the roll of coat and blanket, or sitting quite erect, with an occasional bow forward or to the right or left, like the swaying of a flag on a signal station, or like the careerings of a drunken man. The horse of such a sleeping man will seldom leave his place in the column, though this will sometimes occur, and the man awakes at last to find himself alone with his horse which is grazing along some unknown field or woods. Some men, having lost the column in this way, have fallen into the enemy's hands. Sometimes a fast-walking horse in one of the rear companies will bear his sleeping lord quickly along, forcing his way through the ranks ahead of him, until the poor fellow is awakened, and finds himself just passing by the colonel and his staff at the head of the column! Of course, he falls back to his old place somewhat confused and ashamed, and the occurrence lends him just excitement enough to keep him awake for a few minutes.

It is seldom that men under these somnambulic circumstances fall from their horses, yet sometimes it does happen, and headlong goes the cavalier upon the hard ground, or into a splashing mud-puddle, while general merriment is produced among the lookers-on. But as no one is seriously injured, the "fallen brave" retakes his position in the ranks and the column proceeds as though nothing had happened. We had all these experiences in one form or another in our raid, and on reaching camp we found that several men had lost their caps by the way.

The day following our arrival at camp the general in command issued his complimentary message, namely:

Headquarters Army of Virginia,
Washington, July 21.

To Hon. E. M. Stanton, Secretary of War:

Sir: The cavalry expedition I directed General King to send out on the nineteenth instant has returned.

They left Fredericksburg at seven P. M., on the nineteenth, and after a forced march during the night made a descent at daylight in the morning upon the Virginia Central Railroad at Beaver Dam Creek, twenty-five miles north of Hanover Junction and thirty-five miles from Richmond. They destroyed the railroad and telegraph line for several miles, burned the dépôt, which contained forty thousand rounds of other musket ammunition, one hundred barrels of flour, and much valuable property, and brought in the Captain in charge as a prisoner.

The whole country round was thrown into a great state of alarm. One private was wounded on our side. The cavalry marched eighty miles in thirty hours.

The affair was most successful, and reflects high credit upon the commanding officer and his troops.

As soon as full particulars are received I will transmit to you the name of the commanding officer of the troops engaged.

I am, Sir, very respectfully,
Your obedient servant,
John Pope,
Major-General Commanding.

The above order was received with great gladness by the boys of the Harris Light, and Kilpatrick had just reasons to feel proud of his brave boys and their noble deeds. As we had done so well in this branch of business, it was natural for the commanding general to be looking out for more similar jobs for us, and, indeed, they came.

July 24.—Kilpatrick was again launched out with his men on another raid upon the Virginia Central Railroad, which, this time, we struck at Anderson Turnout. However, we did not reach the railroad before we had surprised a camp of Rebel cavalry, with which we had a sharp skirmish on the south bank of the North Anna River. But having the advantage of the enemy, we defeated them, captured their camp, with several prisoners and horses. A large quantity of camp and garrison equipage fell into our hands, which we burned. Unfortunately for us we did not come just in time to take the cars, but we created an alarm quite as extensive as that which prevailed at Beaver Dam, on our former visit. The Richmond Examiner, commenting upon the affair, gave the following truthful rendering:

ANOTHER SCARE ON THE CENTRAL ROAD.

"When the train from the west on the Central Railroad reached Frederick's Hall, a station fifty miles from this, it was met by a rumor that the Yankee cavalry had made another raid from Fredericksburg, and had possession of the track at Anderson Turnout, ten miles below Beaver Dam, and thirty miles from Richmond. The telegraph wire not being in working order, there was no means at hand of ascertaining the truth of this report. Under the circumstances the conductor, not choosing to risk the passengers and train, took an extra locomotive and ran down to Anderson's on a reconnoissance. When he reached this place he found the report of the Yankees at that point correct, but they had left several hours previous to his arrival. He learned the following particulars:

"At a quarter past nine A. M., just a quarter of an hour after the passage of train from Richmond, the Yankee cavalry, several hundred in number, made their appearance at the Turnout. Having missed the train, they seemed to have no particular object in view, but loitered about the neighborhood for a couple of hours. They, however, before taking leave, searched the house of Mr. John S. Anderson, which is near the railroad, and took prisoner his son, who is in the Confederate service, but at home on sick furlough. They also took possession of four of Mr. Anderson's horses. They made no attempt to tear up the railroad, having no doubt had enough of that business at Beaver Dam last Sunday. They did not interfere with the telegraph wire through prudential motives, shrewdly guessing that any meddling with that would give notice of their presence.

"Of the movements of our troops occasioned by this second impudent foray it is unnecessary to say any thing. The Central train reached this city at eight o'clock, three hours behind its usual time."

It is evident that we are greatly embarrassing the Rebel travelling public by our raids, destroying public property, capturing prisoners and horses, and gaining some valuable information. We have learned from contrabands and other sources that Rebel forces in considerable numbers are being transported westward over this route. Some grand movements are undoubtedly on foot. We have received word that on the fourteenth General John P. Hatch, with all his cavalry, was ordered by General Banks to proceed at once upon Gordonsville, capture the place and destroy all the railroads that centre there, but especially to make havoc of the Central road, as far east as possible, and west to Charlottesville. For some reason General Hatch was too slow in his movements, and General Ewell, with a division of Lee's army, reached the place on the sixteenth, one day ahead of Hatch. Thereupon Hatch was ordered to take from fifteen hundred to two thousand picked men, well mounted, and to hasten from Madison Court House, over the Blue Ridge, and destroy the railroad westward to Staunton. He commenced the movement; but after passing through the narrow defiles of the mountains at Swift Run Gap, he felt that there was no hope of accomplishing any thing, and returned. General Pope immediately relieved him from command, and appointed General John Buford, General Banks' chief of artillery, in his place.

After some months had elapsed, the following correspondence between General Hatch and his former command will partly vindicate, if it does not fully justify, his course:

Second Cavalry Brigade, Third Army Corps,
Near Fort Scott, Va., —— 1862.

To Brigadier-General John P. Hatch:

General: The accompanying sabre is presented to you by the officers of the First Vermont and Fifth New York Cavalry.

We have served under you while you commanded the cavalry in Virginia—a period of active operations and military enterprise—during which your courage and judgment inspired us with confidence, while your zeal and integrity have left us an example easier to be admired than imitated.

We, who have passed with you beyond the Rapidan and through Swift Run Gap, are best able to recognize your qualities as a commander.

Accept, therefore, General, this testimonial of esteem offered long after we were removed from your command,—when the external glitter of an ordinary man ceases to affect the mind, but when real worth begins to be appreciated.

On behalf of the officers of the Fifth New York,

Robert Johnstone,
Lieutenant-Colonel, Fifth New York Cavalry.

To the Officers of the Fifth New York and First Vermont Regiments of Cavalry:

Oswego, N. Y., —— 1862.

Gentlemen: A very beautiful sabre, your present to myself, has been received. I shall wear it with pride, and will never draw it but in an honorable cause.

The very kind letter accompanying the sabre has caused emotions of the deepest nature. The assurance it gives of the confidence you feel in myself, and your approval of my course when in command of Banks' Cavalry, is particularly gratifying. You, actors with myself in those stirring scenes, are competent judges as to the propriety of my course, when it unfortunately did not meet with the approval of my superior; and your testimony, so handsomely expressed, after time has allowed opportunity for reflection, more than compensates for the mortification of that moment.

I have watched with pride the movements of your regiments since my separation from you. When a telegram has announced that "in a cavalry fight the edge of the sabre was successfully used, and the enemy routed," the further announcement that the First Vermont and Fifth New York were engaged, was unnecessary.

Accept my kindest wishes for your future success. Sharp sabres and a trust in Providence will enable you to secure it in the field.

Your obedient servant,
John P. Hatch,
Brigadier-General.

August 5.—The Harris Light was again sent out on a reconnoissance to the Central Railroad, which we struck on the sixth, about ten o'clock A. M., at Frederick's Hall. The dépôt, which contained large supplies of commissary and quartermaster stores, was burned. The telegraph office was also destroyed, with considerable length of wire, while the railroad track was torn and otherwise injured, principally by the fires we built upon it. In a factory near the station were found huge quantities of tobacco. The men took as much as the jaded condition of their horses would permit, and the remainder was wrapped in flames.

All this was accomplished without loss on our side. These daring and successful raids made Kilpatrick very conspicuous before the army and country. He was complimented by the general commanding both in orders and by telegraph, and his name became a synonym of courage and success. This gave wonderful enthusiasm to his men, and their devotion to him was unbounded. Wherever he led us we gladly went, feeling that however formidable the force or dangerous the position we assailed, either by main force we could overcome, or by stratagem or celerity we could escape. This gave our young hero a double power.

August 8.—To-day Kilpatrick was ordered with his regiments to reconnoitre in the direction of Orange Court House. He advanced by way of Chancellorsville and old Wilderness Tavern; but on approaching the Court House we found it occupied by a heavy force of the enemy. It is evident that the Rebel army is advancing with a show of fight towards the upper fords of the Rapidan, where, we understand, Generals Buford and Bayard are picketing. After ascertaining all we could about present and prospective movements, we returned to our old camp, having made a swift and tedious march.

BATTLE OF CEDAR MOUNTAIN.

On the ninth was fought the memorable battle of Cedar or Slaughter's Mountain, in which both sides claimed the victory. The Confederates certainly had the advantage of position, having taken possession of the wooded crest before the arrival of our advance; and they also greatly outnumbered the Union ranks. But their loss was nearly double our own, and nearly the same ground was occupied by the combatants at night, which each held in the beginning of the fight. The cavalry was not conspicuously engaged in this bloody fray, except such portions of it as were escort or body-guard to officers in command, and among these some were killed. The main cavalry force watched the flanks, doing good service there.

August 10.—At an early hour of the day the Harris Light was ordered to report at Culpepper Court House, and we were soon on the march. On arriving

41

at our destination we found the place well nigh filled with our wounded from the battle of yesterday. It is estimated that not less than fifteen hundred of our men were killed and wounded, about a thousand of the latter having found a refuge here. The seventh part of the casualties of a battle, on an average, will number the killed and mortally wounded; the others claim the especial attention of their comrades. It is heart-sickening to witness their bloody, mangled forms. All the public buildings and many private residences of this village are occupied as hospitals, and the surgeons with their corps of hospital stewards and nurses are doing their work, assisted by as many others as have been detailed for this purpose, or volunteer their services. The Rebel wounded who have fallen into our hands receive the same attention that is bestowed upon our own men, many of them acknowledging that they are far better off in our care than they would be among their confederates.

These hospitals are all much more quiet than one would naturally suppose. How calmly the brave boys endure the wounds they have received in defence of their beloved country! Only now and then can be heard a subdued sob, or a dying groan; while those who are fully conscious, though suffering excruciating pain, are either engaged in silent prayer or meditation, or reading a Testament or a last letter from loved ones, and patiently awaiting their turn with the surgeon or the nurse.

In the most available places tables have been spread for the purpose of amputations. We cannot approach them, with their heaps of mangled hands and feet, of shattered bones and yet quivering flesh, without a shudder. A man must need the highest style of heroism willingly to drag himself or be borne by others to one of these tables, to undergo the processes of the amputating blade. But thanks be to modern skill in surgery, and to the discoverer of chloroform; for by these the operations are performed quickly and without the least sensation, until the poor brave awakes with the painful consciousness of the loss of limbs, which no artificer can fully replace. Thus the skill displayed and the care taken greatly mitigate the horrors of battle. Men here are wounded in every conceivable manner, from the crowns of their heads to the soles of their feet, while some are most fearfully torn by shells. It had been thought that men shot through the lungs or entrails were past cure, yet several of the former have been saved, and a few of the latter. Indeed, it would seem as though modern science was measuring nearly up to the age of miracles.

We found that a large force of cavalry was concentrating at Culpepper, awaiting new developments. Reconnoissances are of frequent occurrence, and all of them reveal that the enemy is in motion, concentrating on our front. Our picket lines are made doubly strong, and the utmost vigilance is enjoined. Scouts and spies are on the rampage, and more or less excitement prevails everywhere.

August 16.—To-day a small detachment of cavalry under Colonel Broadhead, of the First Michigan Cavalry, was despatched on a scout in the direction of Louisa Court House. Having penetrated to within the enemy's lines, and not far from the Court House, they made a swift descent upon a suspicious looking house, which proved to be General Stuart's headquarters. The general barely escaped through a back door, as it were "by the skin of his teeth," leaving a part of his wardrobe behind him. His belt fell into our hands, and several very important despatches from General Lee. Stuart's adjutant-general was found concealed in the house and captured. General Pope, in his official reports, speaks of this affair as follows:

"The cavalry expedition sent out on the sixteenth in the direction of Louisa Court House, captured the adjutant-general of General Stuart, and was very near capturing that officer himself. Among the papers taken was an autograph letter of General Robert E. Lee to General Stuart, dated Gordonsville, August fifteenth, which made manifest to me the disposition and force of the enemy and their determination to overwhelm the army under my command before it could be reënforced by any portion of the Army of the Potomac."

Had it not been for the timely discovery of this Rebel order, General Pope's army, only a handful to the multitudes which were gathering against him from the defences of Richmond, would have been flanked and probably annihilated. Assured, however, that reënforcements from McClellan's army could certainly reach him before long, General Pope held his advanced position to the last, our pickets guarding the fords of the Rapidan. On the eighteenth, the entire force of cavalry relieved the infantry pickets, and evident preparations were being made for a retreat. On the day following a sharp skirmish took place with Rebel cavalry which appeared across the narrow, rapid river. In this engagement Captain Charles Walters, of the Harris Light, was killed, and his remains were interred at midnight just as orders were received to retreat on the road to Culpepper.

The cavalry under General Bayard is acting as rear guard to our retreating columns. Stuart's cavalry, with whom we are engaged at almost every step, is vanguard of the Rebel army, which is advancing as rapidly as possible. The prospect before us is exceedingly dark. Nothing is more discouraging to a soldier than to be compelled to retreat, especially under a general whose first order on assuming command contained the following utterances:

"Meantime, I desire you to dismiss from your minds certain phrases which I am sorry to find much in vogue among you.

"I hear constantly of taking strong positions and holding them—of lines of retreat and of bases of supplies. Let us discard such ideas.

"The strongest position a soldier should desire to occupy is one from which he can most easily advance against the enemy.

"Let us study the probable lines of retreat of our opponents, and leave our own to take care of themselves. Let us look before, and not behind. Success and glory are in the advance. Disaster and shame lurk in the rear."

We all felt that the moment we begin to turn our backs to the enemy, that moment we acknowledge ourselves either outgeneraled or whipped, a thing most disheartening, and to which pride never easily condescends. Our only hope was based on early reënforcements. Should these fail us we saw nothing but defeat and disaster in our path.

Burial of Captain Walters at Midnight, During Pope's Retreat.

August 20.—While our cavalry forces were feeding their horses on the large plains near Brandy Station, about six o'clock this morning, a heavy column of Stuart's cavalry was discovered, approaching from the direction of Culpepper. Kilpatrick was ordered to attack and check this advance, which he did in a spirited manner. The Harris Light added fresh laurels to its already famous record, and made Brandy Station memorable in the annals of cavalry conflicts. Stuart's advance was not only retarded, but diverted; and it was made our business to watch closely his future movements.

On the twenty-first we reached Freeman's Ford, on the Rappahannock, which we picketed, preventing the enemy from effecting a crossing. As the fords of the river were generally heavily guarded up to this point, the enemy kept moving up the stream toward our right, evidently designing to make a flank movement upon us.

On the twenty-second a notable cavalry engagement, with light artillery, took place at Waterloo Bridge. During this fight a Rebel shell took effect in our ranks, killing instantly the three horses ridden by the three officers of the same company, dismounting the braves very unceremoniously, but injuring no one seriously. Through the darkness of the night following, Stuart, with about fifteen hundred picked cavalry, effected a crossing of the river, and after making quite a détour via Warrenton, came down unperceived through the intense darkness and the falling rain upon General Pope's headquarters near Catlett's Station. He captured the general's field quartermaster and many important documents, made great havoc among the guards, horses, and wagons, and finally escaped, without injury to himself, with about three hundred prisoners, and considerable private baggage taken from the train. His victory was indeed a cheap one, but we all felt its disgrace, which the darkness to some extent explained, but did not fully excuse.

August 23.—A severe contest occurred to-day at Sulphur Springs. The enemy is pressing us hard at every crossing of the river, and continues to move towards our right. Skirmishing occurs at nearly every hour of the day and night, occasioning more or less loss of life. Yesterday in a skirmish led by General Sigel, who had crossed the river, General Bohlen was killed, and our forces driven back to the north side of the river. While this manœuvring was going on along the Rappahannock, General Lee had despatched Stonewall Jackson, to pass around our right, which he did by crossing about four miles above Waterloo, and, on the twenty-fifth, he struck our forces at Bristoe Station, where a severe contest took place, the losses in killed and wounded being heavy on both sides. But the enemy was successful in taking possession of the railroad; and in the evening a portion of Stuart's cavalry, strengthened by two regiments of infantry, advanced to Manassas Junction, where they surprised and charged our guards, capturing many prisoners, also ten locomotives, seven trains loaded with immense quantities of stores, horses, tents, and eight cannon. They destroyed what they could not take away. The Rebel General Ewell, having followed closely in the track of Jackson, also came upon the railroad in rear of General Pope's army.

Our commander, greatly astonished at this embarrassing juncture of affairs, began to make the best disposition of his forces, to extricate himself from the toils that had been carefully laid for him; still hoping that new forces would come to his aid from McClellan's army via Alexandria. But "hope deferred made his heart sick," and he was compelled to encounter the immense Rebel hosts, not only massed on his front, but also lapping on his flanks, and penetrating, as we have seen, even to his rear. The situation was critical in the extreme; and had not the available forces behaved themselves with undaunted courage and, at times, with mad desperation, the disaster would have been unprecedented.

Several unimportant and yet hotly contested battles were fought at Sulphur Springs, Thoroughfare Gap, Bristoe Station, etc., and early on the morning of the twenty-ninth commenced the battle of Groveton, by some called the second Bull Run. The Rebels were in overwhelming numbers, though driven

45

badly during the earlier hours of the day; and had Fitz-John Porter brought his forces into the action, the victory must have been ours. The cavalry, though quiet most of the day, made an important charge in the evening. The carnage had been terrible, and the fields were strewn with the dead and dying. It is estimated that the casualties would include not less than seven thousand men on our side alone; and it is fair to suppose that the enemy has lost not less than that number.

August 30.—Our lines having fallen back during the night, the battle was renewed to-day on the field of the first Bull Run. But the fates were again against us, and, though not panic-stricken, our men retired from the field at night, until they rested themselves on the heights of Centreville. The enemy did not follow us very closely, not attempting even to cross Bull Run.

On the thirty-first General Pope expected to be attacked in his strong position at Centreville, but the enemy was too cautious to expose himself in a position so advantageous to ourselves, where the repulse of Malvern Hill might have been repeated. Quiet reigned along our entire line during the day.

KEARNY'S DEATH AT CHANTILLY.

September 1.—Becoming aware that a flank movement was in operation, General Pope started his entire army in the direction of Washington. But his army had not proceeded far, before one of his columns, which had been sent to intercept the Little River Turnpike, near Chantilly, encountered Stonewall Jackson, who had led his weary, yet intrepid legions entirely around our right wing, and now contested our farther retreat. General Isaac J. Stevens, commanding General Reno's Second division, who led our advance, at once ordered a charge and moved with terrible impetuosity upon the foe; but he was shot dead, on the very start, by a bullet through his head. His command was thereupon thrown into utter disorder, uncovering General Reno's First division, which was also demoralized and broken.

Just at this critical moment, General Philip Kearny, who was leading one of General Heintzelman's divisions, advanced with intrepid heart and unfaltering step upon the exultant foe. This was during a most fearful thunder-storm, so furious that with difficulty could ammunition be kept at all serviceable, and the roar of cannon could scarcely be heard a half dozen miles away. The Rebel ranks recoiled and broke before this terrible bolt of war. Just before dark, while riding too carelessly over the field and very near the rebel lines, Kearny was shot dead by one of the enemy's sharpshooters. His command devolved upon General Birney, who ordered another charge, which was executed with great gallantry, driving the enemy from the field, and defeating the great flanker in his attempts farther to harass our retreating columns. But our success had been dearly bought. Two generals had been sacrificed, and Kearny especially was lamented all over the land. Of him the poet sings:

"Our country bleeds
With blows her own hands strike. He starts, he heeds
Her cries for succor. In a foreign land
He dwells; his bowers with luxury's pinions fanned,
His cup with roses crowned. He dashes down
The cup, he leaves the bowers; he flies to aid
His native land. Out leaps his patriot blade!
Quick to the van he darts. Again the frown
Of strife bends blackening; once again his ear
War's furious trump with stern delight drinks in;
Again tho Battle-Bolt in red career!
Again the flood, the frenzy, and the din!
At tottering Williamsburg his granite front
Bears without shook the battle's fiercest brunt.
So have we seen the crag beat back the blast,
So has the shore the surges backward cast.
Behind his rock the shattered ranks re-form;
Forward, still forward, until dark defeat
Burns to bright victory!
Fame commands
The song; we yield it gladly; but the glow
Fades as we sing. The dire, the fatal blow
Fell, fell at last. Full, full in deadliest front
Leading his legions, leading as his wont,
The bullet wafts him to his mortal goal!
And not alone War's thunders saw him die;
Amid the glare, the rushing, and the roll,
Glared, crashed, the grand dread battle of the sky!
There on two pinions,—War's and Storm's,—he soared
Flight how majestic! up! His dirge was roared
Not warbled, and his pall was smoke and cloud;
Flowers of red shot, red lightnings strewed his bier,
And night, black night, the mourner.
Now farewell,
O hero! In our Glory's Pantheon
Thy name will shine, a name immortal won
By deeds immortal! In our heart's deep heart
Thy statued fame, that never shall depart,
Shall tower, the loftier as Time fleets, and show

How Heaven can sometimes plant its Titans here below."

General Pope, during all the day, and most of the night, hastened his retreat, and on the second of September, his broken and demoralized columns found rest and rations within the fortifications which guard the approaches to Washington. Thus ended General Pope's brief and trying career as commander of the Army of Virginia. Here he resigned his command, and was succeeded by General McClellan.

Chapter VI - Rebel Invasion of Maryland

1863.—Result of Pope's Campaign.—Best and Recruit at Hall's Hill.—"My Maryland:" Its Invasion.—Offensive Policy of the Rebellion.—Pennsylvania and the Whole Country Aroused.—Battle of South Mountain.—Harper's Ferry.—Colonel Miles.—His Treachery and Death.—Bloody Battle of Antietam.—Drilling Recruits.— The Harris Light again at the Front.—At Chantilly.—Sudley Church.—Leesburg.— McClellan again Relieved from Command.

By the almost continual fighting of General Pope's campaign, our ranks had been greatly depleted. Of the cavalry in general one correspondent makes the following remark: "They picket our outposts, scout the whole country for information, open our fights, cover our retreats, or clear up and finish our victories, as the case may be. In short, they are never idle, and rarely find rest for either men or horses." We had felt the influence of this wear and tear so sadly, that our once full and noble regiment was now reduced to about three hundred and fifty men, scarcely one third of our original number. Nearly every regiment of cavalry which had participated in the misfortunes of the campaign, had suffered a like decimation. To replenish our weakened ranks and to infuse new vigor and discipline into the various commands, became a question of no little moment. Consequently a large number of regiments, under the direct supervision of General Bayard, were ordered to Hall's Hill, about ten miles from Washington, where we established camps of instruction and drill. During the disasters of the Peninsular campaign, and the subsequent defeats and retreats from the Rapidan to the Potomac, the country had awakened to the importance of increasing the army by new organizations, and of filling up the broken ranks by fresh levies of recruits. This feeling was greatly intensified by the exposure of Washington to the victorious and advancing enemy, and by the invasions of Northern soil, which the triumphs of the Rebellion made imminent. Hence multitudes of recruits were pouring into Washington principally, and into other places, gladly donning the uniform, and eager to learn the duties, of the soldier. Camps of instruction were, of course, necessary. And as the attention of young men was turning very favorably to the cavalry service, our camps at Hall's Hill were the scenes of daily arrivals of fine specimens of patriots, whose hands were warmly grasped by us; and gladly we initiated them into the mysteries of this new science. We were not a little elated at the epithet of "Veteran," which these recruits lavished upon us. The experiences and labors of our old camps "Oregon" and "Sussex" were repeated with somewhat of new combinations and interests, as we sought to prepare ourselves and others more thoroughly than before to meet the foe in coming campaigns.

We had scarcely reached our new camps and entered upon our new labors, when we learned that General Lee was marching his confident hosts into Maryland. This movement at first was regarded as a feint only, with the intention of uncovering Washington; but as column after column was known to have crossed the Potomac, and to be advancing through the State with more or less rapidity, the tocsin of alarm was sounded everywhere, and a general movement was made to repel the invaders. Pennsylvania was thoroughly aroused, and her loyal and true governor issued a proclamation calling upon all the able-bodied men of the Commonwealth to organize for defence. The militia promptly responded to the call, and military preparations were going on, not only in the old Keystone State, but throughout the land.

Up to this time the attitude of the Rebels had been defensive, but their recent great victories had led them to change their tactics, and thinking that ultimate success was almost within their grasp, they now assumed the offensive policy. Aside from this consideration they doubtless hoped to awaken in the Border States a sympathy and an enthusiasm on their behalf, which thus far they had failed to create; and that their brilliant march northward would not only carry a strong political influence, but that their ranks would be greatly swollen by accessions of recruits from those States. This indication of Rebel thought is evidently found in the address which General Lee issued to the people of Maryland on the eighth day of September. In it are found the following sentences:

"The people of the Confederate States have long watched with the deepest sympathy the wrongs and outrages that have been inflicted upon the citizens of a Commonwealth allied to the States of the South by the strongest social, political, and commercial ties, and reduced to the condition of a conquered province. * * *

"Believing that the people of Maryland possess a spirit too lofty to submit to such a Government, the people of the South have long wished to aid you in throwing off this foreign yoke, to enable you again to enjoy the inalienable rights of freemen, and restore the independence and sovereignty of your State.

"In obedience to this wish, our army has come among you, and is prepared to assist you with the power of its arms in regaining the rights of which you have been so unjustly despoiled."

But the fond hopes which prompted this address were destined to be blasted. Lee's advancing columns met no resistance, and marched directly upon Frederick City, where recruiting offices were opened under the superintendence of General Bradley T. Johnson, who had left this city, at the beginning of the war, to serve in the Rebel army. But the Confederate chiefs were disappointed. The number who were marshalled under their stars and bars did not exceed the number of those who, tired of training in Rebel gray, deserted their banner.

The enemy's peaceful march through the State and its quiet possession were not of long duration; and the invaders soon found other work to do, than to make political orders and harangues, and to increase their ranks by recruits. From Washington the Union army began to advance with considerable strength and determination, compelling General Lee to relinquish his design of penetrating into Pennsylvania. Initiatory steps were now being taken for a great battle, the first encounter of which took place, under General Pleasonton, who commanded our cavalry during this campaign, at the Catoctin Creek, in Middletown, Maryland. The enemy's rearguard, consisting of cavalry, was struck with some force, the prelude of the battle of South Mountain, at Turner's Gap. The enemy having taken possession of this mountain pass, was driven from it only after the most obstinate resistance and severe loss, and forced to leave only before superior numbers. This occurred on the fourteenth; and the victory, though somewhat dearly bought, inspired our troops with new courage, and gave them a foretaste of better days.

HARPER'S FERRY AND ANTIETAM.

But during the day we have received sad tidings from Harper's Ferry, a point of no little importance to the invaders. Unfortunately for us the place was under the command of Colonel Miles, who, for his drunkenness and general incompetency, had made himself conspicuous during the first battle of Bull Run. Why such a man was left in command of at least ten thousand men, and at a place of so much interest, cannot well be accounted for.

Aware as he must have been several days ago, that this position was a coveted prize and would undoubtedly be assailed, he neither retreated, nor fortified himself as he easily could have done to hold out for a long time against a superior force. Nothing but imbecility or treachery could have controlled his conduct. On the eleventh his command was increased largely by a force under General Julius White, who had evacuated Martinsburg on the approach of Stonewall Jackson.

50

But to-day he was attacked from various positions, and his forces driven; and on the fifteenth, being attacked from at least seven commanding positions, early in the day the white flag was raised, which the enemy failing to see, continued to fire for several minutes, during which time Colonel Miles was killed, some say by a Rebel shell, others assert by some of his own men. By this shameful surrender there fell into the hands of the enemy nearly twelve thousand men, half of them New Yorkers, who had just entered the service; also seventy-three guns good and bad; thirteen thousand small arms; two hundred wagons, and a large supply of tents and camp equipage.

Stonewall Jackson, who had commanded the expedition from Frederick to Harper's Ferry, now moved forward to join Lee's main army, which he did on the sixteenth. From South Mountain General McClellan began to collect his forces well in hand and to move towards Boonsborough. Here General Pleasonton again struck the Rebel cavalry rearguard, capturing two hundred and fifty prisoners and two field-pieces. Infantry supports were following our cavalry very closely, and, after marching about twelve miles, they discovered the Rebels in force posted on the south bank of Antietam Creek, just in front of the little village of Sharpsburg. Our troops entered into bivouacs for the night, expecting to attack the enemy early next morning. But the morning and most of the day passed in idleness, while the Rebels were fortifying their positions, and gathering their forces which had been more or less scattered. Had McClellan ordered an advance that morning early, the sixteenth of September, 1862, would have witnessed a comparatively easy and complete victory.

At four o'clock P. M., General Joseph Hooker was sent out on the right. Moving at a sufficient distance to keep out of sight of the Rebel batteries, he forded the Antietam, and, soon afterward turning sharply to the left, came down upon the enemy near the road to Hagerstown. But darkness soon coming on put a speedy end to the conflict.

September 17.—This day has witnessed the grand and glorious battle of Antietam, the particulars of which I need not record. It is enough to say, that the daring of our men and their heroic deeds upon this field, wiped out forever, in Rebel blood, the disgrace and foul stain cast upon our arms in the momentous military blunders and defeats which have followed us since the beginning of this great American conflict.

The losses were heavy on both sides, but the enemy was fairly beaten, and driven from his chosen positions; and night closed the most sanguinary day ever known to the American continent. McClellan ought to have followed up his victory early next morning, but hesitating, the enemy made good his escape across the Potomac, leaving only his dead and desperately wounded, the latter numbering about two thousand, in our hands.

October 4.—We are still in our camps at Hall's Hill, teaching and learning the tactics of war. To-day Kilpatrick detailed me to act as drill-master, and gave me the command of a detachment of recruits. This gives me a new phase of army experience, and though it has its difficulties, as one will always find when he endeavors to control "men of many minds," yet I find a good exercise of my little knowledge of human nature, and realize that the influence of my new labor upon myself is very salutary. I had thought that I was master of all the preliminary steps of the science and art of a soldier's discipline, but in endeavoring to teach the same to others, I have learned so much myself, that it now seems to me that what I knew before was the merest rudiment. This I learn is the experience of others who are engaged in similar work. Helping others has a wonderful reflex influence upon ourselves. I often wonder if this may no explain in part the philosophy of that passage of Holy Writ, which says, "It is more blessed to give than to receive." In this exercise of drilling, and in the comparative monotony of camp life, we spent the month of October.

All was quiet along the entire lines of the great armies. Our ranks had been greatly swollen by new accessions; yet General McClellan was constantly calling for reënforcements, and all kinds of supplies, alleging that the army was in no condition to move. At length about the twenty-sixth of October a feeble advance was made across the Potomac. Several days were spent in putting the Federal army on the sacred soil and under marching orders. No opposition was encountered in the march. Our forces moved along the east side of the Blue Ridge, the enemy still occupying the Shenandoah Valley, and moving southward on a line parallel with our own.

November 2.—The Harris Light broke camp at Hall's Hill and advanced to the Chantilly Mansion, bivouacking on its beautiful grounds. This property is said to be owned by one of the Stuarts, who is reported to be a quartermaster-general in the Rebel service. Pleasant as was the place, with its fine walks, bordered with flowers and evergreen shrubbery; its fruitful gardens and groves, the cold of the night made our stay not the most agreeable. The next morning we pursued our line of march to Sudley Church, near Bull Run, where we encountered a strong force of Stuart's cavalry. After a sharp conflict, in which Yankee ingenuity and grit were fairly tested, the chivalry retired southwestwardly, acknowledging themselves badly defeated.

November 4.—To-day the regiment was ordered to move to Leesburg, near which we pitched our shelters. This is an old, aristocratic village, the shire-town of Loudon County. It is situated in a lovely valley, at the terminus of the Loudon and Hampshire Railroad, and is only about two miles from the Potomac, and an equal distance from Goose Creek, which is a considerable stream. Though this county sent many brave men into the Union ranks, probably more than any other county of the same population in Virginia, yet Leesburg is almost a fac-simile of Charlestown, the capital of Jefferson County, the scene of John Brown's execution, where all the people, including women and children, are "secession to a man."

All this while the Grand Army of the Potomac was moving southward at a snail's pace; and on the seventh of November, just after reaching Warrenton, General McClellan was relieved from command, and directed to report to the authorities by letter from Trenton, New Jersey. Thus ended another indecisive campaign, which though it had witnessed a greater victory than ever won before, yet had failed to reap the fruits thereof.

Chapter VII - McClellan Succeeded By Burnside.

1862—Burnside's First Campaign.—Army of the Potomac in Three Divisions.— Advance from Warrenton to Falmouth.—General Stahel's Raid to the Shenandoah.— Laying Pontoons across the Rappahannock under Fire.—Battle of Fredericksburg— Daring Feats and General Heroism.—Death of General Bayard.—The Hospitals.— Sanitary and Christian Commissions.—Camp "Bayard."—Camp-Fires.—Winter Quarters.—Friendly Relations of Pickets.—Trading.—Pay-Day.—"Stuck in the Mud."

Upon General Ambrose Burnside fell the choice of the Executive for commander of the great Union army. He assumed it with great reluctance and unfeigned self-distrust, and only as a matter of obedience to orders. This change in the commanding officer, deleterious and dangerous as it might be upon the morale of the army, was nevertheless considered necessary and expedient.

Having secured, by somewhat formidable forces, the principal gaps or passages of the Blue Ridge, which had been occupied by the enemy since their advance into the Valley, General Burnside began to make preparations to move his army to Fredericksburg, as being the most feasible and direct line from Washington to Richmond. To mask as long as possible his real design, he threatened an attack upon Gordonsville; but General Lee, by the aid of his emissaries and raiders, soon ascertained his plans, and moving his army across the Blue Ridge, through the western passes, he took his position on the south bank of the Rappahannock, to prevent Burnside's crossing.

November 8.—The Harris Light broke camp at Leesburg early in the morning, and advanced to White Plains, where we encountered and defeated a detachment of Rebel cavalry, driving them towards the mountains. Continuing our journey through this pleasant valley between the Blue Ridge and the Bull Run mountains, we soon joined our main army, whose headquarters were at Warrenton. This is the most beautiful village in this region of country, situated on the crest of fruitful hills, and elegantly laid out. It is the shire-town of

Fauquier County. Here a few days were consumed in effecting the alterations incident upon a change of commander, and on the fourteenth the Army of the Potomac was constituted into three grand divisions, to be commanded respectively by Generals Sumner, Franklin, and Hooker. The following day Warrenton was abandoned, and the army swept down towards the Rappahannock. The sight was a grand one. On our march, orders were received from President Lincoln enjoining a stricter observance of the Sabbath in the army and navy, than had been done before. As a general thing the Sabbath had not been regarded as any more than any other day. Indeed, very few men in the rank and file kept any calendar of time, and seldom knew the date or day. This was occasionally the case even with officers. The only possible way of keeping pace with flying time in the army, is by writing a diary. But even when it was known that the Sabbath had been reached, no regard was taken of its sacred character. One of the causes of our disaster at the first battle of Bull Run was supposed by many to be, that we had desecrated the holy Sabbath by our attack. However true or false such a view may have been, the order we received to-day from Washington was universally felt to be opportune.

Two days' march brought our advance to Falmouth, and on the twenty-first General Patrick, our provost-marshal general, was directed to repair to Fredericksburg under a flag of truce, and request the surrender of the city. The authorities replied, that while its buildings and streets would no longer be used by Rebel sharp-shooters to annoy our forces across the river, its occupation by Yankee troops would be resisted to the last. Had the means of crossing the river been at hand, General Burnside would have made hostile demonstrations at once; but through some misunderstanding between himself and General Halleck, at Washington, the pontoons were not in readiness.

November 28.—A strong force of Rebel cavalry, under General Wade Hampton, dashed across the river at some of the upper fords, raided up around Dumfries and the Occoquan, captured several prisoners and wagons, and returned to their side of the river without loss. As a sort of offset to this, on the twenty-ninth, General Julius Stahel, who commanded a brigade of cavalry at Fairfax Court House, commenced an expedition of great daring and success, to the Shenandoah Valley. Having advanced to Snicker's Gap in the Blue Ridge, a strong Rebel picket-post was captured by our vanguard. Pressing forward on the main thoroughfare, they soon reached the Shenandoah river, and were not a little annoyed by Rebel carbineers, hidden behind old buildings across the stream. Captain Abram H. Krom, commanding a detachment of the Fifth New York Cavalry, and leading the advance, dashed across the river, though deep and the current swift, closely followed by his men. On reaching the opposite bank, a charge was ordered, and executed in so gallant a manner that several Rebels were made prisoners, and the remainder of the squad was driven away at a breakneck speed. Our men pursued them in a scrambling race for nearly three miles, when they came upon a Rebel camp, which was attacked in a furious manner. Our boys made noise enough for a brigade, though only a squadron was at hand. The enemy attempted a defence, but utterly failed. Reënforcements coming to our aid, the Rebels were thoroughly beaten and driven away, leaving in our hands one captain, two lieutenants, thirty-two privates, one stand of colors, and several wagons and ambulances. Most of these were laden with booty taken by White's guerillas in a recent raid into Poolesville, Maryland. Sixty horses and fifty heads of cattle were also captured in this gallant charge. With all their spoils the expedition returned, via Leesburg, arriving at their camps in safety.

But all eyes were turned expectantly towards Fredericksburg, with its two vast armies preparing for a grand encounter. Nearly all the citizens of the city had left their homes and fled southward. While General Burnside waited for his pontoons, General Lee was fortifying the Heights in rear of the city, and concentrating his forces for the anticipated onset. This state of things was greatly regretted.

December 11.—The laying of the pontoons commenced in the night, but the task was only partially performed when daylight made the sappers and miners at work a fair mark for the sharpshooters, who were hidden among the buildings which lined the opposite shore, and whose numbers had largely increased within a few days. Battery after battery was opened on Falmouth Heights, until not less than one hundred and fifty guns, at good range, were belching fire and destruction upon the nearly tenantless city, and still the sharpshooters prevented the completion of the pontoons, and disputed our crossing. At this critical moment the Seventh Michigan regiment of infantry immortalized their names. Failing, after some entreaty, to secure the assistance of the engineer corps to row them across, they undertook the perilous labor themselves, and amid the rattling of bullets and the cheers and shouts of our own men, they reached the opposite shore, with five of their number killed, and sixteen wounded, including Lieutenant-Colonel Baxter. They immediately dashed through the streets of the city, and being quickly reënforced by other regiments, they soon cleared the rifle-pits and buildings adjacent to the stream of all annoyance. Foremost among the noble men who performed this heroic work was the Rev. Arthur B. Fuller, chaplain of the Sixteenth Massachusetts infantry, who was killed by a rifle-shot.

Our pontoons were now laid in quietness to the city; and about three miles below General Franklin laid his pontoons without opposition. Several bridges were thus constructed, and before night the main body of infantry and cavalry filed across the river, preparatory to a grand engagement. On the twelfth General Bayard moved his cavalry down the river six miles, and was posted on picket. Several shots were exchanged with the Rebel pickets during the day, and the demon of fight seemed to exist everywhere.

December 13.—The night had been cold, and the morning was dimmed by a heavy fog which covered friend and foe. But orders for an attack upon the formidable works of the enemy had been given, and even before the mist arose, General Gibbon opened fire with his heavy artillery, which was responded to, but without much effect, owing to the fog, which, however, disappeared about eleven o'clock. The engagement now became general, and the fighting was of a character more desperate and determined than ever known before.

The line of Rebel fortifications was so far back from the river, that our artillery, posted on the Falmouth Heights, was out of range, and made more havoc in our advancing ranks than in the ranks of the enemy, until the fire was silenced by order of General Burnside. About one o'clock, one of the most brilliant movements of the day was performed by General George G. Meade's division, which by a terrific charge, gained the crest of the hill, which was near the key of the position. But not being sufficiently supported, they were compelled to retire, bringing away several hundred prisoners with them.

Another masterpiece of gallantry was presented nearer the town, at Marye's Heights, where General Meagher's Irish Brigade repeatedly charged the Rebel works, until at least two-thirds of his stalwart men strewed the ground, killed and wounded. Brigade after brigade was ordered to take these heights, and though their ranks were mown down like grass before the scythe, in the very mouth of Rebel guns the effort was again and again made. Midway up the Heights was a heavy stone wall, behind which lay the hosts of the enemy, who delivered their fire with scarcely any exposure, sweeping down our columns as they approached. This hillside was completely strewn with our dead and disabled, and at length our assailing ranks retired, compelled to abandon their futile and murderous attempts. But in the language of General Sumner, "they did all that men could do." This could be applied to all the troops engaged. Night at length threw her sable mantle over the bloody field, covering in her sombre folds the stiffened corpses and mangled forms of not less than fifteen thousand dead and wounded, including the casualties of both armies.

Not one of all our dead fell more lamented than Major-General George D. Bayard, who was struck by a shrieking shell, dying early in the evening. He was only twenty-eight years of age, of prepossessing appearance and manners, with as brave a heart as ever bled for a weeping country, and a capacity of mind for military usefulness equal to any man in the service. Gradually he had arisen from one position of honor and responsibility to another, proving himself tried and true in each promotion, while his cavalry comrades especially were watching the developments of his growing power, with unabating enthusiasm. But "death loves a shining mark," and our hero, with his own blood, baptized the day which had been appointed for his nuptials. The recital of his early death brought tears to many eyes, and caused many a loving heart to bleed.

"Death lies on him like an untimely frost—
Upon the sweetest flower of all the field."

The night following this bloody conflict was horrible in the extreme. Every available spot or building in the city was sought for a hospital, to which the wounded were brought on stretchers by their companions. Now and then there came a poor fellow who was able to walk, supporting with one hand its bloody, mangled mate. At times two men might be seen approaching through the darkness, supporting between them their less fortunate comrade, whose bloody garments told that he had faced the foe. But many of our hospitals proved to be very unsafe refuges, into which Minié balls and broken shells would come rattling, and in some instances destroying the precious lives that had escaped—though not without suffering—the terrible and deadly shock of battle. Many of the wounded were taken across the river, and made perfectly safe and as comfortable as circumstances would permit. The Sanitary and Christian Commissions rendered very effective service, enshrining themselves in the memory of a grateful people. Their deeds of charity and mercy can never be forgotten. By their timely supplies and personal labors many lives were saved, and thousands of the wounded were comforted.

December 14.—The light of this holy Sabbath was hailed with gladness by many a poor soldier, who had suffered from the chill of the night alone upon the bloody field. The weather, however, is unusually clement for this season of the year. A little firing occurred this morning, but no general engagement resulted. This was greatly feared, for had General Lee advanced upon us, it is difficult to see how our men, though somewhat covered by the fire of our batteries from Falmouth Heights, could have recrossed the stream without fearful loss. But both armies spent most of the holy day in the sacred task of caring for the wounded and burying their dead. Monday was also spent mostly in the same employment, and in the night, so skilfully as to be unknown even to the Rebel pickets, our whole army was withdrawn to the north side of the river in perfect order and without loss. Our pontoons were then taken up. General Burnside was not willing to remain totally idle, and, after some time had elapsed, he planned another grand movement, which, with more or less opposition from his subordinates, who did not confide in his judgment, he endeavored to execute. But he had just taken the first step in the programme when he was signaled to desist by a telegram from the President, who had been informed that the temper of the army was not favorable to a general move under its present commander.

With the battle of Fredericksburg terminated the campaign of 1862, and the two great armies established their winter quarters facing each other along the line of the Rappahannock. Our camps extend for several miles along the northern shore above and below Falmouth, and the enemy occupy the south bank above and below the Heights of Fredericksburg. Indeed, nearly the whole territory between the Rappahannock and the Defences of Washington, a dark, forsaken, wilderness region, with only here and there a plantation or a village, was soon converted into a vast camping ground, and became the most populous section of Virginia.

To avoid the distant transportation of forage, the greater portion of the cavalry is encamped near Belle Plain, where government transports land with supplies from Washington. The Harris Light has established its camp on the Belle Plain and Falmouth Turnpike, about four miles from the former place, and has named it "Bayard," in honor of our lamented commander, whose fall at Fredericksburg is still a subject of universal sorrow.

It is wonderful to witness how the forests are disappearing in and around our camps. From morning till night the chopmen's axes resound from camp to camp, echoing dolefully along the river-shore and far back into the dense, dark woods. Soon after the battle of Fredericksburg, as we had no quarters, and nothing but worn and torn shelter-tents, our only way to prevent freezing at night was to cut and heap together a large number of logs, which, though green, when fully ignited made a rousing fire. These fires, numerously built in rows throughout the streets of our camps, presented, especially at night, a most beautiful and lively scene. The few trees which still remained as shelters were generally lighted up by our fires into grand chandeliers, reflecting upon our white tents a weird light of gold and green, which might have furnished the pen of the romancer, and the pencil of the artist, their most interesting plots and designs.

Around these fires gathered the comrades of many a march and battle, to discuss the experiences of the past, to applaud or censure certain men and measures, and to lay plans, and to entertain rumors with regard to future operations. The gallantry and merits of companions fallen in strife were presented by those most intimate with them; and otherwise dreary hours were pleasantly whiled away with narratives of personal encounters, of terrible sufferings of prisoners while in the hands of the enemy, and of hair-breadth escapes. These accounts were generally enlivened with extra coloring drawn from the enchanting and fairy-like scenes which surrounded the speaker, and an entire group was thrilled and electrified until frequently the night was made to ring with uproarious applause. Occasionally the friends and home scenes we have left behind us became the subjects of conversation, and it is astonishing how that word "home," with its hallowed associations, touches the tender feelings of our hearts. These colloquies often ended with the good old hymn, "Home, sweet home," and with the sound of the last bugle-call we hastened to our rest, to spend, it may be, a miserable night of cold and storm. No soldier can ever forget these camp and bivouac scenes, for they are deeply photographed upon his memory. He will often recall their ludicrous as well as romantic side, when the mud was knee-deep and over, up to within a few feet of the fire, compelling him often to stand so near the burning pile as to set his clothes on fire. In very cold weather he would freeze one side while the other burned, unless he frequently performed that military feat, changing "his base of operations." If the wind blew, making his fantastic gyrations among the tents, so that you never knew whence he would come nor whither he would go, you were sure to get your face smoked horribly.

With thousands of camps thus circumstanced, it may be conjectured that no little amount of fuel would suffice us. At first the trees were cut down without much regard to the height of the stumps, but as the forest receded from the camps, making transportation difficult, the stumps were dug up by the roots, leaving the ground perfectly smooth, and made ready for the ploughman, whenever our swords are beaten into ploughshares and our battle spears into pruning hooks. And besides the consumption of wood for fires, no little amount is used for the construction of our houses or huts. Nearly every man has suddenly become a mason or a carpenter, and the hammer, the axe, and the trowel are being plied with the utmost vigor, if not with the highest skill. Many of us, however, are astonished at the ingenuity that is displayed in this department. Large logs, notched at the ends so as to dovetail together, and sometimes hewn on the inside, compose the body of the hut. By the careful application of mud—that Virginia mortar or plaster with which every soldier is so familiar—to the crevices between the logs, a very comfortable structure is made ready for its covering and occupancy. Shelter-tents, buttoned or sewed together, form the roof, which, by the aid of talmas or ponchoes, is generally made water-proof.

Three or four men usually unite in the construction of a hut, and share one another's skill and stores. If they can afford it, they purchase of the sutlers small sheet-iron stoves, which will keep them very comfortably warm, and afford them an opportunity to do their own cooking on extra occasions, such as come with the issues of supplies from the Christian or Sanitary Commissions, or the reception of boxes from friends at home. The ordinary cooking of a company is done by men detailed for that purpose. Often good fire-places and chimneys are erected in the tents. These are sometimes made of sticks of wood laid in thick mud, or of stones or bricks taken from the foundations and remains of buildings that have been destroyed in the neighborhood of our camps. Every means is resorted to which Yankee ingenuity can devise to make our soldier-homes as comfortable and convenient as possible. Punch says, "that a Yankee baby will creep out of his

59

cradle, take a survey of it, invent an improved style and apply for a patent, before he is six months old," and this he said some time ago; what he would say now, we cannot tell. If a house has been abandoned by its inmates anywhere within our lines, it is taken as prima facie evidence that the owners must be Rebels—and it matters but little whether they are or not so long as the house stands alone; and in nearly as short a period of time as it takes to tell the story, the building is torn in pieces, and the materials are used in the construction of our huts and the stables of our horses.

The dying year left us engaged in these labors.

January 1, 1863.—The Harris Light was ordered to the Rappahannock, where we were posted on picket near Port Conway.

The Federal and Rebel pickets have mutually arranged that there shall be no firing on either side, unless an advance is undertaken. This agreement is of course among ourselves, neither approved nor disapproved at headquarters. For several days the most perfect harmony has prevailed between the blue and the gray. Yankees and Johnnies wash together in the same stream, procure water to drink and for culinary purposes from the same spring, and, curious to relate, often read the news from the same papers. Squads of soldiers from both armies may be observed seated together on either side of the Rappahannock, earnestly discussing the great questions of the day, each obstinately maintaining his views of the matters at issue.

On one occasion a soldier from our ranks took from his pocket a copy of the New York Herald, and read the Union account of one of the great battles to an attentive crowd of Rebel soldiers. When he had concluded, up sprang one of the chivalry, who brought to view a dingy copy of the Richmond Examiner, and proceeded to read his side of the story. No one was offended, and all relished the comparison of views, and then began to discuss the merits of the two accounts.

Cavalry Pickets Meeting in the Rappahannock.

During all these interviews trading was the order of the day, and a heavy business was carried on in the tobacco, coffee, and hard-tack line. There was also a special demand on the part of the Rebels for pocket-knives and canteens, these articles evidently being very scarce in Dixie.

January 12.—The weather has been very uneven since the year began. Wind, rain, sleet, and snow, singly and combined, have been our portion, and as a natural consequence, oceans of mud have thus far given Camp Bayard a most unwelcome appearance. Our only remedy is to corduroy our streets, which we do by bridging them with the straightest timber we can find. Usually this is pine, with which thousands of acres of Virginia are covered. As it is mostly of a recent growth, averaging about six inches in diameter, and shooting up to an immense height before you can reach the branches, it is well suited to our purpose.

Rough as these corduroyed streets are, they are very passable, and prevent us from sinking with our horses into a bottomless limbo. On the fourteenth of the month our picket details returned to camp, after being several days on duty. The weather is becoming delightful. The sun is often so brilliant and warm that we are compelled to seek shelter in our tents or in the fragrant shades of the woods. We are reminded of pleasant April weather in Northern New York. Under this régime of old Sol, the roads are rapidly improving, and should no adverse change occur, we may look for some important army movement.

January 21.—To-day we received two months' pay, and, as is usually the case on pay-day, the boys are in excellent spirits. Whatever trouble or difficulty the soldier may have, pay-day is a wonderful panacea, at least if his pay-roll and accounts are all satisfactory and right. But the men do not all make the same use of their money. Many on receiving the "greenbacks" hasten to Adams' Express or despatch an agent, and send home all the money we can spare. Some repair at once to their tents and enter upon gambling schemes with cards generally, or other games; and it is no uncommon thing to hear that some one has lost all he had, and has gone so far even as to borrow more, in less than twelve hours of the time he was paid. A small portion of the men visit the sutlers, those army vampires, whose quarters are converted into scenes of dissipation, drunkenness, and folly. Men whose families at home are waiting for means to live, thus waste all their wages, disgrace themselves, and cast their dependents upon the charities of the cold world.

January 22.—For about two days the army has been prepared for an advance across the Rappahannock. To-day the grand movement was commenced. Several regiments, supposing that they never again would need their winter huts, have burned or otherwise demolished them. But the weather, which was fine at the outset, has suddenly changed, and about ten o'clock at night there poured upon us, untented and unprotected, a furious storm of rain, sleet, and snow, making our condition almost unendurable. We are now left in a bed of almost fathomless mire. None of the men who flounder through these oozy roads, under the inclement sky, will ever forget the "Muddy March." We had scarcely reached the river-shore before we were compelled to return. In one instance a piece of artillery with its horses had to be abandoned, submerged so deeply in the mud that it was considered impracticable to extricate them. Men are frequently compelled to assist one another, unable to proceed alone. The ground is covered with snow, and yet the mud is so deep that it is almost an impossibility to move artillery or supplies. All our forage and rations are brought from Belle Plain on horses and pack-mules, all wheeled vehicles being entirely shipwrecked.

The Rebels appear to understand what had been our designs, and know fully the cause of our failure in the expedition. Consequently, to tantalize us, they have erected an enormous sign-board on their side of the river, but in full view of our pickets, bearing the inscription: "Stuck in the mud!"

General Burnside, beset on every hand with misfortunes and disasters, tendered his resignation, but was simply relieved, as at his own request, from the command of the Army of the Potomac.

Chapter VIII - Organization of a Cavalry Corps.

1863.—General Hooker assumes Command of the Army of the Potomac. — Demoralization.—Reorganization.—A Cavalry Corps.—General George D. Stoneman in Command.—Death of Sergeant May.—Forests of the Old Dominion.—The Cavalryman and his Faithful Horse.—Scenes in Winter Quarters.—Kilpatrick.—His Character.—Qualifications of the True Soldier.—A New Horse.—A Mulish Mule.— Kilpatrick's Colored Servants in Trouble.—Terrific Hail-Storm.—Major E. F. Cooke Honored.—Colonel Clarence Buel.

On the twenty-sixth of January, General Joseph Hooker assumed command of the Army of the Potomac, whose vicissitudes and defeats have well-nigh broken its spirit and wiped out its efficiency. The patriotic fire is burning dimly in shrines where it has blazed brightly before. The tide of military life has possibly reached its lowest ebb, and the signs of the times are ominous of ill. Desertions are reported to be fearfully large. For this many of our friends at the North are responsible. Not only do their letters speak discouraging words to the soldier, but many of them sent by express citizens' clothes, with which many of the boys quickly invest themselves, throwing away the blue, and thus disguised find their way to their false friends at home. I esteem him false to me who would thus rob me of my honor. I would rather say, "despoil me of my life, but my integrity never." Discouraging as all this depression of mind and dispersion of comrades may be, many still remain steadfast at their trust and unflinchingly go ahead in the discharge of their duty.

General Hooker's first work seems to be in the direction of checking this loosening of discipline, and in reorganizing and strengthening the bands of military order. As the infantry needed but little further solidification, the commander-in-chief turned his attention to the cavalry. In the possible efficiency of this arm of the service the general seems to have full faith. But it is currently reported that the general has said "that he has yet failed to see or hear of a dead cavalryman." Of course this cannot be strictly true, for we could cite him multitudes, including our noble Bayard, whose bravery and sacrifice of themselves upon their country's altar, are worthy of recognition at the hand of their commander. But it is quite evident that the cavalry has not yet come up to the beau-ideal of the general. And, indeed, it has been a source of wonderment to us, that while the efficiency of the infantry is known to depend largely upon its organization into brigades, divisions, and corps, with their general commander, the same may not be true of the cavalry.

General Bayard, the great cavalry chief of the Army of the Potomac during General Burnside's administration, made several efforts at consolidation, resulting, however, in no very permanent changes. It was reserved for General Hooker to bring about the desired result; and, at last, the Cavalry Corps of the Army of the Potomac is organized, with General George D. Stoneman for its commanding officer. By this change regiments which have been scattered here and there on detached service are brought together, and made to feel the enthusiasm which numbers generally inspire, especially when those numbers are united into a system, with a living head, whose intelligence and authority control the whole.

Under this new régime some very beneficial changes have been wrought. Schools or camps of instruction have been established, with a more rigid discipline than before, and boards of examination, with all the experience of the past before their eyes, have been organized. Old and incompetent officers have been dismissed, or have slunk away before this incisive catechism, giving way generally to intelligent, young, and efficient men, who, placed at the heads of regiments and brigades, give promise of success in the struggles that await us.

The Rebel cavalry under Stuart has long been organized into an efficient body, which, at times, has sneered at our attempts to match them; and yet they have been made to feel, on some occasions, that we are a growing power, which time and experience may develop into something formidable. But the general successes of the Rebel army have made them all very insolent, in the hope that final victory is already in their grasp.

February 11.—My old friend and comrade, Sergeant Theodore May, of Pittstown, New York, died this afternoon at two o'clock, after a brief illness, of typhoid fever, which is a great scourge throughout the army. The death of this valiant fellow-soldier casts a deep gloom over the entire command, in which he has so faithfully served. When we entered the army together at the organization of the regiment, he came a perfect stranger, but his gentle manners and soldierly deportment soon made for him hosts of warm friends. By his gallantry on the field of battle, as well as by the gentleness of his manners and his unblemished conduct in camp, he has won the respect, and even admiration, of all who knew him.

The patriotic motives which induced Sergeant May to quit his pleasant home in the beautiful valley of the Tomhannock, for the privations, hardships, and dangers of military life, have always proved him to be a true and warm sympathizer in his country's cause. It was evidently not the mere love of adventure, or the mere pageantry or glory of war, that led him to make the great sacrifice. He has been with us in every conflict, and shared with us the varied fortunes of the Harris Light. His death, which he would rather have met on the field of strife, battling manfully against traitors, was reserved for the calm and quiet of the camp, where he spent his last moments urging his comrades to "cheer up and fight on," offering as his dying reason, that "our cause is just, and must triumph." Such a death is a rich legacy to a command. "He being dead, yet speaketh." We would emulate his virtues.

February 12.—On recommendation of Lieutenant Frederick C. Lord, I was to-day appointed by Colonel Kilpatrick First Sergeant of Company E, vice Henry Temple, promoted to Sergeant Major. My appointment is to date from the first of January, making me a very desirable New Year's gift, which I shall strive to honor.

February 22.—Snow has been falling uninterruptedly the livelong day, and yet the boys have been unusually merry, as they were wont to be on this anniversary before the war. Our celebration has been on a scanty scale, and yet we have felt the patriotic stimulus which comes from the great men and days of the past. And truly, the birth of the great Washington gives birth to many interesting thoughts, especially at this period of our history. A national salute has been fired from our fortifications on the Potomac, and the whole country round about us has been made to reverberate with the sound that welcomes in the day.

But all these patriotic manifestations have not prevented the snow-storm and the cold. When we left our home in the North for what was termed "the sunny South," we little expected to find such storms as this here. While the summers are much cooler than we expected to find them, the days being generally fanned by a beautiful sea-breeze, the winters exceed for cold our highest expectation. The cold is not continuous, but very severe. We have seen the soft ground and water-puddles freeze sufficiently in one night to bear a horse; and in several days and nights the frost has penetrated the earth several inches deep. The snow-storm of to-day is as severe as most storms experienced in the North. The wind has howled from the north-west, burdened with its cold, feathery flakes, which to-night lie at least twelve inches deep in places undisturbed. It is such a storm as our suffering pickets, and indeed our entire army, cannot soon forget.

It may be that the vast forests of Virginia have much to do with its peculiar temperature. As we travel from place to place we are strongly impressed with the vastness of the wilderness, which covers thousands of acres of as fine arable soil as can be found on the continent. How different is this from the notions we had formed of the Old Dominion, while reading of its early settlements, and of its great agricultural advantages. But when we look into its system of land-owning, and find that one individual monopolizes a territory sufficient for a dozen farms, and consequently neglects eleven twelfths of his acres; and then look into its even worse system of labor, we need search no farther for the causes of this backwardness in agricultural pursuits. The implements made use of here on the plantations are such as were rejected by New England farmers over half a century ago; and the methods of cultivation are a century behind the times. Slavery and land-monopoly are the incubus. Who does not sincerely hope that the time is not far distant, when the rich acres of this great State shall be properly shared by its inhabitants, and when, freed from a burden and curse which have long paralyzed their energies, instinct with new life and enterprise, the people will realize the dignity of labor? Then will the almost interminable forests disappear, and in their stead the industrious yeoman will behold his rich fields of waving grain. Then, too, along the now comparatively useless streams and swift water-courses, will spring up the factory and the mill, whose rolling wheels and buzzing spindles will bring wealth and prosperity to the nation. We are convinced, from what we have seen, that Virginia has water-power enough to turn the machinery of the world. With these changes the school-house will be found by the side of every church, and intelligence and virtue will bless the home of the Presidents. We have also many times been led to think, while lying in these chilly woods, that a greater warmth would be imparted to the atmosphere if the forest-trees were felled and the land put under cultivation,—a change sufficiently great to be appreciable throughout the State.

"UNCHRONICLED HEROES."

Sunday, March 1.—The usual Sunday morning inspection was omitted on account of rain. Rain, rain had fallen for many days almost incessantly. The regiment has been earnestly at work throughout the day in building stables for the horses, which have suffered greatly from being kept standing too long in the mud. Under these circumstances our horses are afflicted with the scratches, many of them so badly as to render them unserviceable, and occasionally they lose their lives.

By this cause and through hard work my little black mare, which I drew by lot at Camp Sussex in the autumn of 1861, has at last succumbed, and, with a grief akin to that which is felt at the loss of a dear human friend, I have performed the last rite of honor to the dead. The Indian may love his faithful dog, but his attachments cannot surpass the cavalryman's for his horse. They have learned to love one another in the most trying vicissitudes of life, and the animal manifests affection and confidence quite as evidently as a human being could. The cavalier, it is true, is often compelled to drive at a most fearful rate, as when bearing hurried despatches, or making a charge, frequently causing almost immediate blindness to the animal. Or, may be, he continues on a march for many days and nights in succession, as on a raid, averaging at least sixty-five miles in twenty-four hours, with little water and less forage; unable to remove the saddle, which has to be tightly bound, until the animal is so badly galled that the hair comes off with the blanket at its first removal. Sufferings like these often cause the death of a large proportion of a command; and to a careless looker-on these things would appear to be mere neglects. But these cruel military necessities only develop more perfectly the rider's sympathy for his suffering beast, and bind them in closer and more endearing bonds.

Some men had rather injure themselves than have their horses harmed, and the utmost pains are taken to heal them in case they are wounded. Each regiment has its veterinary surgeon, whose skill is taxed to the utmost in his branch of the healing art.

Among the most touching scenes we have witnessed, are those in which the mortally wounded horse has to be abandoned on the field of carnage. With tearful eyes the rider and perhaps owner turns to take a last look of the "unchronicled hero," his fellow-sufferer, that now lies weltering in his blood, and yet makes every possible effort to follow the advancing column. The parting is deeply affecting.

Often the cavalryman finds no object to which he may hitch his horse for the night save his own hand; and thus with the halter fast bound to his grasp he lies down with a stone, or perhaps his saddle, for a pillow, his faithful horse standing as a watchful guardian by his side. At times the animal will walk around him, eating the grass as far as he can reach, and frequently arousing him by trying to gain the grass on which he lies; yet it is worthy of note, that an instance can scarcely be found where the horse has been known to step upon or in anywise injure his sleeping lord. Such a scene the poet undoubtedly had in his mind when he sang:

"The murmuring wind, the moving leaves
Lull'd him at length to sleep,
With mingled lullabies of sight and sound."

Such experiences as these had taught me to love my faithful and true friend. But I found I was not the only man in the command who was bereaved of his first love. Only a few horses of the original number which we drew still remain, and several of them are either partially or totally blind, though yet serviceable. The hardships of the camp and the campaign are more destructive of animal than human flesh. Men are often sheltered from the storm when the horses are exposed, and the men are sometimes fed when the horses have to go hungry. In battle the horse is a larger mark than the man, and hence is more frequently hit, so that more than twice the number of horses fall in every engagement than men. The cavalryman is more shielded from the deadly missile than the infantryman. The horse's head and shoulders will often receive the bullet which was intended for the rider's body. This is true also of the elevated portions of the saddle, with the rolls of blankets and coats and bag of forage. A difference has also been noticed between the casualties in cavalry and infantry regiments under equal exposure. This difference is wholly explained when we consider the jolting and swift motion of the man as his horse leaps forward in the fray, making him a very uncertain mark for the enemy.

BRIGHT DAYS.

March 3.—This is the first bright day we have seen in more than three weeks. The mud around our camps, especially in the neighborhood where we water our horses, is terrible, and the roads are almost bottomless. However, long trains of forage and commissary-wagons may be seen passing to and fro, with horses and mules in mud from "stem to stern." Cavalcades of mudded horses and riders traverse the camps and adjoining fields in various directions. Large flocks of crows—the most soldier-like bird in the world—with their high-perched vedettes when alighted, and their military line of march when on the wing, afford some lessons of diversion and instruction. It would seem as if all the ravens of the United States had congregated here, having been attracted by the carrion of battle-fields and the refuse of camps. Turkey buzzards, birds which are always on the wing, and that none of us ever yet saw alighted, wheel through the air like eagles, gazing down upon us with seeming defiance. The sights are of daily occurrence.

KILPATRICK.

To-day several details were made from the regiment for brigade headquarters, where Kilpatrick, the senior colonel in the brigade, now commands. In the afternoon we raised the "stars and stripes" in front of his tent, after which three cheers were given for the flag and three for the Union. Kilpatrick was then called upon for a speech, and responded in his usually felicitous style. He is certainly an orator as well as a warrior. He speaks, too, as he fights, with dash and daring. What he has to say he says with such perspicuity that no one doubts his meaning. Frequently there are flashes of eloquence worthy of a Demosthenes. His voice and diction seem to be well-nigh faultless. His speech to-day elicited frequent outbursts of applause, and the men cheered him enthusiastically at the close, and left his quarters with a deeper affection for him than before. Strict as he is to enforce discipline, and thorough, yet he is not severe; and the men love him for his personal attention to their wants, and for his appreciation of their labors. If he gives us hard work to do in march or battle, he endures or shares with us the hardship. If by the losses of men he has sustained he is truly entitled to the nickname of "Kill Cavalry," which has been quite generally accorded to him, his men know that these casualties have fallen out in the line of duty, in bold enterprises that cost the enemy dearly, the wisdom of which will ever exculpate our loved commander from the imputation of rashness with which, by uninformed parties, he is sometimes charged.

In preparation for, and during, a battle, none can excel him. His plans are quickly made and executed, while all possible contingencies seem to have been foreseen. His selection of positions and disposition of forces always exhibits great sagacity and military genius. He generally holds his men under perfect control. His clarion voice rings like magic through the ranks, while his busy form, always in the thickest of the fight, elicits the warmest enthusiasm. His equanimity of mind seems never to be overcome by his celerity of motion, but are equally balanced. Rarely is so great prudence found blended with so undaunted courage. He has an indomitable will that cannot brook defeat. The word impossible he never knows, whatever difficulties intervene between him and duty. He feels like Napoleon, "that impossible is the adjective of fools." Added to all these mental qualifications, is that perfect physique, which makes Kilpatrick the model soldier. As an equestrian we have never seen his superior. He rides as though he had been made for a saddle. Rocks, stumps, fallen trees, brooks, and fences are nothing before him. His well-trained steeds understand him perfectly, and are never at a loss to know what is meant by the sharp spurs on their sides, whatever obstacles stand in their path. We have seen him leap over barriers where only few could follow him. To accomplish such feats the horse must have confidence in the rider as well as the rider in the horse. While in a charge, Kilpatrick has more the appearance of an eagle pouncing upon his prey, than that of a man pouncing upon a man. Then, too, he has a wonderful power of endurance. Though somewhat slender in form and delicate in mould, with complexion and eyes as light as a maiden's, yet it would seem as though his bones were iron and his sinews steel, while the whole is overlaid with gold. He is certainly compactly built. He has undoubtedly his faults, but his men fail to see them, so that to them he is as good as perfect. What so young a champion of the right may yet achieve for his country, is a matter of much hopeful conjecture among us. He is now only twenty-five years of age, having had his birth in the beautiful valley of the Clove, in Northern New Jersey, in 1838. He entered the Military Academy at West Point on the twentieth of June, 1856, and graduated with honors in 1860, just in time to be ready for the great conflict then impending. He was present at Baltimore when the mob endeavored to stop the trains for Washington, and the blood of Massachusetts men was spilt upon the streets. He there exhibited that bold intrepidity which has ever characterized his actions. He was wounded at the battle of Big Bethel, one of the first engagements of the war, where as a lieutenant he commanded Duryea's Zouaves, June eleventh, 1861. He had just recovered from his wound when he entered upon the organization of the Harris Light, and became its lieutenant-colonel.

March 5.—We had regimental drill at the usual time this morning. I rode my black pony recently drawn in place of my little black mare, deceased. This was his first experience in cavalry discipline; and I infer that the men in the front rank of the platoon, which I commanded, hoped it might be his last entry; for it must have been most emphatically evident to those who followed him that he was determined to introduce a new system of tactics, in which heels were to go up in no gentle manner at every change of movement. He is certainly the most ungovernable horse on drill I ever mounted; and nothing but long marches and raids can effectually subdue his kicking propensities. I am encouraged, however, with the consideration that such fiery metal, when properly controlled and moulded, is usually very valuable.

The rain fell so fast on the sixth, that we were prevented from drill, and recall was sounded immediately after drill-call.

Sunday, March 8.—Details from the regiment were ordered out on picket. The night had been stormy, but the day has been lovely. At such times, were it not for the mud, we would feel that we are very comfortably circumstanced. On the eleventh, in the morning, the ground was covered with snow which had fallen in the night. A brilliant sun soon dissolved the pure mantle and left us in much mire. But our attention was diverted from the going by a novel scene which we were called to witness in camp. The regiment was instructed in the best method of packing a mule, by one who has had experience in the business. The most mulish mule in the whole braying family was selected for the operation, and if we did not have some tall fun I will admit that I am no judge. A hog on ice or a bristling porcupine are bad enough, but an ugly mule outstrips them all. It seems as if the irascible animal tried to do his prettiest, flouncing around in a most laughable manner, pawing and kicking at times furiously. But the desperate Yankee teacher was not to be outwitted, and conquered him at last, when the pack was satisfactorily poised, and the ornamented mule was promenaded about camp as in triumph.

We are informed that it is the intention of the authorities to have pack-mules used in the cavalry corps henceforward in place of army wagons. The reason of this change seems to be to facilitate rapid movements or forced marches. It is the prevailing opinion, however, that the experiment will prove a failure. Too many mules would be required for this purpose, and our forage and rations would be very insecure, especially from the storms. But we will see how the thing works. At times it may be expedient.

March 12.—I had the misfortune to have my quarters burned this morning while getting out a detail for picket. All my extra clothing, equipments, and some little mementoes or valuables were speedily converted into ashes. But I immediately went to work, and with some kind assistance, which every brother-soldier is so ready to bestow, I put up a new establishment which in every respect is superior to the old. Our homes, it is true, are easily destroyed, but they are as easily replaced.

March 13.—Details from the regiment, with pack-mules, were sent out to the Rappahannock, to carry rations and forage to our pickets. The mule-train looks oddly enough, and yet through these muddy roads it seems to be a necessity.

March 14.—To-day I am doing regimental guard duty. The guard has been not a little amused by the arrest of Kilpatrick's colored servants. It was their misfortune to be discovered by Captain Southard, the officer of the day, while engaged in a fierce contest, in which their heads were used as the chief weapons of attack and defence. The blows they dealt upon each other were most terrible, reminding one of the battering-rams of old, used for demolishing the walls of forts or cities. Such ancient modes of warfare, of course, could not be tolerated here, especially as no order for battle had been promulgated from headquarters, and the captain arrested the offenders and brought them to the guard-house, where they were placed in my charge. I immediately ordered them out under guard to police camp as a punishment for their bad conduct.

While thus engaged, Kilpatrick happened to see them, and, not wishing to have his faithful servants subjected to such humiliating labor, issued an order for their immediate release from durance vile, asserting that he would be responsible for their fighting in the future, if at least they did not put their heads together more than half a dozen times a day.

The day following this laughable farce, in the afternoon, we experienced one of the most terrific storms ever known in this part of the country. The day had been quite pleasant until about two o'clock, when dark clouds began to obscure the sky, and the wind shifted from the south to the north-west. At four o'clock the elements were ready for battle, and a fierce engagement commenced. Gleaming and forked lightnings cleft the canopy, while booming thunder shook the trembling earth. The artillery of Heaven had not long been opened before the musketry commenced, and down poured a shower of hail, which came near demolishing our tents, and brought suffering and sorrow upon all unsheltered heads. Mules brayed horribly, vying with the hoarse, muttering thunder, making the camp most hideous and lonely. The wind and cold increased with every passing hour, the hail fell faster and more heavily, and night came suddenly down to hide, though not to prevent, the storm. The night was one of great suffering, especially on the lines of picket—it was bad enough anywhere.

March 23.—A beautiful sabre was presented to Major E. F. Cooke this afternoon, by the members of his old company, for his gallantry and soldierly character, which have earned his promotion. Captain O. J. Downing, of company B, made the presentation speech, in which he beautifully alluded to the happy relation which always exists between a faithful commander and his men. As a token that such relation existed between the major and those whom he had often led through perilous scenes and conflicts, their gift was presented. An appropriate response was made by the major, in which he very humbly attributed his military success thus far to the bravery of the noble men who had always stood by him, and whose gift he accepted not only as a mark of their appreciation of himself as a man, but of their devotion to the cause which he hoped, by the edge of the sabre and trust in Providence, we may yet win.

March 24.—Kilpatrick's brigade was reviewed this morning by General Gregg, who commands the Second division of the cavalry corps. Kilpatrick commands the First brigade, which is composed of the First Maine, the Tenth New York, and Harris Light. On the twenty-fifth General Gregg again reviewed us. We were ordered to turn out in "heavy marching orders," that is, with all our clothing, rations, forage or grain, and fully equipped. For some reason inspections and reviews are frequent of late. The Harris Light maintains its established reputation, as being second to none in the corps, for its efficiency in drill and discipline, and in its general appearance. The men take pride in keeping up the morale of the regiment.

March 28.—Colonel Clarence Buel is paying us a visit to-day. This gallant and noble officer, who organized and formerly commanded the Troy company of the Harris Light, has recently been promoted to the colonelcy of the Hundred and Sixty-ninth New York Infantry. The colonel has taken a temporary leave of absence from his new command for the purpose of making us a friendly call; and he is again surrounded by his old tried friends and comrades. Company E hails with pleasure its former loved captain, and though sad at his loss, still rejoices in his well-earned and merited promotion. All the men of the company showed their respect and admiration for him by falling into line upon the announcement of his arrival in camp, and thus greeted the Christian soldier. It was a very delightful and enjoyable occasion.

As a soldier, Colonel Buel stands among the bravest and the best. Always attentive to the wants of his command, his men are always the last to be out of supplies of rations or clothing. He generally exercised that fatherly care over us which called forth in return a filial love. He is dignified, and yet perfectly affable. As a commander, he is intrepid and cool, and manages his troops with admirable skill. He possesses a naturally well-balanced mind, thoroughly cultivated, and a heart always full of Christian hopefulness and benevolence. We wish him great success in his new field of labor and responsibility.

Chapter IX - Rebel Chiefs and Their Raids.

1863.—Rebel Raids by Stuart, Imboden, and Fitz-Hugh Lee.—John S. Mosby, Guerilla Chief.—His Character.—His Command.—Daring and Plunder.—Aided by Citizens.— Condition of the Country Favorable for their Depredations.—Our Picket Lines too Light.—Attacks on Pickets at Herndon Station, Cub Run, and Frying-Pan Church.— Miss Laura Ratcliffe, Mosby's Informant.—Mosby at Fairfax Court House.—Capture of General Stoughton.—Fight at Chantilly.—Mosby lauded by His Chiefs.—Mosby beaten at Warrenton Junction.—Severely whipped at Greenwich, where he loses a Howitzer captured from Colonel Baker at Ball's Bluff.

The Rebel cavalry has been very active all winter, as may be seen by the many raids which they have made, beginning as far back as December twenty-fifth, when their chief, J. E. B. Stuart, anxious to obtain something suitable with which to celebrate the holidays, crossed the Rappahannock, advanced on Dumfries, where it would seem that our boys, freezing dumb (Dumfries), suffered the raider to capture not less than twenty-five wagons, and at least two hundred prisoners. Moving boldly northward, he struck the Orange and Alexandria Railroad, burning the bridge across the Accotink Run, and from Burke's Station he swung around Fairfax Court House, and returned, by long, circuitous route, into their lines with their hard-earned spoils.

A lull of operations followed this bold holiday enterprise, until the sixteenth of February, when a party of General John D. Imboden's rangers, in the Shenandoah Valley, made a rapid raid to Romney, farther west, where they captured several men, horses, and wagons, having taken our forces entirely by surprise. The success which characterized these forays was not only disgraceful to ourselves, and very disheartening, but it gave the Rebels an audacious effrontery and malignant boldness, which led them into more frequent and reckless movements. But our men were a little more on the alert, and thus averted, to a great extent, the injury which was intended.

February 25.—To-day Fitz-Hugh Lee, almost in the very face of our pickets, crossed the Rappahannock near Falmouth, attacked by surprise a camp, where he captured one hundred and fifty prisoners, but was not able to return without some loss. The next day General W. E. Jones marched with a brigade into the Valley, attacked and routed two regiments of General Milroy's cavalry, and, with slight loss from his command, escaped with about two hundred prisoners. The most daring, however, of all these raids was made by Major White, with his band of Loudon County rangers, which differs not much from guerillas, into Maryland, where they captured a few prisoners, but spent most of their time and strength in plunder. Poolesville was the scene of their depredations.

It did seem as though nearly every Rebel cavalry officer had been touched with a magic wand which filled him with the most weird and romantic views of warfare, and led him into enterprises almost as wild as any of Dick Turpin's. Fauquier County was the theatre of several of these movements by Captain Randolph, of the Black Horse Cavalry. And in these days appeared another partisan, whose name for the first time flashes out in big capitals in the official as well as other bulletins, amid most startling manœuvrings: it is John S. Mosby. To the Harris Light this gentleman was not wholly unknown, and we distinctly remember the time when he was a prisoner in our hands. It appears that he was then sent to Old Capitol Prison at Washington. Not long thereafter he was released; and, being bent on revenge, and naturally fitted for guerilla operations, he soon received permission from his chief, to operate on an independent plan.

This Mosby, as we have been informed by an acquaintance of his, a Rebel soldier who has known him from early life, has always been a sort of guerilla—deserting from his father's house in mere boyhood—fighting duels as a pastime—roving the country far and wide in search of pleasure or profit—a thorough student of human nature and of the country in which he operates—bold and daring to a fault and romantic in his make—and finding now his chief delight in the adventures of guerilla life.

His commission is a roving one, and his command seems to be limited neither to kind or number. Many of his men are citizens, who spend a portion of their time in their ordinary business, and who hold themselves in readiness for any movements indicated by their commander-in-chief. Occasionally he is accompanied and assisted in his forays by daring men from various

73

commands, who are at home on leaves of absence or furloughs, while a few seem to be directly and continually under his control. The principal stimulus of the entire party (except the bad whiskey which they are said to use), is the plunder which they share. It is their custom at times to parole their prisoners and send them back to our lines, though often, when large numbers are taken, they are sent to Richmond; but all horses and equipments, which now command enormous prices in Dixie, are the property of the captors.

The region of the country they have chosen for their operations is certainly well adapted to facilitate their designs. Deep ravines traverse the country, skirted with dense, dark foliage, which affords them shelter, and through which they pass like so many wild turkeys or wild boars, knowing, as they do, all the roads and by-paths. Indeed, some of their parties are dwellers in these regions, and are acquainted with every nook and corner, where they can hide securely with their prey and elude their pursuers. When the immediate neighborhoods of their depredations do not offer a sufficient asylum, they fly to the fastnesses and caverns of the Bull Run Mountains.

Then, too, there is a certain degree of carelessness on the part of our own men, which merits censure and causes trouble. For instance, they frequently call at the homes of bitter Rebels for the purposes of pleasure, or to get articles of food, which they purchase or take, and while at these places they are too free to talk about the condition of our army, the position of our picket lines and posts, etc.—information which is grasped with wonderful avidity and as readily transmitted to Mosby and his men. Scarcely does any important event transpire among us, that is not fully understood immediately by the Rebel families within our lines, and is very easily borne to those outside the lines between two days. Thus movements even in contemplation have been heralded before the incipient steps had been taken, and consequently thwarted. Our only safety from this source of trouble would be to drive out of our lines all Rebel families, thus preventing the means of communicating the news to the outer world.

Another simple statement will explain the chances of the enemy and the causes of many of our casualties. Our picket-lines are too much extended, covering too wide a territory to make them as strong as they should be. Only a brigade is doing the work of a division, and consequently the picket-posts are not sufficiently near each other. Thus, in the night, it requires no very great dexterity to creep through the bushes between the pickets unobserved, and, once within our lines, any amount of mischief may be done by the miscreants. The method indicated here is usually the one employed by these active guerillas, and it forms the chief stratagem of all their movements upon us. Their first important attack upon our pickets took place on or about the tenth of January. A small Federal picket was doing duty at Herndon Station, on the Loudon and Hampshire Railroad. Mosby determined to effect their capture.

Led by a skilful guide, he dismounted his command some distance from the picket-lines. Then they all crept cautiously between the vedettes, until they reached the rear of the post, and from that direction advanced upon the unsuspecting boys, whose forms could be distinctly seen by the flaring light of their bivouac fire. While the pickets were thus a fine shot and mark for the enemy, the attacking force was concealed perfectly by the darkness of night and the shades of the thick pines. A pistol-shot from the guerillas was followed by a charge, when our boys were suddenly surrounded and captured.

This attack and capture was followed by another similar enterprise a few nights afterwards at Cub Run, near the Little River Turnpike. The picket relief was captured by a charge made in their rear, and only the two vedettes made their escape. Later in the same night a similar assault was made upon our post at Frying-Pan Church. Not far from this church resides a Miss Laura Ratcliffe, a very active and cunning Rebel, who is known to our men, and is at least suspected of assisting Mosby not a little in his movements. The cavalry brigade doing picket duty at this point is composed of the First Virginia (many of whose men were raised in these parts), the First Vermont, the Fifth New York, and the Eighteenth Pennsylvania. The latter of these regiments has but recently been mustered into the service, is poorly drilled and worse equipped, and is by no means fitted to picket against so wily a foe as Mosby. Though great caution is exercised by Colonel Percy Wyndham, who is in command of the brigade, to arrange and change the alternation of the pickets, so that the regiments to picket at a given point may not be known beforehand; yet by means of Miss Ratcliffe and her rebellions sisterhood, Mosby is generally informed of the regiment doing duty, and his attacks are usually directed against the unskilled and unsuspecting.

Having approached, under cover of the night above alluded to, within a few hundred yards of the pickets, whose position and strength he knew very well from information received by the neighbors, the horses were left in charge of one man, while the party skulked along through the thick underbrush, until they could approach the post from the direction of the Union camp. The picket relief was mostly quartered in an old house near by, with a single sentinel stationed at the door. Seeing the Mosby party approaching, he supposed that they were a patrol, and consequently allowed them to come within a few paces of the house before he challenged them. But it was now too late; and springing forward like panthers, the guerillas presented their pistols at his head, ordering a surrender. The house was immediately surrounded and the assailants began to fire through the thin weather-boarding upon the men shut up within. This fire, however, was vigorously returned for a time, but yielding at last to superior numbers, who had greatly the advantage, the whole party was compelled to surrender.

The success with which Mosby carried on his operations made him a sort of terror to our pickets, while it attracted to him from all quarters of Rebeldom a larger and more enthusiastic command. They became wonderfully skilled and bold, as may be seen by the following daring exploit. On the night of the eighth of March, during rain and intense darkness, Mosby led a squadron of his conglomerate command through the pines between the pickets near the Turnpike from Centreville to Fairfax Court House. Striking through the country, so as to avoid some infantry camps, he soon reached the road leading from Fairfax Station to the Court House. Moving now with perfect confidence, as no pickets along this route would suspect the character of such a cavalcade several miles inside our lines, about two o'clock in the morning he entered the village and began operations. The first thing was to capture the pickets stationed along the streets in a quiet manner, so as to arouse no one from their slumbers, and this was easily accomplished. The way was now fully open to the Confederate band. Divided into parties, each with its work assigned, they quickly accomplished the mischief they desired.

Mosby, with a small band, proceeded to General Stoughton's headquarters, in the house of a Dr. Gunnel. Dismounting, he soon stood knocking at the door. A voice from an open window above demanded their business at such an unseasonable hour. "Despatches for General Stoughton," responded Mosby. The door was quickly unlocked, and the guerilla chief stood by the bedside of the sleeping general, who had but a few moments before retired from a dancing and convivial party. Fancy now the reënactment of the scene in old Ticonderoga fort, when Ethan Allen, by stratagem, stood in the presence of His Majesty's sleeping commander.

Stoughton was soon apprised of the character of his nightly visitors, and quickly making his toilet, he was hurried away with a portion of his escort, and several other prisoners, including Captain Augustus Barker, of the Fifth New York Cavalry. Fifty-eight of the finest horses from the officers' stables were also captured; and Mosby retraced his sinuous route through our lines of pickets so rapidly, that he escaped all his pursuers.

The morning light of the ninth of March revealed the boldness and success of the raiders, and no little excitement prevailed. Several parties of cavalry were ordered out in pursuit of the flying partisans, but all returned at night unsuccessful. This was an occasion for great humiliation on the part of our troops, stationed about the Court House, while in Washington and throughout the nation not a little humor was drawn from the remark made by the President when some one told him of the loss we had sustained; "Yes," he characteristically replied, "that of the horses is bad; but I can make another general in five minutes."

Suspicious that Rebel citizens within our lines were more or less implicated in this and other raids, quite a number of arrests were made among them, which cleared the country of the most flagitious cases. However, it is very probable that some innocent ones were made to suffer, while the most guilty were allowed to escape.

March 23.—The pickets near Chantilly had been quiet for several days, but toward night a company of cavaliers, mostly dressed in blue uniforms, emerged from a piece of wood within a mile of the Chantilly mansion, and moved directly toward the picket post stationed near a small run on the Little River Turnpike. The picket, supposing them to be Union troops, watched their approach without suspicion; and when they had come within a few feet of him they introduced themselves by shooting him through the head. The alarm being thus given, the nearest reserve made a sudden descent upon the attacking party, which proved to be Mosby's, and the guerillas retreated for some distance up the turnpike, closely pursued. Having followed them about three miles, they came to a barricade of trees which had been fallen across the road. Back of this obstruction Mosby had formed a large part of his command, and our column was stopped by a heavy fire from carbines and pistols in their front and also by a flank-fire from the woods. At this inopportune moment Mosby made a charge which broke our column. The boys were driven back at a furious rate, and had not strength to rally. Some horses giving out, the hapless riders were captured.

But as Rebels and Yankees were uniformed much alike, it gave some of our boys an opportunity for stratagem. For instance, one of our fellows finding himself overtaken by the enemy, began to fire his pistol in the direction of his flying comrades (with care not to harm them), but with sufficient vim to be taken by the enemy, in their haste, as one of their number. In this way they passed him by, and he effected his escape.

This scrambling race continued for about three miles, back to the ground where the affair commenced, when our men were reënforced by the reserve from Frying-Pan Church. The Mosbyites were now compelled to halt, and a charge made upon them drove them back up the pike. They were pursued several miles, but night came on and our men were compelled to return. Three of our men were killed, and about thirty-five were taken prisoners, including one lieutenant. Several horses were also taken away. The enemy suffered no appreciable loss.

Mosby's plans were certainly made with great wisdom and forethought, and executed with a dash and will which were at times very astonishing. His men must have been warmly attached to him as their leader, while the gain they made by their plunder greatly increased their zeal. The command was truly unique in its leader, its composition, and its modus operandi, while its results, assisted as they were by the topography of the country, and the Rebel sympathizers within and just without our lines, attracted no little attention. The orders of General Stuart and even those of General Lee associated the name of Mosby with consummate daring and continual success, stimulating the band to greater deeds. We append one specimen of those orders, furnished us by one of their own number:

Headquarters, Cavalry Division,
Army of Northern Virginia, March 27, 1863.

Captain—Your telegram, announcing your brilliant achievements near Chantilly, was duly received and forwarded to General Lee. He exclaimed upon reading it, "Hurrah for Mosby! I wish I had a hundred like him!"
Heartily wishing you continued success, I remain your obedient servant,

J. E. B. Stuart,
Major-General Commanding.

Captain J. S. Mosby, commanding, etc., etc.

But it is not often permitted one man always to prosper in his enterprises, and even the wonderful Mosby was destined to meet equals, and to be worsted in engagements. Later in the season, while General Stahel's cavalry division was picketing the line of the Orange and Alexandria Railroad, Mosby made a sudden descent one morning upon the First Virginia Cavalry at Warrenton Junction. Unfortunately, these Union Virginians, who were one of the best regiments in our service, were just then unprepared for any such manœuvring. They had just been relieved from duty, and were taking their rest. Many of the men were lounging about under the shade of trees, or quartered for the time in a few block buildings situated in an angle formed by the two railroads. Their horses were mostly "unsaddled and unbridled, and hence not fit for a fight," while many of them were grazing loosely and quietly in the adjoining fields. Mosby advanced upon them from the direction of Warrenton—was at first mistaken for a squadron of our own cavalry, which had been sent out on a scouting expedition. The error was soon corrected by a fierce charge made by the guerillas. Such of the men as were roaming about the premises, mostly unarmed, of course immediately surrendered; but about one hundred of them fled for refuge in one of the largest buildings, resolved to sell themselves (if it came to that) at the dearest price. And now commenced a fearful struggle. The Confederates would ride up near the windows and discharge their pieces at the men within, while the brave fellows inside, commanded and inspired by Major Steele, one of the bravest of the brave, defended themselves with a noble determination. All efforts of Mosby to make them surrender were in vain. Finding at last that he could not intimidate them with bullets, he ordered the torch to be applied to a pile of hay near by, and the house was set on fire.

Just at this juncture of affairs a strong party of Mosby's gang, having dismounted from their horses, rushed against the door of the building with such force as to burst it open. Surrounded now by the flames, which were spreading rapidly, and attacked with desperation by the foe, the whole party was compelled to surrender.

Flushed with success, the guerillas were making preparations to retire from the field with their booty, when the Fifth New York Cavalry, which had been bivouacked in a grove not far from Cedar Run Bridge, arrived at the Junction, whither they had been attracted by the firing, and immediately fell upon the foe like an avalanche. Major Hammond commanded in person. Mosby was heard to exclaim, "My God! it is the Fifth New York!" A hand-to-hand encounter now took place, in which bravery was fired with desperation, and Yankee sabres were used with fearful effect. The Rebels soon broke and fled in every direction, demoralized and panic-stricken, leaving behind not only the captures they had made, but many of their own number. Some Rebel heads were fearfully gashed and mangled, one of them exhibiting his lower jaw-bone not only dislocated, but almost entirely severed with one determined blow from the strong hand of a cavalryman.

General Stahel, in his despatch to General Heintzelman, says: "The Rebels, who fled in the direction of Warrenton, were pursued by Major Hammond, Fifth New York Cavalry, who has returned, and reports our charge at Warrenton Junction as being so terrific as to have thoroughly routed and scattered them in every direction. I have sent in twenty-three prisoners of Mosby's command, all of whom are wounded—the greater part of them badly. Dick Moran (a notorious bushwhacker) is among the number. There are also three officers of Mosby's. The loss of the enemy was very heavy in killed, besides many wounded, who scattered and prevented capture. I have no hopes of the recovery of Major Steele, of the First Virginia. Our loss is one killed and fourteen wounded."

Templeman, one of Stonewall Jackson's best spies, was killed; and the partisans confessed themselves thoroughly whipped. They were wont to call this their first retreat, in which they did some tall running. The following complimentary order was issued:

Headquarters Stahel's Cavalry Division,
Fairfax Court House, Va., ——, 1863.
SPECIAL ORDERS NO. 80.

When soldiers perform brave deeds, a proper acknowledgment of their services is justly their due. The commanding general, therefore, desires to express his gratification at the conduct of the officers and men of Colonel De Forest's command, who were engaged in the fight at Warrenton Junction, on

Sunday, ——, 1863. By your promptness and gallantry the gang of guerillas who have so long infested the vicinity has been badly beaten and broken up. The heavy loss of the enemy in killed, wounded, and prisoners, proves the determination of your resistance and the vigor of your attack. Deeds like this are worthy of emulation, and give strength and confidence to the command.

By command of
Major-General Stahel.

Thoroughly as Mosby had been whipped on this occasion, and diminished as was his command, it was not long before he was again heard from. It must be confessed that he possessed remarkable recuperative powers. His qualities of heart and mind seemed to attach his men to him peculiarly, while his mode of warfare was calling many young and daring Virginians to his standard. By this means his numbers were soon recruited, and he was again on the rampage. At this time the government was sending supplies to the army on the Rappahannock viâ the Orange and Alexandria Railroad. Each train was in charge of a guard, and all the principal bridges and exposed places on the route were under pickets. Besides this, frequent patrols were sent from one picket post to the other, so that the entire road was under a close surveillance. One morning, between seven and eight o'clock, the cavalry pickets and reserves about Catlett's Station were startled by artillery firing just below them on the railroad. A train laden with rations and forage had just passed on its way to the Rappahannock. It was soon ascertained that during the night the guerillas had carefully unfastened one of the rails in the woods, and by means of a wire attached to it and extended to some distance from the road, in a manner to be unobserved by the patrols, a man concealed behind a tree had drawn the rail out of place just as the engine was approaching it, throwing it off the track. A mountain howitzer, which had been placed in position, immediately plunged a shell through the engine, and at the same time a charge was made upon the guard. This consisted mostly of men whose term of service expired that very day, and their resistance amounted to nothing. They soon fled in shameful confusion, leaving the ground to the Rebels, who, after taking such plunder as they could carry, fired the train, and then started on the road to Haymarket.

But the cavalry had been aroused, and detachments of the First Vermont and Fifth New York, each in separate routes, commenced a vigorous pursuit. Mosby, who commanded in person, evidently had not reckoned on so sudden and sharp an encounter. He had not proceeded two miles before he espied the boys in blue eagerly flying after him. His howitzer was quickly brought into position, and a shell was accurately thrown among his pursuers, suddenly dismounting one of the officers, whose horse was killed. But the detention of the column was only temporary, the boys being determined once more to cross sabres with the chivalry. The nature of the ground was unfavorable for a cavalry charge, and the enemy showed no disposition to fight, but fled as rapidly as possible, firing an occasional shell, but without inflicting any injury. Eagerly the boys spurred on their chargers, and were soon joined by the Vermonters, who added fresh excitement to the chase.

Mosby, finding himself too closely followed for his comfort, and knowing that something desperate must be done, determined to sell his howitzer as dearly as possible. Having reached the head of a narrow lane, near the house of a Mr. Warren Fitzhugh, he wheeled the piece into position and commenced a rapid fire. There was no way for our boys to reach the howitzer except through the lane, the whole length of which was raked by every discharge. "That gun must be captured," exclaimed Lieutenant Elmer J. Barker, of the Fifth New York, "and who will volunteer to charge it with me?" About thirty brave fellows responded promptly, and suiting the action to the words, "charge, boys!" he rushed furiously forward at their head, while the fields rang with their maddening yell. But the brave lieutenant fell severely wounded before a murderous discharge of grape and canister, which killed three of his men and wounded several. The lieutenant's faithful horse was also mortally wounded. But before the piece could be reloaded with its only one remaining shell, the surviving comrades were crossing sabres with the gunners over the gun. The conflict here was desperate, but of short duration. Mosby's lieutenant, Chapman, fought with the rammer of the gun, but fell wounded and was captured. At length those who could not escape surrendered, and the howitzer was ours. It bore an inscription which showed that it had been captured by the Rebels from the lamented Colonel Baker, at Ball's Bluff.

Among the enemy's wounded and captured was a Captain Hoskins, formerly of the British army, who had run the blockade and espoused the Rebel cause. He received his death-wound as follows: having wounded a private soldier in a hand-to-hand encounter, he roughly cried out, "Surrender, you d——d Yankee!" "I'll see you d——d first," was the characteristic reply, while the Yankee boy lodged a pistol ball in the captain's neck, from which he did not long survive. An interesting diary was found in Captain Hoskins' possession, describing mainly his private life since entering Mosby's command.

Mosby himself barely escaped being captured on this occasion, and he carried the mark of a sabre-cut on his arm. The fight had been desperate on both sides, but the guerillas were badly worsted, and driven away as far as the jaded condition of our horses would permit us to pursue them. In their flight the spoils, which had been taken from the captured train, were left behind, strewn in every direction. This fight occurred near the little village of Greenwich, and gave Mosby a blow quite as severe as any he had ever received.

Chapter X - Chancellorsville and Stoneman's Raid.

April 1.—April-fool day always brings its trains of fun and broods of annoyances, the boys being determined to make the most of it. The usual plan is to induce a comrade to believe that either the colonel, his captain, or lieutenant, wants to see him. This scheme is generally successful; for the victim dare not refuse to report whenever called for, and as he is unable to learn whether he is really wanted or otherwise, he finds it necessary to call upon his superior to ask his pleasure. Receiving the assurance that nothing is wanted of him, he sees that he has been "sold," and returns to his comrades in the midst of their hilarity at his expense. But he is generally determined to have revenge, and to get the "laugh" on them before the day is spent. Sometimes these jokes are carried rather too far for sport, and recoil upon their perpetrators with unpleasant force.

But, then, this soldier-life of ours is so grave and solemn that our buoyant natures seek relief in all such means as the above. The bow, always bent to its utmost tension, would soon break or become useless; it must be straightened to send the arrow. So our natures would break were they not elastic, and were there no opportunities for reaction as well as action. Then, too, there is a kind of monotony to our life in winter-quarters, to which it is difficult to accustom ourselves. And he who can suggest any thing laughable is a great benefactor to his comrades; for then the monotony is broken, and we enjoy a little sprinkling of variety, which is truly said to be "the spice of life." A good joke, that runs through the command like a bubbling brook along the flowering meadows, is worth more to us than a corps of nurses with cart-loads of medicine.

On the second of April, from nine to eleven o'clock in the morning, we had a mounted brigade-drill. Colonel Kilpatrick was in command. He appeared well pleased, at the close, with the proficiency of his men, and they are all enthusiastic over him. There seems to be a wonderful unanimity of feeling in the brigade, all regarding Kilpatrick as the right man in the right place.

April 6.—To-day the Cavalry Corps, consisting of twenty-five regiments, well filled and drilled, was reviewed by President Lincoln and Generals Hooker and Stoneman. A salute of twenty-one guns was fired upon the arrival of the Presidential party. The review took place on Falmouth Heights, in full view of the Rebel encampment in rear of Fredericksburg. The scene we presented to our enemies must have been grand, for we appeared in our best uniforms and with flying colors. It was an occasion not to be forgotten, the sight being one of the most magnificent many of us ever saw. The column was between three and four hours passing in review. It seemed to do us all good to get a glimpse of the solemn, earnest face of the President, who reviewed us with apparent satisfaction.

April 7.—Picket details returned from the river to-day. In the afternoon several horse-races came off near our camp, between the First Pennsylvania, the First New Jersey, and Harris Light. One of Kilpatrick's favorite horses was badly beaten, much to his mortification, owing, as was alleged, to the stupidity of the rider, who was sent off the ground in disgrace. We are frequently training our horses for swift motions, and teaching them to jump ditches and fences. These are occasions of excitement and amusement. Men are frequently thrown from their horses while endeavoring to jump them beyond their ability, though seldom is any one hurt. Much practice is necessary to make perfect in this exercise.

The papers bring us good news of a "Great Union Victory in Connecticut." Such victories, though bloodless, have a powerful influence upon the rank and file of the army. Every ballot cast to sustain the administration is equal to a well-directed bullet against the foe.

April 8.—The brigade was called out this morning on the old drill-ground to witness a somewhat sad and novel scene, namely, the branding and drumming out of service of two deserters from Company K. The command was formed into a hollow square, facing inward. Upon the arrival of the blacksmith's forge, the deserters were partially stripped of their clothing, irons were heated, and the letter "D" was burnt upon their left hip. Their heads were then shaved, after which they were marched about the square under guard, accompanied by a corps of buglers playing "the rogue's march." It was a humiliating and painful sight, and undoubtedly it left its salutary impression, as it was designed, upon all who witnessed it. A deserter should be regarded as only next to a traitor, and when the military law against such offenders is enforced with becoming rigor, we will probably have fewer infractions. This part of our army discipline has thus far been evidently too loosely administered, giving occasion for demoralization.

In the afternoon we enjoyed a very pleasing change of programme, when true merit was rewarded. A beautiful sabre was presented by the officers of the brigade to Kilpatrick. Affairs of this kind are much enjoyed by the major part of the command; and when night came on we all felt that to-day, at least, we have learned that "the way of the transgressor is hard," and also that

"Good actions crown themselves with lasting days;
Who deserves well needs not another's praise."

April 9.—To increase the variety of our experience, and to give it a pleasing tone, Kilpatrick's brigade-band made its first appearance in front of headquarters this evening. They discoursed national airs in a manner that thrilled and elated us, making the welkin ring with their excellent music. As the last echoes of a plaintive air died over the distant woods, and I crept into my lowly quarters for my rest, the poet's verse seemed full of hallowed potency:

"Music exalts each joy, allays each grief,
Expels diseases, softens every pain,
Subdues the rage of poison and of plague."

April 11.—An exciting game of "base-ball" was played to-day near our camp, between boys of the Fourteenth Brooklyn and the Harris Light. The contest resulted in a drawn game, so that neither could claim the victory. Our time, of late, is slipping rapidly along. The weather is warm and beautiful, the mud is disappearing, and flowers and birds remind us that winter is over and gone. For several weeks preparations have been evidently made for the opening of the Spring campaign. Each branch of the service has been thoroughly recruited and drilled, and the entire force is computed to be at least one hundred and twenty-five thousand strong. All seem to be anxious for a good opportunity to advance upon the enemy.

April 13.—On the evening of the twelfth, at regimental inspection, orders were received to be ready for march at daylight the next day. Consequently, early this morning our winter-quarters were abandoned, and General Stoneman, at the head of about thirteen thousand cavalry, took up a line of march in the direction of the upper fords of the Rappahannock, in the neighborhood of the Orange and Alexandria Railroad.

General Hooker's order to his cavalry-chief had the ring of bright metal in it, and contained the following terse sentences:

"Let your watchword be fight, and let all your orders be fight! FIGHT! FIGHT! bearing in mind that time is as valuable to the Federal as the Rebel authorities.

"It devolves upon you, General, to take the initiative in the forward movement of this grand army; and on you and your noble command must depend, in a great measure, the extent and brilliancy of our success. Bear in mind that celerity, audacity, and resolution are every thing in war; and especially is it the case with the command you have, and the enterprise on which you are about to embark."

We moved at a sufficient distance from the Rappahannock to screen our columns from the enemy's posts of observation. We marched to the vicinity of Elkton, where we bivouacked for the night. The next morning we resumed our march, and soon struck the railroad at Bealeton, where we met and drove a detachment of Rebel cavalry. After a sharp skirmish they fell back to Beverly Ford, where their crossing was covered by artillery and sharpshooters. A neat little fight enabled us to advance carbineers down to the ford, which we held, though subjected to the fire of rifled cannon on the opposite bank.

At another of the numerous fords of the river (Sulphur Springs), which was not guarded, an entire division was forded across before night. But during the night a heavy rain-storm set in à la Virginie, which so suddenly raised the stream, that the order for crossing more troops was not only countermanded, but the forces already across were ordered to return. This was not very easily done. Meanwhile the separated division, by rapid movement and some fighting through the rain, had swung down the river to Beverly Ford, where they commenced recrossing, without pontoons, and with the ford unfordable. The enemy, taking advantage of this unhappy predicament, attacked the rearguard with furious determination, killing and capturing quite a number. As our artillery could not be brought into position, the only help we could afford to our unfortunate comrades was to play on the Rebels with our carbines, which kept them somewhat at bay. In the haste and difficulty of crossing, where horses were compelled to swim a considerable distance through the strong current, several animals and men were drowned and borne down the stream. It was certainly a very sad experience—a disheartening commencement of operations.

April 16.—The Harris Light was relieved from picket, and moved to Bealeton, leaving Beverly Ford at four o'clock A. M. The roads are almost impassable. The rain has continued almost uninterruptedly for forty-eight hours, making our sojourn in these parts very disagreeable. But, notwithstanding the mud, on the seventeenth a squadron of the Harris Light, composed of Companies E and F, in command of Captain Charles Hasty, left our bivouac at Bealeton, early in the morning, with instructions to proceed to Warrenton, and, if possible, to occupy the place until four o'clock P. M. When we had approached to within three miles of the place the Captain learned that the famous Black Horse Cavalry, under Captain Randolph, was in possession of the village, and would undoubtedly give us a splendid entertainment.

The boys were unanimously pleased at the prospect of an opportunity to cross sabres with those heroes of Bull Run, and, concluding from their worldwide reputation that nothing short of a desperate fight would ensue, we made preparations accordingly. The squadron was formed in column of platoons, and two detachments, consisting each of a sergeant and eight men, were instructed to advance upon the town from two parallel streets, thus giving our small force the appearance of being only the vanguard of a very large army. It was my privilege to command one of these detachments; and, on entering the village, we found the foe formed into line of battle on Main street, with the apparent intention of giving us a warm reception. They had been notified of our approach by a sentinel posted in a prominent church-steeple, and were, therefore, ready for us. We immediately drew sabres and bore down upon them with the usual yell; and, strange as it may seem to those who laud the daring of the Southern Black Horse, they advanced to receive us, fired a few shots, unsheathed their bloodless sabres, but wheeled about suddenly and dashed away to the rear at a breakneck pace, without even halting to pay us the compliment of an affectionate farewell. Actually it seemed as though they did not so much as look behind them until fairly out of the range of our best carbines. It was quite evident to us that they agreed perfectly with that most ungallant poet, who sings:

"He who fights and runs away,
Will live to fight another day."

The beautiful and aristocratic village was now in our possession. Being informed that the proprietor of the Warrenton House was a conspicuous Rebel, Captain Hasty decided to try his hospitality and sound his commissary department. Accordingly he accosted the chivalrous gentleman, and ordered a dinner for the entire squadron. When all had partaken freely of the good things provided, our Rebel landlord showed signs of uneasiness in his desire to ascertain who would foot the bill. After a while the Captain politely directed him to charge it to Uncle Sam. This ended all controversy on the subject. We left Warrenton in accordance with instructions, at four o'clock, and, well satisfied with our excursion, rejoined the regiment during the following night.
April 18.—The enemy "opened the ball" this morning by shelling the cavalry pickets in the woods near Rappahannock Station. Under this fire we advanced some distance toward the river, and then retired slowly with a view of drawing the Rebels across to our side. But they were too wily to be caught in such a trap, and our attempt failed. A stream is a great barrier, between two contending forces, and no careful leader will place his men with a stream behind them, unless he is quite certain of victory. We had a sad lesson of this in the battle of Ball's Bluff.
On the day following this useless cannonade, each regiment of the corps had dress-parade at six o'clock P. M. Orders from General Stoneman were read by the adjutants of their respective regiments, informing them that the entire cavalry force would move at an early hour next day. A portion of the evening

was spent in preparation. However, when in the bivouac, as we have been for some time, it takes but a few moments to prepare for a move. All surplus baggage, which naturally accumulates during winter-quarters, has been disposed of, either by sending it home, or to some quartermaster dépôt, established for the purpose, as at Alexandria, or by destruction; and each man carries only what little articles he can stow away in his saddle-bags and roll up in his blanket. His inventory might run as follows: A shirt, a pair of socks (and often he has only those he wears), a housewife or needle-book, paper and envelopes, a tin cup, and bag which contains his coffee and sugar mixed together. Some men carry a towel and soap. The great effort is to learn to get along with the very least possible.

At first the soldier thinks he must have this article of luxury and the other, until he finds that they are positive burdens to himself and horse, and gradually he throws off this weight and that incumbrance, until his entire outfit is reduced to nearly "the little end of nothing, whittled to a point!" Possessed of a coffee-bag and cup and a hard-tack or biscuit, the most essential things, he seldom now borrows much trouble about the rest of men and things.

April 20.—We commenced march at four o'clock]this morning on the road to Sulphur Springs. Scarcely had we gone out of our bivouacs before a drenching rain-storm set in, and continued incessantly until we were forced to halt, the mud being really oceanic. The day being quite warm, we experienced but little discomfort from the wet until night. The weather then became cold, and every thing being so wet, it was difficult to make fires; consequently we had a very tedious night. A fellow considered himself fortunate, if, after toiling long through the cold and dark, he could succeed to cook a little coffee. But the soldier will have his coffee, if it be possible, and then he is quite contented with his lot.

On the twenty-first, all we could do was to change our position, to get out of the very deep mud, which one night's treading of the horses' feet produced. On the following day in the afternoon the Cavalry Corps moved from Waterloo Bridge to Warrenton Junction. The day was pleasant, though the roads are still in a fearful condition. Our infantry is engaged in repairing the railroad to Rappahannock Station. We are evidently on the eve of some important movements.

Before night, many of the boys were made glad by the reception of a large mail from the North, which is the first we have received since we left our winter-quarters on the thirteenth instant. Nearly every man had a letter, and there was general contentment all around. The mail-bag is always a welcome visitor, especially in times like this, and it is not the least of the instrumentalities which mould our character and give tone to our morale.

April 23.—Another drenching rain set in this morning and continued without cessation throughout the day. We were all drowned out of our little shelter-tents, and many preferred to take the chastisement face to face with the merciless elements. We were a sorry looking company of men, drenched with the rain, bespattered with mud, and chilled with the cold. Our fires, well-nigh quenched by the falling floods, were of very little use to us. Men and horses all suffered together. Thus far the month has been very wet, and this April is certainly entitled to be classed among the Weeping Sisters.

We spent the dreary night hoping for a better morrow. But the twenty-fourth followed the example of its predecessor, and rain poured upon us in torrents. The yielding clay of this region of country is soon trodden into a soft mud, under so many hoofs, until it seems quite impossible to find a dry spot large enough to lie down upon at night. This makes our bivouacs very dreary and uncomfortable. And yet under these melancholy circumstances we are not totally bereft of pleasant entertainment. The woods and fields in this vicinity abound with quails and rabbits, whose presence has been the cause of some excitement and not a little fun.

Ever and anon a sportive cavalier starts up a nimble rabbit and chases the frightened little creature through the camp, crying at the top of his voice, "stop him! stop him! catch that rabbit," etc. Poor pussy comes flying down the road, pursued by a throng, of men, while the shouts are caught up and repeated along the entire line of escape, men jumping up at every bound of the animal, and joining in the sport. Occasionally the rabbit is so perfectly surrounded as to be compelled at last to surrender, when the trembling prisoner is caught, but carefully treated. At this time of the year they are so very small and lean as to be scarcely eatable, and yet now and then they are shot, as well as quails, to increase our commissary supplies, and the cooks display considerable skill in dressing and preparing them à la Delmonico.

Cavalry Scouting Party Halting for the Night.

April 27.—Colonel Davies, after quite a lengthy absence from us, rejoined the regiment at ten o'clock A. M. He reported having a narrow escape from guerillas near Elkton, where he was fired at and pursued for some distance, while on his way from Falmouth. Details were ordered out immediately to those infested regions, with instructions to capture every thing in the shape of a bushwhacker. Captain Coon, of the Connecticut squadron, was put in command of the reconnoitring party. We had a rich and delightful ride, but did not succeed in overhauling the offenders.

On the twenty-eighth the first battalion of the Harris Light, commanded by Captain Samuel McIrvin, was ordered to reconnoitre as far as Brentsville. We went via Elkton and Bristersburg, at which places we captured several guerillas, who were not looking for us. The first part of the day was very pleasant, but from eleven o'clock till night we had a continually drizzling rain, which made our march exceedingly disagreeable.

We had but just halted for the night, when an order was received from a messenger, to rejoin the regiment without delay. Through the rain, mud, and darkness we hastened back to Catlett's Station, where we found every thing in motion, preparing for some grand movement.

With the gray light of the morning of the twenty-ninth, after marching most of the night, we reached the banks of the Rappahannock at Kelly's Ford. In addition to the Cavalry Corps we found here the Fifth, Sixth, Seventh, and Twelfth Corps of the Army of the Potomac, making preparation to cross the river. The Engineer Corps soon laid the pontoons, and the grand columns effected a passage without material resistance or difficulty.

STONEMAN'S RAID.

We are credibly informed that other columns of our army are crossing the river at other points, and that a great battle is imminent. There has been occasional skirmishing, on the front, during the day. The Rebels, however, seem to have been taken wholly by surprise and are not making the demonstrations we had good reason to anticipate; but we shall be greatly disappointed if they do not soon awake, and come to their work.

The going is far from pleasant, though to-day the weather is favorable. The streams are dreadfully swollen and nearly all bridgeless, compelling us to ford them. This process, through the cold, high water, is attended with more or less difficulty and suffering.

Soon after crossing the river the Cavalry Corps broke away from the infantry, in the direction of Stevensburg; and it is rumored among us that a grand raid upon the enemy's communications is contemplated, while the two armies engage in deadly combat, it is thought not far from the river.

April 30.—This afternoon our column reached the Rapidan at Raccoon Ford, and began to cross over. The water being much above the fording mark and very rapid, we had an exciting time. Several horses and men were swept down the stream by the swift current and were drowned; and none of us escaped the unpleasant operation of getting wet.

After reaching the high plateau on the south bank of the river, the entire corps were formed in line of battle, in which hostile position we were ordered to spend the night. For more thorough protection, pickets had been sent out in every direction, and posted with much care. It was a season of considerable anxiety to all, and of great fatigue especially to those of us who had been in the saddle several consecutive days and nights. Standing to horse as we were compelled to do, very little rest could be obtained, though many were so exhausted, that, dropping to the earth, with bridle and halter in hand, they fell asleep, while their comrades wished for the morning, which came at last.

After our frugal breakfast, which consisted mostly of hard-tack and coffee, a thorough inspection of the command was made, and all men reported to have unserviceable or unsafe horses, were sent to the rear. The weather is perfectly charming to-day, although quite too warm, in the midday heat, to be comfortable marching.

May 2.—Early in the morning our column reached the railroad, in the rear of General Lee's army, and, with slight opposition from scattered pickets, the work of destruction began. Culverts and bridges, telegraph lines and posts, disappeared like the smoke of their burning.

KILPATRICK AT LOUISA COURT HOUSE.

While this work was going on, Kilpatrick was ordered to lead the Harris Light into Louisa Court House, which he did in a gallant manner. The inhabitants, taken by surprise, were greatly terrified at our approach and entry into the place, but finding themselves in the hands of men, and not fiends, as they had been wont to regard us, and receiving from us neither disrespect nor insult, soon dispelled their needless fears. We remained in town until two o'clock P. M., tearing up railroad track and destroying railroad property, as well as commissary and quartermaster stores found in public buildings.

At the hour above named we were ordered out to support the First Maine Cavalry in a spirited skirmish with Rebel cavalry. In this engagement our Troy company had one sergeant wounded, and one corporal and four men taken prisoners.

By eleven o'clock at night General Stoneman's forces had reached the neighborhood of Thompson's Cross Roads, where the command was broken up into several independent expeditions to scour the country in every direction, and to destroy as completely as possible all the enemy's means of supply. Colonel Percy Wyndham, with the First New Jersey and First Maine, was sent south to Columbia on the James River, to destroy the great canal which feeds Richmond from the west. Lieutenant Colonel Davis, with the Twelfth Illinois, was despatched to the South Anna River, in the neighborhood of Ashland Station, on the Fredericksburg and Richmond Railroad, to destroy the important bridges in that vicinity. General Buford was to march westward and do all the mischief he could. But it was reserved to Kilpatrick to advance upon Richmond, enter the Rebel capital, if possible, and lay waste the public property and communications there.

Sunday, May 3.—We marched steadily after leaving General Stoneman, long into the night, halting only long enough for a little refreshment and rest. At two o'clock this afternoon the command, which consists only of about three hundred men, well mounted, was marched into a pine thicket, where we were ordered to destroy or throw away all our extra clothing and blankets, with every thing which we could possibly spare, to lighten the burdens of our horses. This halt in the shade of the pines was very refreshing both to men and beasts. The sun is very warm and shelter is very agreeable.

Leaving the fragrant shade, we moved on until night. We are now within fifteen miles of Richmond, where vigilance is the price, not only of liberty, but of life. Sergeant Northrup, while on a scout to the front, was fired upon by a guerilla undoubtedly, and wounded. Colonel Kilpatrick and Major Henry E. Davies, Jr., slept on their arms in the road with the men. Very little sleep was had through the night, but what we did get was precious.

At two o'clock on the morning of the fourth we resumed our hazardous journey toward the rebellious city. Had it not been for the intrepidity of our leader, and the utmost confidence of the men in his ability to accomplish whatever he undertook, it would have been impossible to proceed. Fearing as we did the desolation and sorrows of "Libby Prison," ignorant of the forces we might soon encounter, and the ambuscades that might be laid for us, we nevertheless pushed bravely on, because we were bound to follow our chief, be the consequences what they might.

Soon after day-break we came down upon Hungary Station, on the Fredericksburg and Richmond Railroad. Here we destroyed the telegraph lines, tore up the track, and burned the dépôt. Near the station we ran into the enemy's pickets, the first we have encountered since leaving our main column. Only two of them were discovered, and they fled so rapidly that it was useless for us to try to overtake them with our jaded horses. They kept generally about three hundred yards ahead of us, and as we had orders to fire on no one unless positively necessary, they proceeded unmolested, in the direction of Richmond.

Having arrived within five miles of the city, we advanced more cautiously. There was good reason for this, for our condition was critical. There we were, only a remnant of a regiment, many miles away from any support, with no way to retreat, as we had burned all the bridges and ferries in our rear, nearer to the Confederate capital than ever any Union troops were before, and ignorant of the forces that garrisoned it. Still on we moved, looking only to our leader, who seemed especially inspired for the work assigned him.

We soon arrived in sight of the outer line of fortifications, and moved steadily upon them. To our surprise, we found them unmanned, and we safely passed in towards the second line of defence. We had scarcely entered these consecrated grounds, when General Winder's assistant adjutant-general pompously rode up to the head of our column, and inquired, "What regiment?" Astonishment and blight accompanied the answer of Kilpatrick, who said, "The Second New York Cavalry," adding, "and you, sir, are my prisoner."

Ceremonies were short, and Kilpatrick very quickly appropriated Winder's favorite charger, upon which the captured adjutant was mounted when he made his fatal challenge.

We continued still to advance, until the smoke from workshops, and the church steeples were plainly visible, and we began to think that we were about to enter Richmond without opposition. We were now within two miles of the city, and yet we halted not until we had reached the top of a hillock just before us. Here was an interesting scene. There stood a handful of cavalrymen, far within the fortifications of a hostile city, almost knocking at the door of her rebellious heart. On every hand were frowning earthworks, and just ahead of us the coveted prize.

But just at the foot of the hill on which we stood, we discovered a battery of artillery, drawn up in the road, supported by infantry, ready to receive us. It became evident that we had advanced as far as prudence would permit us. We had also reached and secured the road to the Meadow Bridge across the Chickahominy, over which we were expected to escape, and which it was very desirable to destroy. These facts or circumstances decided the direction of our march. We moved leisurely on our way, the cavalry refusing to give us even the semblance of a pursuit.

Having crossed Meadow Bridge, it was set on fire. Following the railroad a little distance, a train of cars was met and captured, much to the astonishment of the bewildered conductor, who was in charge of government stores en route for Richmond. After firing the cars, the engine was set in motion under a full head of steam, and the blazing and crackling freight went rushing on until it reached the burning bridge, when the whole thing well-nigh disappeared in the deep mud and water of the sluggish stream.

No particular line of escape seemed to have been agreed upon. Our main object was to do all the mischief in our power to the Rebel cause. The men were much exhausted for want of rations and rest, but you could not hear a word of complaint from one of them. They were all inspired with the greatness of the deeds which they were required to perform, feeling much as Napoleon's legions must have felt, when he said to them: "The eyes of all Europe are upon you." Sustained by such considerations, and cheered by the voice and still more potent example of their leader, they pressed onward, resolved to do all within their power, and then, if the worst came, they could go to "Libby" or "Belle Isle," with the pleasing consciousness that they had done their duty.

All night we marched with only an occasional and brief rest. On the morning of the fifth we arrived at the Pamunkey River. Here we captured a Rebel train laden with commissary stores, just the prize we coveted. After appropriating a generous supply for the day, the remnant was reduced to ashes. All the serviceable animals captured were added to our cavalcade, and the prisoners paroled and sent on their way rejoicing. The river was crossed on a one-horse platform ferry-boat, whose capacity was only twenty horses and their riders. Considerable precious time was consumed in this tedious operation. When the last man had reached the desired shore, the ferry-boat was destroyed, and the column resumed its line of march.

About four o'clock in the afternoon a cold rain-storm set in, borne on the flapping wings of a chilly wind. Cold, hungry, and fatigued, we still pressed onward, suffering not a little. Fearful of encountering heavy forces of the enemy on the main thoroughfares, we filed along the by-ways and neglected paths, where we were frequently immersed in almost impenetrable bushes dripping with rain.

May 6.—To-day we crossed the Mattapony, at Aylett's, burning the ferry behind us. We then took the road to Tappahannock, a small village on the Rappahannock. We had not proceeded far in this direction before we met and captured another wagon-train, laden with ham and eggs and other luxuries, which had been smuggled across the Rappahannock. This, of course, was thoroughly confiscated, appropriated, and destroyed. A consultation of officers was here instituted, and it was decided to try to reach Gloucester Point, opposite Yorktown, which we knew was in possession of Union forces.

Not far from King and Queen Court House we captured and burned a dépôt of ordnance and several wagons. We have been much annoyed by bushwhackers on the way to-day. Their plan is to hide in the thick bushes, and fire upon the rear of our column as we pass, in places where it is not possible to pursue them without much loss of time, which is too precious to be wasted thus. Several men and horses have been wounded by these skulkers during the day. As night was settling down upon us, we discovered a body of cavalry in our front, and quickly made preparations to meet them. Kilpatrick deployed skirmishers and advanced in column of squadrons. Our supposed enemies were also prepared for fight, and a spirited conflict was anticipated. Several shots were exchanged, when the contending parties discovered their mutual mistake. Our opponents proved to be the Twelfth Illinois, which, after leaving the main column at Thompson's Cross Roads, had swept down through the enemy's communications about Ashland Station, destroyed several important bridges and some stores, and was now, like ourselves, endeavoring to reach Gloucester Point.

This rencounter was very pleasing. Our column was greatly increased and encouraged. We needed this stimulus exceedingly, for we had been marching all day through a cold drizzling rain, which had dampened our ardor somewhat, and chilled our blood. Many of our horses had given out by the way, and were killed to prevent their falling into the enemy's hands. A few days of rest and care will so recruit such horses that they become again serviceable. Their places were filled by those horses and mules which were brought to us by the contrabands, which all along our journey flocked to our standards, and by such other animals as were captured by our flankers and advance guards. Exhausted as most of us were, no bivouac fires were kindled until we reached our lines of pickets from Gloucester Point, where we were received by our Union comrades in the midst of demonstrations of admiration and joy. Here we had a splendid rest.

May 7.—This morning, after a more sumptuous breakfast than we had had for many days, we crossed the York River to Yorktown, where we encamped. We are now, as it may well be supposed, the "lions of the day." Nothing is too good for us. We have the freedom of the town, and the subject of our raid is the theme of private and public speculation.

In our travels we have captured and paroled over three hundred prisoners, burned five or six railroad bridges, destroyed all the ferries on our route, captured and demolished two wagon-trains, burned five or six dépôts of stores, destroyed one railroad train, besides stations and telegraph offices, and have torn several miles of track. We have taken over one hundred and fifty horses, some of them the finest in the country.

The following extract from the Yorktown Gazette will more fully explain the importance of our expedition:

"We have heard startling accounts of the prodigies of valor performed by Stuart's Cavalry in Virginia, and the bands of Morgan in the West. That they showed true valor, nice discretion, and great powers of endurance, we will not for a moment question. But the exploits of our cavalry, in the late expedition in the rear of Lee's army, surpasses any thing ever achieved on this continent. Especially are the adventures of the Second New York (Harris Light Cavalry) and the Twelfth Illinois almost incredible. But they bear with them trophies that fully confirm the record of their daring.

"They penetrated within the outer lines of fortification at Richmond, to within less than two miles of the city, and captured prisoners and trophies there. They cut all the communications between that city and Lee's army, travelled two hundred miles, and lost only thirty men. Many of them have changed horses a number of times on the route. Whenever theirs got tired, they laid hold of any thing that came in their way that suited them better. The contrabands flocked to them from every quarter. They would take their masters' teams from the plough and their best horses from the stables. Some of them were almost frantic with delight on the appearance of the Yankees. Over three hundred found their way to this place. Their services are all needed at this present time."

The following report of Brigadier-General King will be read with interest:

Yorktown, Virginia, May 7, 1863.

To Major-General Halleck:

Colonel Kilpatrick, with his regiment (the Harris Light Cavalry) and the rest of the Twelfth Illinois, have just arrived at Gloucester Point, opposite this post.

They burned the bridges over the Chickahominy, destroyed three large trains of provisions in the rear of Lee's army, drove in the Rebel pickets to within two miles of Richmond, and have lost only one lieutenant and thirty men, having captured and paroled upwards of three hundred prisoners.

Among the prisoners was an aid of General Winder, who was captured with his escort far within the entrenchments outside of Richmond.

The cavalry have marched nearly two hundred miles since the third of May. They were inside of the fortifications of Richmond on the fourth; burnt all the stores at Aylett's Station, on the Mattapony, on the fifth; destroyed all the ferries over the Pamunkey and Mattapony, and a large dépôt of commissary stores near and above the Rappahannock, and came here in good condition. They deserve great credit for what they have done. It is one of the finest feats of the war.

Rufus King,
Brigadier-General Commanding Post.

Another print contained the following remarks:

Two regiments of Stoneman's Cavalry, the Second New York (Harris Light Cavalry) and the Twelfth Illinois, after accomplishing the duty assigned them of cutting the railroads near Richmond, made their way through the country to this place. The boldness and success of their movements surpass any thing of the kind ever performed in this country.

Various opinions are entertained with regard to General Stoneman's expedition as a whole, some believing it to have been a grand success, and others a conspicuous failure. The former look only at what was actually accomplished, the latter only at what they think might have been done. While all admit that the destruction of property and the severance of communications were a serious blow to the enemy, most persons agree that the General made a mistake in dividing his command. Had he kept his forces together he was amply sufficient to have broken all railroad and telegraphic connection between Lee and Richmond at least for a whole week, and he could have routed any cavalry force which could have been brought against him. As it was, by dividing his strength, he made each party too weak to effect very great damage, and exposed them to great danger of capture.

The following is a summary, in tabular form, as clipped from the New York Herald, of the work accomplished by General Stoneman's expedition:

Bridges destroyed	23	
Culverts destroyed	7	
Ferries destroyed	5	
Railroads broken, places		7
Supply-trains burned	4	
Wagons destroyed	122	
Horses captured	200	
Mules captured 104		
Canals broken 3		
Canal-boats burned	5	
Trains of cars destroyed		8
Storehouses burned	2	
Telegraph-stations burned		4
Wires cut, places	5	
Dépôts burned 3		
Towns visited 25		
Contrabands liberated 400		

Besides the destruction of large quantities of pork, bacon, flour, wheat, corn, clothing, and other articles of great value to the Rebel army.

BATTLE OF CHANCELLORSVILLE.

But it must be borne in mind that General Stoneman's grand raid and ride were only the background of a bloody tableau in the wilderness country around Chancellorsville. The last days of April witnessed the stratagem and skill of General Hooker, in his advance upon the enemy's position. A feint of crossing his entire army to the south side of the Rappahannock below Fredericksburg completely deceived the enemy, who at once withdrew his forces from the upper fords of the river. This was Hooker's desire and expectation.

Three corps, commanded respectively by Generals Howard, Slocum, and Meade, had been sent up the river, but marched at a sufficient distance from the hostile southern bank to avoid all observation. Arriving at Kelly's Ford, they began to cross, though it was in the night, and the men were compelled to wade in water up to their armpits. The moon, which shone brightly, assisted them most of the night, but went down before the entire force had crossed, when crossing had to be suspended until morning. Pontoons were brought up and laid, and so the remainder of the infantry and the cavalry corps crossed pleasantly.

The column advanced towards the Rapidan, and Generals Howard and Slocum's commands crossed this stream at Germania Mills, and General Meade's at Ely Ford, below, and then all marched on roads which converge to the Chancellorsville House, a large brick edifice, which was used as a mansion and tavern, situated in a small clearing of a few acres, and which, with its few appendages of outbuildings, constituted the village known by that name. Other forces, including General Pleasonton, with nearly a brigade of cavalry, who guarded the flanks of the advancing columns, had crossed the river, and taken their position near Chancellorsville.

By this wily movement General Lee's position on the Rappahannock had been entirely flanked; and, flushed with incipient success, General Hooker followed his great captains, and in the evening of the thirtieth of April he established his headquarters in the historic brick mansion above described. So completely absorbed was our general with the brilliancy of his advance that, in the moment of exultation, he forgot the dangers of his situation, and issued the following congratulatory order:

Headquarters Army of the Potomac,
Camp near Falmouth, Virginia, April 30, 1863.

It is with heartfelt satisfaction that the commanding general announces to the army that the operations of the last three days have determined that our enemy must either ingloriously fly or come out from behind his defences and give us battle on our own ground, where certain destruction awaits him. The operations of the Fifth, Eleventh, and Twelfth Corps have been a succession of splendid achievements.

By command of Major-General Hooker.

S. Williams, Assistant Adjutant-General.

It would seem as if the general had overlooked the fact that his army had but eight days' supplies at hand; that a treacherous river flowed between him and his dépôts; that he was surrounded by a labyrinth of forests, traversed in every direction by narrow roads and paths, all well known to the enemy, but unknown even to most of his guides; and that many of his guns of heaviest calibre, and most needed in a deadly strife, were on the other side the river. General Lee had undoubtedly been outgeneraled by Hooker in this movement, but he appeared not to have been disconcerted. Leaving the Heights of Fredericksburg with a small force, he advanced towards Chancellorsville.

May 1.—The first collision between the contending forces took place to-day. General Sykes, with a division of regulars, was despatched at nine o'clock in the morning on the Old Pike to Fredericksburg. He was followed by a part of the Second Corps. Sykes had not proceeded far before he encountered Lee advancing, and a sharp contest ensued, with heavy losses on both sides. The Rebels having the best ground, and being superior in numbers, compelled our men to fall back, which they did in tolerable order, bringing away every thing but their dead and badly wounded. But the enemy followed our retreating column, though cautiously, and filled the woods with sharpshooters. They also planted their heavy batteries on hills which partially commanded the clearing around the Chancellorsville House. This gave them great advantage. They were also greatly elated with the success which had crowned the first onset. This was Hooker's first misfortune or mistake. The first blow in such an engagement is quite as important as the last. This first movement ought to have been more powerful, and ought to have given to our men a foretaste of victory. But we had lost prestige and position which undoubtedly weakened us not a little. The night following passed quietly away, except that the leaders were laying their plans for future operations.

About eight o'clock on the morning of the second, it was reported that a heavy column of the enemy was passing rapidly toward our right, whither the Eleventh Corps had been stationed. This movement was hidden by the forests, though the road over which the column passed was not far from our front. A rifled battery was opened upon this moving column, which, though out of sight, was thrown into disorder, at which time General Birney made a charge upon them with such force as to capture and bring away five hundred prisoners. By successive and successful advances, by sunset our men had broken this column and held the road upon which they had been marching to some scene of mischief. But the evil was not cured, as other roads more distant and better screened were followed by the wily foe.

Just before dark Stonewall Jackson, with about twenty-five thousand veterans, fell like a whirlwind upon the Eleventh Corps, which he had flanked so cautiously and yet so rapidly that our German comrades were taken by surprise while preparing their suppers, with arms stacked, and no time to recover. It is not at all wonderful that men surprised under these circumstances should be panic-stricken and flee. Let the censure rest not upon the rout, but upon the carelessness that led to the surprise.

Whole divisions were now overwhelmed by the Rebel hordes, that swept forward amid blazing musketry and battle-shouts which made the wilderness resound; and a frantic stampede commenced which not all the courage and effort of commanding generals, or the intrepidity of some regiments could check, and which threatened to rout the entire army. This unforeseen disaster changed the whole programme of the battle and greatly disheartened our men. However, the ground was not to be abandoned so ingloriously, and though our lines were broken, and the enemy had gained a great advantage, heroism was yet to manifest its grand spirit, and to achieve undying laurels. The sun had gone down, refusing to look upon this Union defeat and slaughter, but the pale-faced moon gazed with her weird light upon the bloody scene, while the carnage still continued.

With the disaster of the Eleventh Corps General Sickles, who was stationed in the front and centre of our lines and had been preparing to deal a heavy blow upon the enemy, was left in a critical position. His expectation of assistance from General Howard was not only cut off, but he was left with only two divisions and his artillery to meet the shock of the advancing hosts. General Pleasonton, with his small force of cavalry, being under Sickles' command, was ordered to charge the proud columns of the enemy, with the hope of checking them until our batteries could be suitably planted.

Pleasonton, addressing Major Keenan of the Eighth Pennsylvania Cavalry, said, "You must charge into those woods with your regiment, and hold the Rebels until I can get some of these guns into position. You must do it at whatever cost."

"I will," was the noble response of the true soldier, who, with only about five hundred men, was to encounter columns at least twenty-five thousand strong, led by Stonewall Jackson! The forlorn charge was made, but the martyr-leader, with the majority of his dauntless troopers, soon baptized the earth upon which he fell, with his life blood. But the precious sacrifice was not in vain. The Rebel advance was greatly checked, as when a trembling lamb is thrown into the jaws of a pursuing pack of ravenous wolves.

The two determined generals improved these dear-bought moments in planting their own batteries, and getting in readiness also several guns which had been abandoned by the Eleventh Corps in its flight. All these guns were double-shotted, and all due preparation was made for the expected stroke. It was a moment of trembling suspense. Our heroes waited not long, when the woods just in front of them began to swarm with the advancing legions, who opened a fearful musketry, and charged toward our guns. Darkness was falling; but the field where the batteries were planted was so level that the gunners could do wonderful execution. And this they did. The Rebel charge had just commenced when our guns simultaneously opened with a withering fire, which cut down whole ranks of living flesh like grass. As one line of embattled hosts melted away, another rushed forward in its place to meet the same fate. Three successive and desperate charges were made, one of them to within a few yards of the guns, but each was repulsed with terrible slaughter. In many places the dead were literally in heaps. Our resistance proved successful.

A little later in the night, and right in front of these batteries, fell Stonewall Jackson, mortally wounded by our scathing fire, as was at first supposed, but more likely by the fire of his own infantry, as one of their writers alleges. Speaking of Jackson, he says, "Such was his ardor, at this critical moment, and his anxiety to penetrate the movements of the enemy, doubly screened as they were by the dense forest and gathering darkness, that he rode ahead of his skirmishers, and exposed himself to a close and dangerous fire from the enemy's sharpshooters, posted in the timber.

"So great was the danger which he thus ran, that one of his staff said: 'General, don't you think this is the wrong place for you?' He replied quickly: 'The danger is all over; the enemy is routed. Go back, and tell A. P. Hill to press right on.' Soon after giving this order General Jackson turned, and, accompanied by his staff and escort, rode back at a trot, on his well-known 'Old Sorrel,' toward his own men. Unhappily, in the darkness—it was now nine or ten o'clock at night—the little body of horsemen was mistaken for Federal cavalry charging, and the regiments on the right and left of the road fired a sudden volley into them with the most lamentable results. Captain Boswell, of General Jackson's staff, chief of artillery, was wounded; and two couriers were killed. General Jackson received one ball in his left arm, two inches below the shoulder joint, shattering the bone and severing the chief artery; a second passed through the same arm, between the elbow and wrist, making its exit through the palm of the hand; a third ball entered the palm of his right hand, about the middle, and, passing through, broke two of the bones.

"He fell from his horse, and was caught by Captain Wormly, to whom he said, 'All my wounds are by my own men.'"

The loss of this heroic chieftain, this swift flanker and intrepid leader, was undoubtedly the greatest yet felt by either army in the fall of a single man. Some report that, on hearing of the sad fall of his chief Captain, General Lee exclaimed, "I would rather have lost twenty thousand men!"

Admitting that the Rebels gained in this battle a great victory, its advantages were dearly purchased by the loss of Thomas Jonathan Jackson. About midnight a fierce charge was made by General Sickles' forces, which proved successful, enabling our boys to recover much of the ground formerly occupied by the unfortunate Eleventh Corps, and they brought back with them some abandoned guns and other valuable articles from the débris, which the Rebels had not time or disposition to disturb.

General Hooker then ordered this exposed position to be abandoned, and by daylight our lines were falling back in good order towards Chancellorsville, but were closely pursued by the enemy, who filled the woods. Several determined charges were made upon our retreating columns, which, however, were repelled mostly by the fire of our artillery, which mowed down hundreds as they rushed recklessly almost to the cannon's mouth. But these batteries had been played and worked so incessantly for the last twelve hours, that ammunition began to fail, and General Sickles sent a message to Hooker that assistance must be granted him, or he would be compelled to yield his ground. The officer who brought the despatch, found General Hooker in a senseless state, surrounded by his hopeless attendants, while general confusion had possession of the headquarters. A few minutes previous to this a cannon-ball had struck the wall of the mansion upon which the General was incidentally leaning, the concussion felling him to the floor. For some time he was supposed to be dead, but soon giving signs of returning consciousness, General Couch, who was next in rank, refused to assume command, and hence about one hour of precious time was lost. This was a fatal hour. Had General Hooker been able to receive Sickles' message, and ordered a heavy force to his assistance, it is thought that a great disaster could have been prevented, and probably a victory might have been gained.

But the golden opportunity, which is seldom duplicated in a given crisis or a life-time, was lost; and the enemy, though somewhat disorganized and badly disheartened by our well-managed batteries, had time, during this lull, to recover strength. They then advanced again with such power as to compel our men to retire from Chancellorsville toward the Rappahannock, leaving the brick mansion a mass of ruins, made such by the fire of the enemy.

By noon General Hooker had recovered his consciousness sufficiently to order the movements of his troops. The fighting on his front was now nearly over, but his position was critical. General Sedgwick, who had been directed to cross the Rappahannock below Fredericksburg, with orders to advance thence against all obstacles until he could fall upon General Lee's rear, while the grand army engaged him in front, found it impossible to proceed as rapidly as was expected of him, and was finally repulsed with such slaughter and pursued with such vigor as to be compelled to recross the river, leaving at least five thousand of his men killed, wounded, and captured in the hands of the enemy.

No alternative seemed now left to the Army of the Potomac but to beat a retreat and recross the river. On the evening of the fifth, General Hooker held a council of war with his commanders, at which, however, nothing was decided upon; but in the night he took the responsibility of ordering all his forces to recross the Rappahannock, which they did in good order and without molestation; and thus ended the disastrous battle of Chancellorsville, with a loss of about eighteen thousand men on each side, and our remaining troops returned to bivouac on their old camping-ground on the north bank of the river near Falmouth.

This retrograde movement was undoubtedly considered to be necessary in consequence of the impending storm, which set in about four o'clock of the afternoon of the fifth, and rendered the march and night exceedingly disagreeable. The river was swollen so rapidly as to set adrift several of our pontoons, and the act of recrossing, though orderly, was by no means pleasant. The storm was cold and violent, and the roads soon became so bad as to remind the boys of Burnside's unfortunate advance in January. It is supposed by some that the rain explains satisfactorily the conduct of the enemy, who seemed to make no attempt whatever to follow our returning troops.

While yet the rain was drenching our weary boys, on the sixth, General Hooker issued a congratulatory order to them and the country, in which are to be found the following characteristic passages:

"The Major-General commanding tenders to this army his congratulations on its achievements of the last seven days. If it has not accomplished all that was expected, the reasons are well known to the army. It is sufficient to say they were of a character not to be foreseen nor prevented by human sagacity or resources.

"In withdrawing from the south bank of the Rappahannock before delivering a general battle to our adversaries, the army has given renewed evidence of its confidence in itself and its fidelity to the principles it represents. In fighting at a disadvantage, we would have been recreant to our trust, to ourselves, our cause, and our country. Profoundly loyal, and conscious of its strength, the Army of the Potomac will give or decline battle whenever its interest or honor may demand. It will also be the guardian of its own history and its own honor.

"By our celerity and secrecy of movement, our advance and passage of the rivers was undisputed, and, on our withdrawal, not a Rebel ventured to follow.

"The events of the last week may swell with pride the heart of every officer and soldier of this army. We have added new lustre to its former renown. We have made long marches, crossed rivers, surprised the enemy in his intrenchments, and, wherever we have fought, have inflicted heavier blows than we have received. We have taken from the enemy five thousand prisoners and fifteen colors; captured and brought off seven pieces of artillery; placed hors de combat eighteen thousand of his chosen troops; destroyed his dépôts filled with a vast amount of stores; deranged his communications; captured prisoners within the fortifications of his capital, and filled his country with fear and consternation. We have no other regret than that caused by the loss of our brave companions; and in this we are consoled by the conviction that they have fallen in the holiest cause ever submitted to the arbitrament of battle." This order, if not perfectly satisfactory to the country and to the authorities, was generally hailed with applause by the army, which recognized in its sagacious rendering of our difficulties and humiliations the meed of praise awarded where it was due.

General Lee's order respecting this campaign is also very modest and unique, and is worthy of a place in this record. In it he says:

"With heartfelt gratification the General commanding expresses to the army his sense of the heroic conduct displayed by officers and men during the arduous operations in which they have just been engaged.

"Under trying vicissitudes of heat and storm, you attacked the enemy strongly intrenched in the depths of a tangled wilderness, and again on the hills of Fredericksburg, fifteen miles distant, and, by the valor that has triumphed on so many fields, forced him once more to seek safety beyond the Rappahannock. While this glorious victory entitles you to the praise and gratitude of the nation, we are especially called upon to return our grateful thanks to the only Giver of victory for the signal deliverance He has wrought.

"It is, therefore, earnestly recommended that the troops unite on Sunday next in ascribing to the Lord of Hosts the glory due His name. Let us not forget in our rejoicings the brave soldiers who have fallen in defence of their country; and, while we mourn their loss, let us resolve to emulate their noble example. The army and the country alike lament the absence for a time of one [Jackson] to whose bravery, energy, and skill they are so much indebted for success."

The two great armies once more confronted each other from either bank of the river, as they had done during all the winter and spring months. On the seventh of May, President Lincoln visited the camp near Falmouth, conferred with his generalissimo on movements past and future, appeared pleased with the spirit and morale of the troops, and returned to Washington to continue his earnest toil for the nation's life and well-being.

During the month quite a depletion of the rank and file of the army took place, by the mustering out of large numbers of three months' and two years' men. And such had been the depressing influences of Chancellorsville upon the country, that the places of these men were not very easily filled. To the sagacious leaders in political and military circles this state of things was not a little alarming. But to the Rebel leaders the times were affording opportunities for grand schemes, and for the execution of movements most startling.

Chapter XI - From Yorktown to Falmouth.

1863.—Curiosity Satisfied.—Pastimes on the York River.—Religious Services; their Influence.—Raid to Mathias Court House.—Sickness and Recovery.—From Gloucester Point to Falmouth.—Exciting Details.—Correspondence of Mr. Young.— The Press.—With the Army of the Potomac again.—Cavalry Fight at Brandy Station.—Bold Charge of the First Maine Cavalry.—The Chivalry fairly Beaten.— Death of Colonel B. F. Davis, Eighth New York Cavalry.—Interesting Letter of a Rebel Chaplain.—Casualties.—What was Gained by the Reconnoissance.—Pleasonton and Kilpatrick Promoted.—Rebels Raiding in Maryland.

Long raids and general engagements or campaigns are usually followed by a few days of comparative rest. This is necessary both for animals and men. Vacancies which are generally made during such vicissitudes, in the staffs of commissioned and non-commissioned officers, have to be filled, and reorganization takes place. This was the experience of the Army of the Potomac after its Chancellorsville campaign, as well as our own after our return from Richmond.

On the eighth of May, Kilpatrick's command left Gloucester Point in the morning, and, after crossing the York River, amid the cheers of General Keyes' command, we were provided with tents in an encampment within the fortifications of Fort Yorktown. Here was a fine opportunity for repose, which we were all in a condition to relish. Like the prince of poets, we could realize that

Weariness
Can snore upon the flint, when rusty sloth
Finds the down-pillow hard.

On the day following our arrival here, soldiers and citizens from the town were flocking into our camp in droves, from réveille till taps, eager to learn from us the particulars of our recent raid. Groups of attentive hearers could be seen in various parts of the grounds surrounding some of our talkative comrades who discoursed eloquently to them of the sufferings and fatigue, of the daring and danger, of the stratagem and endurance which attended the expedition. No little amount of yarn was spun, and not a little imagination was employed to paint the scenes as vividly as possible.

May 10.—A dress-parade was ordered at ten o'clock this morning, at which time a complimentary order to the regiment from the Secretary of War was read by the adjutant. The occasion was very interesting, and every man seemed to feel proud of himself, his deeds, and especially of his leader. In the afternoon our cup of delight was made to run over by the appearing of our paymaster with his "stamps," as the boys call the greenbacks. "We received two months' pay. The usual scenes of pay-day were reënacted, and the occasion passed away amid the untempered follies of some and the conserving wisdom of others.

The weather is warm and beautiful. Many of us are improving the opportunity of bathing in the York. This, though not a military, is certainly a very salutary, exercise, and one which we very much enjoy. Boat-rides are occasionally participated in, and lots of sport is found in raking the river-bed for oysters. "Two birds are here killed with one stone," for there is pleasure in catching, and a double pleasure in eating, these bivalvular creatures of the brine. Some days we live on little else but oysters—a diet which is very rapidly recuperating our overtasked powers.

Sunday, May 17.—This has been a beautiful day, and this evening a large meeting for religious services was held near the spot where Lord Cornwallis surrendered his sword to General Washington. The place seemed hallowed with the memory of those events; and it certainly ought to have witnessed the surrender of many rebellious hearts to the "King of kings and Lord of lords." The exercises of the meeting were conducted by the officers of the post, and were full of interest.

Wild and rude as soldiers often are, they generally attend with pleasure all religious services when they are pleasantly invited to do so. And I think no one ever beheld more attentive audiences than here. So great is the contrast between the spirit of such a meeting and the general tenor of our work, that the transition is relieving. Then there is so much in the life and character of a true soldier that suggests the experience and principles of a soldier of the Cross, that a versatile and interesting speaker in a religions assembly here finds ample illustrations from our every-day observations for the unfolding of Christian themes. And yet the main influence of Christianity here lies back even of these statements; it is found in the ready response which memory brings from the fireside religion of our homes, and the early instructions of the Sunday-school and church. The "stirring up of our pure minds by way of remembrance," which is done so easily in the company of American soldiers, is one of the most potent elements of heroism and right discipline which can be found.

The history of this country borrows so much light from the cross which Columbus bore as an ensign, and planted here, from the prayers of the Pilgrim Fathers, and from the Christian devotion of Washington and others who laid the foundation of this great Republic, that a true American cannot be destitute of reverence for the religion of the Bible. Hence over us especially these religious assemblies cannot fail to exert a salutary influence. And yet we observe that not more than one regiment in five is provided with a chaplain, or with means of religious instruction. To a certain extent this deficiency is supplied by the benevolent agents of the Christian Commission, who, however, are not able to fill the place of a faithful chaplain. But if it were not for these, many of our sick and dying would be utterly destitute of Christian influence, and our dead would be buried more like dogs than like Christian heroes. We fear that the Government does not properly appreciate the importance of the chaplaincy in the army, and hence does not give sufficient inducement for true men to enter this difficult field of labor. Only a man of stalwart character is fit for the position—a man of physical, mental, and moral daring. And so far as our observations extend, with very few exceptions, this is the class of men who occupy the position of chaplains among us.

May 19.—Several days have been spent pleasantly within Fort Yorktown, and we are becoming somewhat eager for more lively experiences and scenes.

"Variety's the source of joy below,
From which still fresh revolving pleasures flow."

During the day we abandoned Fort Yorktown, and Kilpatrick established a camp for the regiment in the old peach-orchard, famous for the battle which occurred within its limits during McClellan's Peninsular Campaign. It is a lovely spot, which, however, shows signs of the conflict above referred to. There is scarcely a tree but presents marks of the bloody drama, in broken bark and splintered trunk, and in wounded branches which hang danglingly over our heads.

RAID TO MATHIAS COURT HOUSE.

During the day a detail of the regiment, sufficient in number to mount all the serviceable horses, was ordered out in an expedition against Mathias Court House. A detachment of infantry and a battery of artillery accompany the cavalry, and Kilpatrick is in command of the entire force. The line of march is through a rich and beautiful region of country. Mathias county is a lovely peninsula, encompassed by the waters of the Piankatank River, on the north, the Chesapeake Bay, on the east, and Mob Jack Bay, on the south. The North River forms a portion of its boundary on the west, against Gloucester county, and nearly severs it from the mainland.

Kilpatrick was favored with fine weather in his expedition, and returned on the twenty-second crowned with success. A multitude of slaves was liberated, hailing our forces everywhere as their friends and protectors. Large numbers of fine horses and mules, with which that country abounds, were also captured. No Rebel force of any importance was encountered, and the boys greatly enjoyed their visit to the well-stocked plantations of the wealthy farmers, many of whom had never before seen a Yankee.

May 24.—I was taken very suddenly ill during the night. Dr. Kingston came to see me at three o'clock, and so skilfully treated my case, that I was quickly relieved of pain. In three hours from the time the surgeon came to my quarters, I was well enough to be up and on duty, so that at six o'clock I was able to call the roll of my company as usual, and to attend to other duties. The day after my illness I began to make out muster and pay rolls for my company. This work was undertaken by all the first-sergeants of the regiment. But our task is unusually difficult, as nearly all our company-books and papers were captured by guerillas at the commencement of the spring campaign. "Patience and perseverance" is our motto; and yet many times, as we endeavor to unravel the snarls and untie the knots, we find that the above virtues almost forsake us.

May 26.—This afternoon we had mounted regimental drill, and this was followed by dress-parade. Our time is now devoted mostly to drilling, in preparation, as we all think, for some movement.

May 29.—Orders for an advance have at length reached us. At five o'clock this afternoon we struck our tents, broke camp, and crossed the York by ferry, halting for the night near Fort Keyes, at Gloucester Point. There is much discussion among us as to the point of destination, but nearly all agree that we are to rejoin the Army of the Potomac. Soldiers seldom know the object of their movements. All we need is to receive the order or command, and we go, "asking no question for conscience' sake."

May 30.—We moved from Gloucester Point early in the morning, and made a forced march to the Piankatank River. The rising smoke announced to us that the bridge across this stream had been burnt before us. After considerable searching and sounding, a place so nearly fordable was found as to enable a portion of the command to cross over. Others meanwhile constructed a temporary bridge over which they effected a crossing. Guerillas are very numerous in these parts. One of our vedettes was fired upon and wounded by them early this evening. All our attempts to capture such culprits are in vain. The forests are so dense, and ravines so deep and dark, that a man acquainted with every secret nook and corner, can hide away in perfect security, after committing his depredations.

Sunday, **May 31.**—The Troy company is on picket duty to-day. A detachment from the company made a reconnoissance this morning beyond the outposts, and brought in two citizens of a suspicious character. They undoubtedly belong to the gang of bushwhackers that has hung upon our flanks and rear, and inflicted the injuries we have sustained for the past few days. Rich supplies of bacon and corn, of sorghum and honey, are found along our path. The country has never been visited by Federal troops, and is as full of provisions for us as it is filled with consternation and alarm at our approach. We have spent the day in scouting the country.

June 1.—Our march was resumed at an early hour in the morning, and we advanced to Urbanna, a town on the Rappahannock. Here several important captures were made, including Colonel E. P. Jones and Captain Brown, of the Virginia militia. Here we spent the night pleasantly. During the night Kilpatrick managed to establish communication with our gun-boats on the Rappahannock, and in the morning early we were taken across on transports, protected by the gun-boats. After a short halt to feed our horses from the corn-ricks which dot the country, we resumed our march, and with the setting sun reached a place called Litwalton, where we bivouacked for the night.

June 3.—To-day we had a very pleasant march through a pleasant country and with pleasant weather. Richmond Court House was reached for our bivouac to-night; but we left early in the morning of the fourth, and by good marching arrived at Port Conway at four o'clock P. M. Here we unsaddled our horses for the first time since leaving Yorktown, after the marches of six days.

June 5.—We reached Falmouth. Upon meeting our old acquaintances in the Army of the Potomac, cheers upon cheers were heartily vociferated for Kilpatrick and the Harris Light, and our march was a continual ovation.

The following quotations will show the consideration that was accorded to Kilpatrick's movements:

"Colonel Kilpatrick, with the Harris Light Cavalry and the Twelfth Illinois Cavalry, left Yorktown at twelve o'clock Friday night, reaching Gloucester Point at one A. M., and Gloucester Court House at half-past five A. M., Saturday. They left again at eight o'clock, and at four P. M. on the same day arrived at Saluda, leaving there at half-past four Monday morning, and reaching Urbanna at half-past six A. M., where the wharves were found to be partially destroyed by fire.

"The bridge on the Piankatank River, near Dragon Ordinary, had been destroyed by the citizens, and, as there were no fords, a squadron of the Twelfth Illinois swam their horses over the river, while another portion of Kilpatrick's command—the Colonel and his staff-officers assisting—constructed a floating bridge of felled trees and fence-rails in about half an hour, over which the remainder of the cavalry crossed in safety.

"At Saluda the colors of the Twelfth Virginia Infantry were captured by the cavalry. From there the country was scoured for a distance of ten miles, resulting in the capture of horses, mules, and carriages, and in the emancipation of numerous slaves.

"Between Montague and Bowler's Ferry the Rebel pickets were driven in as far as the barricades which they had constructed of felled trees, within three miles of the ferry.

"Occasionally guerilla skirmishing was encountered on the road; but there was no fighting with any considerable force of the Rebels, though they had infantry and artillery at Kings and Queens Court House and about two hundred cavalry at Bowler's Ferry.

"A letter from Stuart was intercepted, addressed to a secessionist named Fontleroy, in Middlesex County, assuring him that he would have a sufficient force of cavalry in that neighborhood by Sunday evening to relieve the anxiety of the people of the county and stop the raids of the Yankees.

"Among the prisoners captured by Kilpatrick's cavalry was Captain Brown, of the Fifth Virginia cavalry, and the guerilla, Colonel E. P. Jones. The only man wounded was Orderly-Sergeant Northrup, of Company G, Harris Light Cavalry, who was hit with a buckshot-charge fired by a bushwhacker.

"The transports Long Branch, William N. Frazier, Star, and Tallaca, under the command of Lieutenant-Colonel Dickinson, of General Hooker's staff, conveyed the cavalry and the captured horses and mules across the Rappahannock from Urbanna to Carter's wharf, six miles higher up than the former place, and subsequently conveyed the contrabands to Aquia Creek.

"The gun-boats Freeborn, Yankee, Anacostia, Jacob Bell, Satellite, Primrose, and Currituck, convoyed the transports up and down the river, and the Jacob Bell covered the landing at Carter's Creek. These vessels of the Potomac flotilla were under the command of Commodore Samuel Magaw.

"There was a small force of infantry under Colonel Dickinson, being picked men; and the cavalry, with the aid of this infantry at Urbanna, despoiled the Rebels between Yorktown and the Rappahannock of nearly one thousand contrabands and about three hundred horses and mules, besides depleting their granaries and poultry-yards.

"Colonel Kilpatrick, Colonel Dickinson, and Commodore Magaw, and those in their commands, are entitled to commendation for the energy exhibited, as is also the engineer corps of the Fiftieth New York, under Captain Folwell, which promptly repaired the bridge at Carter's wharf. Lieutenant-Colonel Dickinson, Captain John B. Howard, acting assistant-quartermaster, formerly of the Brooklyn Fourteenth, and other military gentlemen and civilians, rode out to Saluda, and were hospitably entertained at the residence of the Clerk of the Courts, who tendered his assurances of respect with generous plates of strawberries and cream."

From another periodical we clip the following:

"We have an account of Colonel Kilpatrick's recent successful raid back from Gloucester Point. He crossed the country between the York and Rappahannock Rivers, making an extensive circuit through the garden-spot of Virginia—a section where our troops have never before penetrated. Colonel Kilpatrick made a large haul of negroes, horses, &c., and has arrived safely at Urbanna with them. He spread general terror among the Rebels. His forces were taken across the Rappahannock by our gun-boats, and proceeded at once to our lines."

A brief item from the Troy Times will complete the journal of this important event:

"Colonel Kilpatrick is the hero of another great raid through the enemy's country. At the conclusion of Stoneman's raid, it will be remembered, Colonel Kilpatrick's command remained at Gloucester Court House. Last week he was ordered to again join the main army, and, on the thirtieth ultimo, he started on the march to Urbanna, on the Lower Rappahannock. He returned to the Army of the Potomac on the fifth instant, after travelling over a large extent of territory and destroying an immense amount of property."

A little rest was enjoyed at Falmouth. But our experience convinces us that the cavalryman must write history in haste if he would write as rapidly as it is made.

June 7.—The bugles sounded réveille at three o'clock A. M. "Boots and saddles" followed at four; "lead out" at four-and-a-quarter, and the column was in motion towards Warrenton Junction at four-and-a-half. We went viâ Catlett's Station, which place we reached at two o'clock P. M. Nearly every step of the march was on familiar ground, where we had passed and repassed many times. It seemed like meeting old friends, and nearly every object we saw suggested thoughts and experiences of the past.

Cavalry Fight at Brandy Station, June 9th, 1863.

At Warrenton Junction we rejoined the Cavalry Corps, now under the command of General Alfred Pleasonton.

June 9.—At two o'clock P. M. the whole Cavalry Corps moved from Warrenton Junction towards the Rappahannock. We are marching in two columns, one towards Beverly and the other towards Kelly's, Fords. The Harris Light moves with the latter column. Two brigades of infantry under Generals Ames and Russell accompany the expedition, each with a battery of artillery.

CAVALRY FIGHT AT BRANDY STATION.

Early on the morning of the ninth we arrived at the river, where it was evident we were not expected in force, for we found nothing but a strong picket-guard to contest our advance. A brief though brisk skirmish took place at the ford, but the Rebel pickets were soon driven back and our column began to cross over, the Harris Light being in the van. On reaching the south bank of the stream, the column was re-formed, and we advanced for some distance at a gallop.

The column at Beverly Ford, commanded by General Gregg, had been engaged since early in the morning, and the roaring of light arms and the booming of cannon clearly indicated to us that hot work was being done by our comrades below. It had been hoped that that column would be able to strike the enemy in flank at Brandy Station, in the early part of the day, giving us an opportunity to rake them furiously in front. Hence we were somewhat retarded in our movements, waiting or expecting the combinations and juxtapositions which had been planned. But, failing in this, at length we advanced towards the station, where, at ten o'clock, we engaged a regiment of Stuart's cavalry. As soon as we reached the field which they had evidently selected for the fight, we charged them in a splendid manner, routing them completely, and capturing many prisoners. Light artillery was used briskly on both sides.

By twelve o'clock Pleasonton's entire force had effected a union, after much severe fighting, on the left, and the engagement became general. The infantry fought side by side with the cavalry. There was some grand manœuvring on that historic field, and feats were performed worthy of heroes.

One incident should be particularized. At a critical moment, when the formidable and ever-increasing hosts of the enemy were driving our forces from a desirable position we sought to gain, and when it seemed as though disaster to our arms would be fatal, Kilpatrick's battle-flag was seen advancing, followed by the tried squadrons of the Harris Light, the Tenth New York, and the First Maine. In echelons of squadrons his brigade was quickly formed, and he advanced like a storm-cloud upon the Rebel cavalry which filled the field before him. The Tenth New York received the first shock of the Rebel charge, but was hurled back, though not in confusion. The Harris Light met with no better success; and, notwithstanding their prestige and power, they were repulsed under the very eye of their chief, whose excitement at the scene was well-nigh uncontrollable. His flashing eye now turned to the First Maine, a regiment composed mostly of heavy, sturdy men, who had not been engaged as yet during the day; and, riding to the head of the column, he shouted, "Men of Maine, you must save the day! Follow me!" With one simultaneous war-cry these giants of the North moved forward in one solid mass upon the flank of the Rebel columns. The shock was overwhelming; and the opposing lines crumbled like a "bowing wall" before this wild rush of prancing horses, gleaming sabres, and rattling balls.

On rode Kilpatrick with the men of Maine, and, on meeting the two regiments of his brigade, which had been repulsed and were returning from the front, the General's voice sang out like clarion notes above the din of battle, "Back, the Harris Light! Back, the Tenth New York! Re-form your squadrons and charge!". With magical alacrity the order was obeyed, and the two regiments, which had been so humbled by their first reverse, now rushed into the fight with a spirit and success which redeemed them from censure, and accounted them worthy of their gallant leader. The commanding position was won; a battery lost in a previous charge was recaptured, and an effectual blow was given to the enemy, which greatly facilitated the movements which followed.

But the Rebel cavalry was greatly emboldened and strengthened by reënforcements of infantry which were brought in railroad cars. We, however, continued to press them closely until six o'clock, when, by a grand charge of our entire force, we gained an important position, which ended the contest. Heavy columns of Rebel infantry could now be distinctly seen advancing over the plains from the direction of Culpepper, to the rescue of their fairly-beaten cavalry. But it was too late for them, for we had won a splendid victory, and had gained all the information of Rebel movements which we desired to obtain. Under cover of the night we recrossed the Rappahannock in safety.

The whole command had lost about five hundred men, and we brought over with us one hundred prisoners. In the early part of the engagement fell Colonel B. F. Davis, of the Eighth New York Cavalry, who was instantly killed. His loss was a subject of general lamentation. He had distinguished himself for great sagacity, wonderful powers of endurance, and unsurpassed bravery. He it was who led the cavalry safely from Harper's Ferry just before Miles' surrender of the place, and who, on his way to Pennsylvania, captured Longstreet's ammunition-train.

Among our wounded was Colonel Percy Wyndham. The enemy's killed included Colonel Saul Williams, of the Second North Carolina Cavalry, and Lieutenant-Colonel Frank Hampton, of the South Carolina Cavalry; General W. H. F. Lee and Colonels Butler and Harmon were among their wounded. They acknowledge a loss of six hundred men.

From the Richmond Sentinel we clip the following account of the battle, by a Rebel chaplain:

Camp in Culpepper County,
June 10, 1863.

Tuesday, the ninth of June, will be memorable to General Stuart's command as the day on which was fought the longest and most hotly-contested cavalry battle of the war. At an early hour skirmishing commenced, and soon the commands of Hampton, the two Lees, Robinson, and Jones, were engaged along the whole Culpepper line, from Welford's Ford, on the Hazel, down to Stevensburg. Each command acted nobly, and the Yankees were forced, after a fight of nearly twelve hours, to recross the river with great losses. We have to lament the loss of many gallant officers and privates, some killed and others permanently disabled. The forces under W. H. F. Lee, that worthy descendant of "Old Light Horse Harry," bore no mean part in the fray. We have to regret the temporary loss of our general (W. H. F. Lee), who was wounded in the thigh, and the death of Colonel Williams (of our brigade), than whom a more elegant gentleman or braver soldier never lived.

Being connected with the Tenth Virginia Cavalry, under Colonel J. Lucius Davis, and, therefore, better cognizant of its conduct, it is not invidious to allude to it, though not claiming any superiority over other regiments, all of which did nobly. Early in the morning this regiment was dismounted for sharp-shooting, and, until ordered off, held its ground, though exposed to an incessant and galling fire from the Fifth United States Regulars, who were snugly ensconced behind a stone fence. At this point many of the casualties in our regiment occurred. In the afternoon the Tenth, led by Colonel Davis, made a splendid charge on the Second United States Regulars, who, after a hand-to-hand conflict, broke and fled incontinently. Our General (Stuart), whose praise is not to be despised, paid a high compliment on the field to the Tenth for its conduct in holding Welford's Hill, and for its dashing charge.

I append a list of casualties:

Company A (Caskie Rangers), commanded by Captain Robert Caskie.—Killed: None. Wounded: Second Lieutenant J. Doyle, slightly in head; Private, Eytel, in breast; English, in foot; Hubbell, in breast; Gill, in arm and shoulder; Wilson, in hip. Missing and taken prisoners: Privates Burton, Charles Childress, Joseph Childress, Fulcher, Hudnall, and Parker.—Total, 12.

Company B, Captain W. B. Clements.—Killed: Corporal N. B. Ellis. Wounded: Privates Anderson Foster, severely in thigh; P. J. Cape, in thigh; H. Foster, slightly in foot; R. P. Brewbaker, slightly in head; A. Caton, in hand.—Total, 6.

Company C, commanded by Lieutenant Richardson.—Killed: None. Wounded: Lieutenant N. Richardson, seriously through breast; Sergeant J. Mason, in leg; Corporal Brown, in arm; Privates J. B. King, slightly in thigh; W. B. Saw, seriously in hip; M. Potter, in hand. Missing: J. Shumate. —Total, 7.

Company D, absent on detached service.

Company E, commanded by Captain J. Tucker.—Killed: Private H. T. Bourgois. Wounded: Corporal F. S. Labit, in shoulder; S. H. Lamb, in hand. Missing: Sergeant Peter Smith (wounded and captured); Sergeant Stromburg (wounded and captured); Private Enoch Pelton.—Total, 6.

Company F, commanded by Captain J. H. Dettor.—Killed: G. Wescott. Wounded: Privates John White, in thigh; John E. Edge, in thigh; J. R. Giles, in arm; Sergeant J. Durret, arm.—Total, 5.

Company G, commanded by M. S. Kirtley.—Killed: None. Wounded: Corporal J. M. McConn, seriously in arm; Private Jonathan Shepherd, slightly in head. Missing: Private S. Hartley.—Total, 3.

Company H, commanded by Lieutenant S. K. Newham.—Killed: None. Wounded: Privates James O'Connor, mortally; M. Neff, seriously in leg. Missing: J. P. Martz, R. F. Koontz.—Total, 4.

Company I (Henrico Light Dragoons), commanded by Lieutenant J. H. T. McDowell.—Killed: Private Louis Ottenburg. Wounded: Sergeant S. L. McGruder, slightly in shoulder; Corporal J. C. Mann, slightly in leg; Privates Walter Priest, mortally in breast; George Waldrop, slightly in shoulder; B. J. Duval, slightly in head; W. T. Thomas, in shoulder slightly.—Total, 7.

Company K, commanded by Captain Dickinson.—Killed: None. Wounded: Corporal J. L. Franklin, in right shoulder; Private J. M. Craig, head, left arm severely; R. V. Griffin, right shoulder severely; C. P. Preston, slightly in nose; W. T. Arrington, breast slightly; T. R. Gilbert, left arm slightly. Missing: Sergeant T. S. Holland; Privates E. A. Haines and S. R. Gilbert.—Total, 9.

Total killed, wounded, and missing, 59.

J. B. Taylor, Jr., Chaplain Tenth Virginia Cavalry,
W. H. F. Lee's Brigade.

Two important ends were reached by this advance, namely, first, a cavalry raid contemplated by Stuart, who had massed his forces near Culpepper, was utterly frustrated; and second, General Pleasonton ascertained conclusively that General Lee was marching his army northward, with the evident design of invading the Northern States. Indeed, it was a suspicion of such a movement that led General Hooker to order the reconnoissance.

The day following this glorious fight, in which the men of the North had proved themselves to be more than a match for the boasted Southern chivalry, and had gained a name which placed Pleasonton's command at the head of the world's cavalry forces, Pleasonton was made a Major-General, and Kilpatrick a Brigadier. Their stars were well-deserved and proudly worn.

During the day the Cavalry Corps moved to Warrenton Junction, leaving strong guards at the fords of the Rappahannock to prevent any crossing which might be attempted by the enemy.

June 11.—At two o'clock this afternoon General Gregg inspected our division. The day was beautiful, and the troopers made a splendid appearance. To heighten the interest of the occasion, the colors captured by the Harris Light at

Urbanna, and those taken by the First Maine in their memorable charge at Brandy Station on the ninth instant, were displayed amid the cheers of the enthusiastic cavalrymen, whose past deeds give encouraging promise for the future.

Sunday, June 14.—We are still encamped on the plains near Warrenton Junction. On the twelfth the regiment was inspected by Captain Armstrong, of Kilpatrick's staff. The following day we had an interesting mounted-drill. We cannot keep idle. This afternoon, at two o'clock, we received orders to prepare to move at a moment's notice. Cannonading is distinctly heard in the direction of Warrenton.

For several days it has been expected that General Lee, with his forces, would make his appearance on the banks of the Potomac, somewhere below Harper's Ferry. But as they have failed to do so, the inquiry is very general among us, "Where are they?" and, "What do they intend?" To work out the answer to such interrogations is generally the work of the cavalry; so that, when our orders for readiness to move were received, we saw before us a reconnoissance in force. We understand that already Rebel cavalry is raiding more or less in Maryland, and some exciting times are expected before long.

Chapter XII - Second Invasion of Maryland.—Gettysburg.

1863.—Invasion of the Northern States.—Kilpatrick at Aldie.—The Bloody Battle.— Daring Deeds.—Colonel Cesnola, Fourth New York Cavalry.—Incidents.—Victory.— Advance to Ashby's Gap.—Pleasonton's Official Report.—Rebel Movements on Free Soil.—Difficulties in the North.—The Cavalry Corps Crosses the Potomac at Edward's Ferry.—General Meade succeeds Hooker.—Orders.—Changes in the Cavalry.— Movements.—Kilpatrick's Fight with Stuart at Hanover Junction.—Solemn and laughable Scenes.—Buford's Division Opens the Fight at Gettysburg.—Death of General Reynolds.—First Bay's Repulse.—Second Bay.—Rebel Advantages.—Third Bay.—Last Grand Effort.—Death of General Farnsworth.—The Republic just Saved.

For nearly two days we were prepared to march, and awaiting orders, when at last they came. At about six o'clock on the morning of the sixteenth we took up our line of march, which was mostly along the railroad in the direction of Manassas. Having arrived at these celebrated plains, we struck off a little to the left towards Centreville, where we arrived at ten o'clock, weary with the long journey. Here we ascertained that General Hooker's headquarters are at Fairfax Court House, or in the vicinity, and that his army covers the approaches to Washington.

June 17.—After a refreshing night's rest, we were up early in the morning, and resumed our march at six o'clock, taking the Warrenton Turnpike. Kilpatrick has the advance of the corps. We soon crossed the memorable fields of the two Bull Run battles, passed the famous field of Groveton, and there deflecting to the right, and pushing forward rapidly, we arrived by noon in sight of the hills which partially surround the village of Aldie, on the north side of the Bull Run Mountains. Kilpatrick had been directed to move through Aldie, and thence to and through Ashby's Gap, in the Blue Ridge, learn all he could of the enemy's movements, and, then returning, to rejoin the corps at Nolan's Ferry on the Potomac. Colonel Duffié, with his regiment, the First Rhode Island, was ordered to move through Thoroughfare Gap, and to join Kilpatrick in Pleasant Valley beyond. These plans were laid with the presumption that no very heavy force of Rebels remained north of the Blue Ridge, and none at all north of the Bull Run Mountains. But this was a great mistake.

BLOODY BATTLE OF ALDIE.

James Moore, M. D., Surgeon of the Ninth Pennsylvania Cavalry, thus describes what occurred to Kilpatrick and his command at this place:
"Scarcely had his advance reached the town of Aldie, when it came directly upon the advance-guard of W. H. F. Lee. It was entirely unexpected. No enemy was supposed to be on the Aldie side of the Bull Run Mountains.
"The general rode to the front, ran his eye over the field for a moment, and then rapidly gave his orders. He had taken in the whole field at one rapid glance, and saw the important points that must be gained. The Harris Light Cavalry was directed to charge straight down the road, through the town, gain and hold the long, low hill over which runs the road from Middleburg. With anxious eye he watched the charge, on which so much depended, saw that it was successful, and quickly and resolutely pushed in one regiment after another on the right of the Harris Light, till the high hills far on the right of Aldie were gained.
"This fine disposition was made, and important position won, before the Rebel General Fitzhugh Lee could make a single effort to prevent it, although he had a division of cavalry at his back.
"He soon recovered, however, from the temporary surprise, and for two hours made most desperate efforts to regain the position lost. He struck the right, left, and centre in quick succession, while his battery of Blakely guns thundered forth their messengers of death.
"But all in vain! Kilpatrick's gallant men—the heroes of Brandy Station—met and hurled back each charge, while Randall's battery, ignoring entirely the Rebel guns, sent his canister and shells tearing through the heavy columns of the enemy.

"On this day Kilpatrick did wonders. He fought under the eye of his chief, and where bullets flew the thickest, and where the shock came the heaviest, there rang his cheering voice and there flashed his sabre. His own regiment, the Harris Light, had failed to meet his hopes on the plains of Brandy Station. This was known to the officers of that splendid organization, and on that very morning they had petitioned their general for an opportunity to retrieve their reputation. The opportunity was at hand.

"A large force of the enemy occupied a strong position behind rail barricades encircling large stacks of hay. For a long time Rebel sharp-shooters, from this secure position, had baffled every attempt to advance our lines on the left. The general ordered up a battalion of the Harris Light. Quickly they came! Addressing a few encouraging words to the men, and then turning to Major McIrvin, the officer in command, he said, pointing to the barricades: 'Major, there is the opportunity you have asked for. Go, take that position!' Away dashed this officer and his men. In a moment the enemy was reached, and the struggle began. The horses could not leap the barricade, but the men dismounted, scaled those formidable barriers, and, with drawn sabres, rushed upon the hidden foe, who quickly asked for quarter.

"Another incident occurred worth mentioning. Colonel Cesnola, of the Fourth New York Cavalry, had that morning, through mistake, been placed under arrest, and, his sword being taken from him, was without arms. But in one of these wild charges, made early in the contest, his regiment hesitated. Forgetting that he was under arrest, and without command, he flew to the head of his regiment, reassured his men, and, without a weapon to give or ward a blow, led them to the charge. This gallant act was seen by his general, who, meeting him on his return, said: 'Colonel, you are a brave man; you are released from arrest;' and, taking his own sword from his side, handed it to the colonel, saying: 'Here is my sword; wear it in honor of this day!' In the next charge Colonel Cesnola fell, desperately wounded, and was taken prisoner.

"The Rebel general, being foiled at every point, resolved to make one more desperate effort. Silently and quickly he massed a heavy force upon our extreme right, and, led by General Rosser, made one of the most desperate and determined charges of the day. Kilpatrick was aware of this movement, and satisfied that his men, exhausted as they were, could not withstand the charge, had already sent for reënforcements.

"Before these could reach him the shock came. The First Massachusetts had the right, and fought as only brave men could to stem the tide that steadily bore them back, until the whole right gave way. Back rushed our men in wild confusion, and on came the victorious Rebel horsemen. The general saw, with anguish, his flying soldiers, yet in his extremity retained his presence of mind, and proved himself worthy the star he had won at Brandy Station.

117

"Sending orders for the centre and left to stand fast, he placed himself at the head of the First Maine, sent to his assistance, and coolly waited till the Rebel charging columns had advanced within fifty yards of Randall's guns. He then shouted 'Forward!' and the same regiment that saved the day at Brandy Station was destined to save the day at Aldie. Rosser's men could not withstand the charge, but broke and fled up the hill. The general's horse was killed in the charge, and here the brave Colonel Doughty fell.

"The general determined now to complete the victory, and, mounting a fresh horse, he urged on the First Maine and First Massachusetts, sent orders for his whole line to advance, and then sounded the charge. Lee struggled for a few minutes against this advance, and then ordered a retreat, which ended in a rout. His troops were driven in confusion as far as Middleburg, and night alone saved the remnant of his command.

"This was by far the most bloody cavalry battle of the war. The Rebel chivalry had again been beaten, and Kilpatrick, who was the only general on the field, at once took a proud stand among the most famous of our Union cavalry generals. The fame of our cavalry was now much enhanced, and caused the greatest joy to the nation."

June 18.—General Pleasonton was anxious to press the Rebel cavalry back upon their infantry, to ascertain minutely their movements; hence, to-day, Kilpatrick was ordered to advance through the Bull Run Mountains, and to occupy Middleburg. Jaded as we were, as well as our horses, with the fearful yet glorious labors of the previous day, with mercury up to 98° Fahrenheit in the shade, and 122° in the sun, with an atmosphere unusually oppressive for Virginia, and through dust which many tramping hoofs made almost intolerable, we marched into Pleasant Valley. The outpost of the Rebel cavalry was met near the town, but they were driven from the streets, and we took possession of Middleburg.

About three o'clock in the afternoon a heavy wind arose, betokening rain, which began to fall about five o'clock, mingled with hail. For this atmospheric change we had earnestly prayed. The heat had become so oppressive, and the roads so dusty, as to make our movements very unpleasant and disastrous to men and beasts, especially to the latter.

In this beautiful region of country we spent a few days very pleasantly, recruiting our strength and awaiting orders.

CAVALRY BATTLE AT UPPERVILLE.

June 21.—The Cavalry Corps, with General Pleasonton at its head, moved, at eight o'clock this morning, in the direction of Ashby's Gap, in the Blue Ridge. We had not proceeded far before we encountered the Rebel pickets, which we drove steadily before us. Their strength, however, greatly increased as we advanced. Quite a large force contested our progress when we entered Carrtown, and from this place to Upperville the engagement was a little too heavy to be called a skirmish. Nevertheless, we pushed ahead without being seriously retarded until we reached Upperville. Here our advance was met with great desperation, the enemy charging us handsomely, but with no great damage. When our forces had been properly arranged, and the right time had come, Kilpatrick was ordered to charge the town. With drawn sabres— weapons in which the general always had great confidence, and generally won success—and with yells which made the mountains and plains resound, we rushed upon the foe. The fray was terrible. Several times did the Rebels break, but, being reënforced or falling back upon some better position, again endeavored to baffle our efforts. But they were not equal to the task, and we drove them through the village of Paris, and finally through Ashby's Gap, upon their infantry columns in the Shenandoah Valley. In these charges and chase we captured two pieces of artillery, four caissons, several stand of small arms, and a large number of prisoners.

It was my misfortune, in one of those desperate encounters, to have a favorite horse shot under me. But it was also my fortune to escape from the deadly missiles which filled the air, and from my fallen horse, unhurt. Another animal was soon provided for me from the captures we had made.

Our scouts, during this engagement, had managed to gain an entrance into the Valley, where they ascertained that the Rebel army, in heavy columns, was advancing towards the Upper Potomac.

This fight was of sufficient importance to call forth from the commanding general the following official document:

Headquarters Cavalry Corps,
Camp near Upperville, 5.20 P. M., June 21.

Brigadier-General S. Williams:

General: I moved with my command this morning to Middleburg, and attacked the cavalry force of the Rebels under Stuart, and steadily drove him all day, inflicting a heavy loss at every step.

I drove him through Upperville into Ashby's Gap.

We took two pieces of artillery, one being a Blakely gun, and three caissons, besides blowing up one; also, upwards of sixty prisoners, and more are coming; a lieutenant-colonel, major, and five other officers, besides a wounded colonel and a large number of wounded Rebels left in the town of Upperville. They left their dead and wounded upon the field; of the former I saw upward of twenty.

We also took a large number of carbines, pistols, and sabres. In fact, it was a most disastrous day to the Rebel cavalry.

Our loss has been very small both in men and horses.

I never saw the troops behave better, or under more difficult circumstances. Very heavy charges were made, and the sabre used freely, but always with great advantage to us.

A. Pleasonton,
Brigadier-General.

The day following this decided victory by force of arms, and by the stratagem of scouts, who obtained all needful information as to the intentions of the enemy, the Cavalry Corps retired from Ashby's Gap and established its headquarters at Aldie. Our outposts are near Middleburg. We are now receiving some exciting news from Maryland and the North. It appears that Rebel cavalry was raiding through Maryland, destroying railroads and bridges, telegraph lines and dépôts, and making havoc on the Chesapeake and Ohio Canal as early as the fifteenth instant; and that General Ewell, with a corps of infantry, crossed the Potomac at Williamsport on the sixteenth, and advanced via Hagerstown towards Pennsylvania.

A sad and distressing alarm seems to have aroused the North. General Lee's advance thus far, excepting the repulses of his cavalry on his right flank, has been a perfect success. It is true that Washington, the glittering prize before him, has been protected by General Hooker's cautious movements. But this protection of the Capital has consumed time and given the enemy a decided advantage in other quarters. He had already entered the Free States before we fairly understood his intentions.

Winchester, an important post in the Shenandoah Valley, guarded by General Milroy, was nearly surrounded by the advancing Rebel hordes, before our general even dreamed that he was in jeopardy. The few of our men who escaped from that garrison, were greatly demoralized, while about four thousand were made prisoners, and many heavy guns, small arms, wagons, horses, and stores of all kinds fell into the enemy's hands.

These blunders on our part and losses, together with the prowess and boast of the Rebel legions, gave the malcontents of the North, and political tricksters, a coveted opportunity to rail against the Administration, and to weaken, as far as their influence could be felt, the confidence which had been reposed in it. The President was represented as an imbecile, utterly devoid of statesmanship. The army was berated with no measured terms. Every reverse of fortune was attributed to a want of brains and heart in the heads of departments. The Republic had certainly fallen upon dark days.

General Lee, undoubtedly, expected to make capital out of this state of things, and hoped that by winning a grand victory on Northern soil, so to cripple the Administration and to demoralize the political party in power, that he could secure the aid and comfort of the opposing party, and thus compel the North to submit to any terms of peace which the anomalous Confederacy might dictate. Notwithstanding the threatening posture of military affairs, and that the Government was thoroughly alarmed and ordered out the militia of Maryland, Pennsylvania, New York, Ohio, West Virginia, and other States, the call being faithfully reëchoed by the Governors of those States, the responses were comparatively faint and fell far short of the numbers which had been demanded. New York City alone responded generously. The uniformed and disciplined regiments there generally and promptly went to the contest, and appeared where they were needed. For this the Governor of the State was publicly thanked by the Secretary of War.

June 25.—We are informed that our infantry and artillery, with small detachments of cavalry, are advancing through Maryland to meet and repel the invaders, who are reported to be crossing the Potomac in two heavy columns at Shepherdstown and Williamsport. Every department of the service seems to be in commotion, and great things are expected. A heavy rain set in early this evening.

June 26.—At six o'clock this morning we broke camp at Aldie and advanced towards Leesburg, spending the night near this place. Most of our time has been spent in the saddle. This is becoming not only our seat, but also our bed and pillow.

June 27.—At five o'clock A. M. our corps commenced its march towards Edward's Ferry, on the Potomac. On our way to the ferry we crossed the famous battle-field of Ball's Bluff, where Colonel Baker and many of his gallant Californians became an early and costly sacrifice to the cause of the Union. On reaching the river we found the two pontoon bridges over which already a large portion of our army had passed on before us. They had been much retarded by the heavy rains and mud. The approaches to the pontoons had been so trodden by the myriad feet of men and beasts, and cut by the heavy wheels of laden wagons and artillery, that we found the roads almost bottomless. But as we had seen mud many times before, we moved forward undismayed, though somewhat retarded, and were soon on Northern soil. A somewhat strange feeling came over us on finding ourselves marching mainly towards the North Star to meet the enemy, whereas we had so long been accustomed to look and march only southward for this purpose.

Our march lay through a fine and fertile section of country. The vast fields of grain are ripening for the harvest, and their appearance indicates that thus far the labors of the husbandman have not been in vain. The peacefulness of the fields and flocks presents a striking contrast to the warlike preparations which are now being made for what must be the most decisive and bloody contest of the war. The rebellion seems to have risked its very existence in the coming conflict, which cannot be many days hence. Determination and desperation seem foremost in the movement. On our side a solemn decision seems to be actuating the masses. We know that should the "Stars and Bars" be victorious again, and at this crisis of our national affairs, as they were at the two Bull Run battles, and at Chancellorsville, our "Stars and Stripes" will not only be shamefully humbled, but suffer cruel elimination. In such an event some of our stars must fall and some of the beams of our light must be obscured.

"But conquer we must, for our cause it is just,
And this be our motto, 'In God is our trust.'
And the star-spangled banner in triumph shall wave
O'er the land of the free and the home of the brave."

Sunday, June 28.—All night long we were on the march, arriving in the vicinity of Frederick City early in the morning. The whole country for miles seems to be covered with soldiers. This is one of the most beautiful spots in the world. However, the city does not show the thrift and prosperity which are evidenced in Northern cities enjoying similar advantages. This is the capital of Frederick County, one of the richest in the State. Looking southward from the city we behold an almost interminable stretch of beautiful rolling land, nearly every inch of which is not only arable but richly productive. On the east, at a distance of several miles, the eye rests upon a range of hills which sweep downward toward the Potomac, terminating in the lofty peak called Sugarloaf. Westward rises the loftier chain of the Catoctin, which is but a continuation of the Bull Run Mountains, severed by the river at Point of Rocks. All the highest peaks of these hills and mountains are now used for signal stations, where wave the signal flags by day and flash the signal fires by night. One seldom wearies in watching these operations, though he may not understand their significance.

CHANGE OF COMMANDERS.

This has been a day of much interest among us and of no little excitement—a day of changes and reorganization. An exciting rumor was bandied from man to man this morning, that General Hooker was about to be relieved from the command of the grand army; and the day was only partly spent when the strange rumor resolved itself into the astounding truth. The facts which led to this result may not be perfectly understood among us, but appear to be about as follows: On discovering that the enemy had actually invaded the Northern States, General Hooker requested the authorities to send him all the forces which could be spared from General Heintzelman's command in and about the Defenses of Washington. This was done. But, having crossed the Potomac, General Hooker visited Harper's Ferry with its strong garrison, and immediately urged upon the Government the importance of placing this force also under his command. Upon this subject there sprang up a sharp controversy between Hooker and Halleck. The latter rejoined to the former in these words:

"Maryland Heights have always been regarded as an important point to be held by us, and much expense and labor incurred in fortifying them. I cannot approve of their abandonment, except in case of absolute necessity."

General Hooker's reply to this shows him to have been in the right, and to have comprehended the relative importance of the position in question:

"I have received your telegram in regard to Harper's Ferry. I find ten thousand men here in condition to take the field. Here they are of no earthly account. They cannot defend a ford of the river; and, so far as Harper's Ferry is concerned, there is nothing of it. As for the fortifications, the work of the troops, they remain when the troops are withdrawn. This is my opinion. All the public property could have been secured to-night, and the troops marched to where they could have been of some service. Now they are but a bait for the Rebels, should they return. I beg that this may be presented to the Secretary of War, and his Excellency, the President."

Receiving no direct reply to this announcement, and goaded by the pressure of fast-moving events, our General yielded to do what many of us heartily condemn, by sending the following message:

Sandy Hook, Md.,
June 27, 1863.

Major-General H. W. Halleck, General-in-Chief:

My original instructions require me to cover Harper's Ferry and Washington. I have now imposed upon me, in addition, an enemy in my front of more than my numbers. I beg to be understood respectfully, but firmly, that I am unable to comply with this condition, with the means at my disposal, and earnestly request that I may at once be relieved from the position I occupy.

Joseph Hooker, Major-General.

To-day came the order relieving General Hooker, who issued the following characteristic farewell address to the troops, many of whom were taken, wholly by surprise, and all of them appeared greatly afflicted:

Headquarters Army of the Potomac,
Frederick, Md., June 28, 1863.

In conformity with the orders of the War Department, dated June 27, 1863, I relinquish the command of the Army of the Potomac. It is transferred to Major-General George G. Meade, a brave and accomplished officer, who has nobly earned the confidence and esteem of the army on many a well-fought field. Impressed with the belief that, my usefulness as the commander of the Army of the Potomac is impaired, I part from it, yet not without the deepest emotions. The sorrow of parting with the comrades of so many battles is relieved by the conviction that the courage and devotion of this army will never cease nor fail; that it will yield to my successor, as it has to me, a willing and hearty support. With the earnest prayer that the triumph of this army may bring successes worthy of it and the nation, I bid it farewell.

Joseph Hooker, Major-General.

Such a change of régime on the eve of a great battle, with the command in the hands of one less known and trusted, at first seemed to threaten disaster. But the modest, earnest words with which the new commander framed his first order to the troops allayed all fears, renewed confidence, and greatly attached to him the hearts of his subordinates.

Headquarters Army of the Potomac,
June 28, 1863.

By direction of the President of the United States I hereby assume command of the Army of the Potomac. As a soldier, in obeying this order —an order totally unexpected and unsolicited—I have no promises or pledges to make. The country looks to this army to relieve it from the devastation and disgrace of a hostile invasion. Whatever fatigues and sacrifices we may be called to undergo, let us have in view constantly the magnitude of the interests involved, and let each man determine to do his duty, leaving to an all-controlling Providence the decision of the contest. It is with just diffidence that I relieved, in the command of this army, an eminent and accomplished soldier, whose name must ever appear conspicuous in the history of its achievements; but I rely upon the hearty support of my companions in arms to assist me in the discharge of the duties of the important trust which has been confided to me.
George G. Meade,
Major-General Commanding.

This change of commanders was followed by others in various branches of the service, not excepting the Cavalry Corps. Our force has been increased by General Julius Stahel's division, which has been employed for some time in the vicinity of Fairfax Court House, and along the line of the Orange and Alexandria Railroad. In the reorganization, the corps, which continues under the efficient command of General Pleasonton, is arranged into three divisions, the First, Second, and Third, commanded respectively by Generals Buford, Gregg, and Kilpatrick. A more effective cavalry force was never organized on this continent, and probably on no other.

The Harris Light is assigned to General Gregg's division, which separates us, for the first time, from our former beloved commander. But we are not among those who desire to shirk responsibility for any such cause as this. After the division had been reorganized and reviewed, in the afternoon we took up our line of march to New Market. Some rain fell towards night, which laid the dust and allayed the heat. Men and horses are living well upon the rich products of the country. Upon such supplies we rely mainly, though our trains are not wholly destitute.

We are received with more or less enthusiasm and demonstrations of patriotism in nearly all the towns we visit, making a very striking contrast with our former receptions in cities and towns of Virginia. This gives our men additional courage, and nerves us for the conflicts impending.

June 29.—We have been in the saddle nearly all day, scouting the country in the neighborhood of Westminster. On the morning of the thirtieth, about nine o'clock, the regiment entered this pleasant town, the citizens flocking from all directions to pay us their respects, and to show their devotion to the cause of the Union. After a short halt we advanced to Manchester.

July 1.—To-day we marched to Hanover Junction, Pennsylvania, where we met the enemy's cavalry under General John Jenkins, and, after a spirited skirmish, they were forced to retire.

The Pennsylvanians welcomed us with glad cheers, and showed their appreciation of our presence and services by driving several "huckster's wagons" into our midst, well laden with a great variety of eatables, which were donated to us by the good citizens of the surrounding country. It is true that some of the inhabitants made their gifts very sparingly and not without grudging, while others charged enormous prices for such articles as we were willing to purchase; but justice demands that we state that such inhospitable, unpatriotic, and niggardly souls were the exception.

While here we learned the particulars of important movements made by other portions of our cavalry. Kilpatrick, with his vigorous division, left the vicinity of Frederick on Monday; and, striking northward, he passed through Taneytown, reaching Littletown about ten o'clock at night, where he was received in the midst of great rejoicing. A large group of children and young ladies, gayly attired, on the balcony of a hotel, waving handkerchiefs and flags, greeted their defenders with patriotic songs, while the heroic troopers responded with cheers which made the welkin ring. The command bivouacked in the vicinity of the village, where the citizens brought abundant forage for the horses, and the cavalrymen rested till morning. The march was then resumed in the direction of Hanover.

The column, which was several miles in length, entered this beautiful town, and was passing through, while the citizens were regaling the men sumptuously from their bountifully provided larders, and interchanging friendly and patriotic greetings, neither party suspecting the presence of the enemy. Nearly one half the column had already passed through, when suddenly the quiet, social scene was disturbed by the opening of a Rebel battery concealed on a wood-crowned hill, and so posted as to rake a portion of the road upon which the Union forces entered the town. This was immediately followed by a charge of Rebel cavalry, which had been drawn up in line of battle just behind a chain of hills which ran near and parallel to the highway. There they had quietly waited until the train was passing before them, with the hope that this might be captured or stampeded, and a glorious victory be won. General Stuart commanded in person, and the attack was certainly well planned. But Kilpatrick's boys were not to be disconcerted nor panic-stricken by any such or any other trap. The main force of the charging column happened to be in the rear of the Fifth New York, commanded by Major Hammond. Quick work was necessary. Rapidly moving out of the street into the open park near the railroad dépôt, Major Hammond drew his regiment in line of battle, and in nearly as short time as it takes to record it, charged with drawn sabres the Rebels, who then possessed the town. The charging columns met on Frederick street, where a fierce and bloody hand-to-hand contest ensued. For a few moments the enemy made heroic resistance, but soon broke and fled, closely pursued. They rallied again and again as fresh regiments came to their aid, but they were met, hurled back, and pursued with irresistible onsets, which compelled them to retire not only from the town, but also behind the hills under cover of their batteries.

In less than fifteen minutes from the time the Rebels charged into the village they were driven from it, leaving the streets strewn with their dead men and horses, and the débris which always accompanies such a conflict. The dead of both parties lay promiscuously about the street, so covered with blood and dust as to render identification in some cases very difficult. The blue of the Union and the gray of Rebellion were almost entirely obliterated, and, in many instances, the contending parties mingled their blood in one common pool. This work of destruction had but just commenced when Generals Kilpatrick and Farnsworth, who, though some miles distant at the head of the column when the booming cannon announced the bloody fray, arrived in hot haste and took personal charge of the movements. These were ordered with consummate skill, and executed with promptness and success. Elder's battery, well posted on the hills facing the Rebels, and well supported, soon silenced the guns of the enemy, and drove him in the direction of Lee's main army. He was thoroughly punished for his audacious attack, and left many dead, wounded, and captured. The colors of the Thirteenth Virginia Cavalry were captured by a sergeant of the Fifth New York. About seventy-five prisoners, beside the wounded, fell into our hands, including Lieutenant-Colonel Payne, who commanded a brigade.

The particulars of his capture are worthy of historic record. In one of the charges made in the edge of the town, one of our boys, by the name of Abram Folger, was captured by Colonel Payne, and marched toward the rear. Just outside the town was a large brick tannery, the vats of which were not under cover, and close alongside of the highway. Folger was walking beside the Colonel's orderly. As they approached the tan-vats he espied a carbine lying on the ground. Quick as thought he seized it, fired, and killed Payne's horse. The animal, in his death-struggle, plunged over towards the vats, and Payne was thrown headlong into one of them, being completely submerged in the tan-liquid. Folger, feeling that the Colonel was secure enough for the moment, levelled his piece on the orderly, who, finding that his pistol was fouled and hence useless, attempted to jump his horse over the fence, but not succeeding, surrendered. It happened, however, that Folger had expended the last shot in the carbine on the Colonel's horse; but, as the orderly did not know it, it was just as well for Folger as though more ammunition had been on hand.

The recently-made prisoner was compelled to assist his Colonel from the vat. His gray uniform, with white velvet trimmings, his white gauntlets, and his face and hair had received a brief but thorough tanning. Folger marched the two in front of him to the market-place in the centre of the village, where he delivered his captives to the authorities. In one hand the brave soldier-boy carried his empty carbine, and in the other a good strong stick. It was a most ludicrous and interesting scene. Folger was captured by Payne's command, in Virginia, the winter before this affair, and his feelings may be imagined at having so nicely returned the compliment.

The citizens of Hanover, who so nobly cared for our wounded in the hospitals during and after the battle, and assisted us in burying our dead, will not soon forget that terrible last day of June. Our brave boys, who, though taken by surprise, had so valiantly defeated the enemy, built their bivouac fires and rested for the night on the field of their recent victory. Stuart's cavalry was now losing caste, while our troopers were not only adding fresh laurels to their chaplet of renown, but also new fibres of vitality to the hearts and hands which loved and defended the sacred Tree of Liberty.

General Buford, with his division, had moved from Frederick City directly to Gettysburg, the capital of Adams County, a rural village of about three thousand inhabitants, beautifully situated among the hills, which, though quite lofty, are generally well cultivated. The general found the borough very quiet, and passed through; but he had not proceeded far beyond before he met the van of the Rebel army under General Heth, of Hill's Corps. The dauntless troopers charged furiously the invading hordes, and drove them back upon their supports, where our boys were driven back in their turn before overwhelming numbers. As Providence would have it, our infantry advance, under General James S. Wadsworth, marching from the village of Emmitsburg, hearing the familiar sound of battle, went into a double-quick, and, hastening through Gettysburg, struck the advancing Rebel column just in time to seize and occupy the range of hills that overlooks the place from the north-west, in the direction of Chambersburg.

General John F. Reynolds, a true Pennsylvanian, was in command of our entire advance, which consisted of the First and Eleventh Corps, about twenty-two thousand strong. As General Wadsworth was placing his division in position, General Reynolds went forward quite alone to reconnoitre, when he discovered a heavy force of the enemy in a grove not far distant. Dismounting quickly he crouched down by a fence through which he sought to survey the force and its position by means of his field-glass, when a whistling ball from a sharpshooter's musket struck him in the neck. He fell on his face and baptized with his life-blood the soil which had given him birth. His untimely fall, especially at this crisis and almost in sight of his childhood's home, was generally lamented. His lifeless form was borne away to the rear just as the Rebels in heavy force advanced upon not more than one-third their number. General Abner Doubleday had to assume command of our forces under this galling fire, having arrived with a portion of the First Corps, the remainder of which and the Eleventh Corps, not being able to join them until two hours of fearful destruction had gone on. Our feeble advance was compelled to fall quickly back upon Seminary Hill, just west of the village, and were pursued very closely, so much so that one portion of our line, seeing its opportunity, swung around rapidly, enveloping the Rebel advance and capturing General Archer the leader and about eight hundred prisoners. On the arrival of the Eleventh Corps, General O. O. Howard, being the ranking officer present, assumed command, giving his place to General Carl Schurz. Our men, now emboldened by these fresh arrivals of helpers, and having alighted upon a fine commanding position, renewed the fight with spirit and wonderful success. This prosperous tide of things continued until about one o'clock P. M., when their right wing was assailed furiously by fresh troops, which proved to be

General Ewell's Corps, which had been marching from York, directed by the thunder of battle.

Thus flanked and outnumbered by the gathering hosts, the Eleventh Corps, which was most exposed to the enfilading fire of the newly arrived columns, began to waver, then to break, and soon fled in perfect rout. The First Corps was thus compelled to follow, or be annihilated. The two retreating columns met and mingled in more or less confusion in the streets of the town, where they greatly obstructed each other, though the First Corps retained its organization quite unbroken. In passing through the town the Eleventh Corps was especially exposed to the fire of the enemy, who pressed his advantage and captured thousands of prisoners. Our wounded, who, up to this time, had been quartered in Gettysburg, fell into the enemy's hands, and scarcely one-half of our brave boys, who had so recently and proudly passed through the streets to the battle lines, had the privilege of returning, but either lay dead or dying on the well-fought fields, or were captives with a cruel foe. The number of killed and wounded showed how desperately they had fought, and the large number captured was evidence of the overwhelming numbers with which they had contended.

General Buford, with his troopers, covered our retreat, showing as bold a front as possible to the enemy, who, it was feared, would follow fiercely, as they were very strong and several hours of daylight yet remained. But doubtless fearing that a trap might be laid for them if they advanced too far, they contented themselves with only a portion of the borough, their main force occupying the hills which form a grand amphitheatre on the north and west. It would be difficult to refrain from saying, that those Rebel forces were prevented from advancing by some mighty unseen hand—the hand of Him who "watches over the destiny of nations."

Our feeble and decimated forces took possession of Cemetery Hill, south of the town, and being reënforced by General Sickles' Corps, they began to intrench themselves with earthworks and rifle-pits, to extend their lines to right and left, and to select the best positions for our batteries. This work was continued quite late into the evening, the broad moonlight greatly facilitating the operations.

General Meade, who had selected his ground for the impending battle along the banks of Pipe Creek, and who at one o'clock P. M. was at Taneytown when the news of the fight, and the death of the brave Reynolds at Gettysburg, reached him, despatched General Hancock to the scene of conflict to take command, and to ascertain whether Gettysburg afforded better ground than that which had been selected. Hancock arrived at Cemetery Hill just as our broken lines were hastily and confusedly retreating from the village; our advance, however, had already taken this commanding position and was making some preparation for resistance. The newly arrived general began at once to order the forces which had been engaged and others which were occasionally arriving. He ordered the occupancy of Culp's Hill on our extreme right, and extended the lines to our left well up the high ground in the vicinity of Round Top, a rocky eminence about two miles from Gettysburg, and nearly equi-distant from the Emmitsburg and Taneytown roads. The line having been made as secure as possible, Hancock wrote to Meade that the position was excellent. His despatch had scarcely gone, when he was relieved by General Slocum, a ranking officer, and so, leaving the field, Hancock hastened to report in person to his chief the condition of things at Gettysburg. On arriving, Meade informed him that he had decided to fight at Gettysburg, and had sent orders to the various commands to that effect; then together they rode to Gettysburg, arriving about eleven o'clock at night.

All night long our forces were concentrating before this historic village, where they were all found on the morning of the second of July, except the Sixth Corps, General Sedgwick's, which did not arrive until two o'clock in the afternoon, after marching nearly all the previous night.

SECOND DAY'S FIGHT.

Until three o'clock all was quiet along the battle lines, except an occasional picket or sharpshooter's fire. However, there had been considerable manœuvring. On our left General Sickles, in his eagerness for a fight, had advanced his corps across the Emmitsburg road, and on a wood-crowned ridge in the immediate vicinity of the main portion of the Rebel army. General Meade, in his inspection of the lines, remonstrated against the perilous position which Sickles had taken the liberty to gain. He, however, intimated that, if desired, he would withdraw to the ridge which Meade had justly indicated as the proper place where our forces would be better protected, and would be able to cover Round Top, a point which it was considered essential to retain. General Meade thereupon expressed his fear to Sickles that the enemy would not permit him quietly to retire from the trap in which he had placed his foot; and the last words had scarcely fallen from his lips, when the Rebel batteries were opened with fearful accuracy and at short range, and the infantry came on with their fierce charging yell. General Longstreet was in command.

With so long and strong lines of infantry in his front, which lapped over his flanks on either side, and a fearful enfilading fire from the heavy batteries on Seminary Hill, Sickles and his brave men were torn, shattered, overwhelmed, and with terrible loss and in great confusion, fell back to the ridge from which he ought not to have advanced. In the struggle the Rebels made a desperate attempt to reach and possess Round Top, which they came near doing before General Sykes, who had been ordered to advance and hold it, had gained the elevation. But their failure to possess this coveted prize proved a great disaster; for before they could withdraw their charging columns across the plain between Round Top and the ridge where Sickles stood at the beginning of the fray, they were attacked by General Hancock with a heavy force, and driven almost like chaff before the wind. Their loss was terrible. At the close of this encounter our lines stood precisely where General Meade desired they should be before the fight commenced, with Round Top fully in our possession and now strongly fortified with heavy artillery and good infantry support.

On our right General Ewell had succeeded in pushing back some portions of our lines under Slocum, who occupied Culp's Hill, and some of our fortified lines and rifle-pits were occupied by the Rebels. Night came on to close the dreadful day. Thus far the battle had been mostly in the advantage of the Rebels. They held the ground where Reynolds had fallen, also Seminary Ridge, and the elevation whence the Eleventh Corps had been driven. They also occupied the ridge on which Sickles had commenced to fight. Sickles himself was hors de combat, with a shattered leg which had to be amputated, and not far from twenty thousand of our men had been killed, wounded, and captured! The Rebels had also lost heavily; but, as they themselves believed, they were the winners.

General Lee, in his official report, says: "After a severe struggle, Longstreet succeeded in getting possession of and holding the desired ground. Ewell also carried some of the strong positions which he assailed; and the result was such as to lead to the belief that he would ultimately be able to dislodge the enemy. The battle ceased at dark. These partial successes determined me to continue the assault next day."

During these days of deadly strife and of unprecedented slaughter, our cavalry was by no means idle. On the morning of the first, Kilpatrick advanced his victorious squadrons to the vicinity of Abbottstown, where they struck a force of Rebel cavalry, which they scattered, capturing several prisoners, and then rested. To the ears of the alert chieftain came the sound of battle at Gettysburg, accompanied with the intelligence, from prisoners mostly, that Stuart's main force was bent on doing mischief on the right of our infantry lines, which were not far from the night's bivouac.

He appeared instinctively to know where he was most needed; so in the absence of orders, early the next morning he advanced to Hunterstown. At this point were the extreme wings of the infantry lines, and as Kilpatrick expected, he encountered the Rebel cavalry, commanded by his old antagonists, Stuart, Lee, and Hampton. The early part of the day was spent mostly in reconnoitring; but all the latter part of the day was occupied in hard, bold, and bloody work. Charges and counter-charges were made; the carbine, pistol, and sabre were used by turns, and the artillery thundered even late after the infantry around Gettysburg had sunk to rest, well-nigh exhausted with the bloody carnage of the weary day. But Stuart, who had hoped to break in upon our flank and rear, and to pounce upon our trains, was not only foiled in his endeavor by the gallant Kilpatrick, but also driven back upon his infantry supports, and badly beaten.

In the night, Kilpatrick, after leaving a sufficient force to prevent Stuart from doing any special damage on our right, swung around with the rest of his troopers to the left of our line, near Round Top, and was there prepared for any work which might be assigned him.

THE LAST EFFORT.

Friday, July 3.—The sun rose bright and warm, and looked down upon the blackened corpses of the dead, which were strewn over the bloody earth; upon the wounded who had not been cared for, and upon long glistening lines of armed men, ready to renew the conflict. Each antagonist, rousing every slumbering element of power, seemed to be resolved upon victory or death. The fight commenced early by an attack of General Slocum's men, who, determined to regain the rifle-pits they had lost the evening before, descended like an avalanche upon the foe. The attack met with a prompt response from General Ewell. But after several hours of desperate fighting, victory perched upon the Union banners, and with great loss and slaughter the Rebels were driven out of the breastworks, and fell back upon their main lines near Benner's Hill.

This successful move on the part of our boys in blue was followed by ominous lull or quiet, which continued about three hours. Meanwhile the silence was fitfully broken by an occasional spit of fire, while every preparation was being made for a last, supreme effort, which, it was expected, would decide the mighty contest. The scales were being poised for the last time, and upon the one side or the other was soon to be written the "Mene, Mene, Tekel, Upharsin." Hearts either trembled or waxed strong in the awful presence of this responsibility.

At length one o'clock arrived; a signal-gun was fired, and then at least one hundred and twenty-five guns from Hill and Longstreet concentrated and crossed their fires upon Cemetery Hill, the centre and key of our position. Just behind this crest, though much exposed, were General Meade's headquarters. For nearly two hours this hill was ploughed and torn by solid shot and bursting shell, while about one hundred guns on our side, mainly from this crest and Round Top, made sharp response. The earth and the air shook for miles around with the terrific concussion, which came no longer in volleys, but in a continual roar. So long and fearful a cannonade was never before witnessed on this continent. As the range was short and the aim accurate, the destruction was terrible. But the advantage was decidedly in favor of the

Rebels, whose guns were superior in number to ours, and of heavier calibre, and had been concentrated for the attack. A spectator of the Union army thus describes the scene:

"The storm broke upon us so suddenly, that soldiers and officers—who leaped, as it began, from their tents, or from lazy siestas on the grass—were stricken in their rising with mortal wounds, and died, some with cigars between their teeth, some with pieces of food in their fingers, and one at least—a pale young German, from Pennsylvania—with a miniature of his sister in his hands. Horses fell, shrieking such awful cries as Cooper told of, and writhing themselves about in hopeless agony. The boards of fences, scattered by explosion, flew in splinters through the air. The earth, torn up in clouds, blinded the eyes of hurrying men; and through the branches of trees and among the gravestones of the cemetery a shower of destruction crashed ceaselessly. As, with hundreds of others, I groped through this tempest of death for the shelter of the bluff, an old man, a private in a company belonging to the Twenty-fourth Michigan, was struck, scarcely ten feet away, by a cannon-ball, which tore through him, extorting such a low, intense cry of mortal pain as I pray God I may never again hear. The hill, which seemed alone devoted to this rain of death, was clear in nearly all its unsheltered places within five minutes after the fire began."

A correspondent from the Confederate army thus describes this artillery contest: "I have never yet heard such tremendous artillery-firing. The enemy must have had over one hundred guns, which, in addition to our one hundred and fifteen, made the air hideous with most discordant noise. The very earth shook beneath our feet, and the hills and rocks seemed to reel like a drunken man. For one hour and a half this most terrific fire was continued, during which time the shrieking of shell, the crash of fallen timbers, the fragments of rocks flying through the air, shattered from the cliffs by solid shot, the heavy mutterings from the valley between the opposing armies, the splash of bursting shrapnel, and the fierce neighing of wounded artillery-horses, made a picture terribly grand and sublime, but which my pen utterly fails to describe." Gradually the fire on our side began to slacken, and General Meade, learning that our guns were becoming hot, gave orders to cease firing and to let the guns cool, though the Rebel balls were making fearful havoc among our gunners, while our infantry sought poor shelter behind every projection, anxiously awaiting the expected charge. At length the enemy, supposing that our guns were silenced, deemed that the moment for an irresistible attack had come. Accordingly, as a lion emerges from his lair, he sallied forth, when strong lines of infantry, nearly three miles in length, with double lines of skirmishers in front, and heavy reserves in rear, advanced with desperation to the final effort. They moved with steady, measured tread over the plain below, and began the ascent of the hills occupied by our forces, concentrating somewhat upon General Hancock, though stretching across our entire front. Says a correspondent of the Richmond Enquirer: "Just as Pickett was getting well under the enemy's fire, our batteries ceased firing. This was a fearful moment for Pickett and his brave command. Why do not our guns reopen their fire? is the inquiry that rises upon every lip. Still, our batteries are silent as death!" And this undoubtedly decided the issue—was God's handwriting on the wall. The Rebel guns had been thundering so long and ceaselessly that they were now unfit for use, and ceased firing from very necessity.

"Agate," correspondent of The Cincinnati Gazette, gives the following graphic description of the struggle:

"The great, desperate, final charge came at four. The Rebels seemed to have gathered up all their strength and desperation for one fierce, convulsive effort, that should sweep over and wash out our obstinate resistance. They swept up as before: the flower of their army to the front, victory staked upon the issue. In some places they literally lifted up and pushed back our lines; but, that terrible position of ours!—wherever they entered it, enfilading fires from half a score of crests swept away their columns like merest chaff. Broken and hurled back, they easily fell into our hands; and, on the centre and left, the last half hour brought more prisoners than all the rest.

"So it was along the whole line; but it was on the Second Corps that the flower of the Rebel army was concentrated; it was there that the heaviest shock beat upon, and shook, and even sometimes crumbled, our lines.

"We had some shallow rifle-pits, with barricades of rails from the fences. The Rebel line, stretching away miles to the left, in magnificent array, but strongest here—Pickett's splendid division of Longstreet's corps in front, the best of A. P. Hill's veterans in support—came steadily, and as it seemed resistlessly, sweeping up. Our skirmishers retired slowly from the Emmitsburg road, holding their ground tenaciously to the last. The Rebels reserved their fire till they reached this same Emmitsburg road, then opened with a terrific crash. From a hundred iron throats, meantime, their artillery had been thundering on our barricades.

"Hancock was wounded; Gibbon succeeded to the command—an approved soldier, and ready for the crisis. As the tempest of fire approached its height, he walked along the line, and renewed his orders to the men to reserve their fire. The Rebels—three lines deep—came steadily up. They were in point-blank range.

"At last the order came! From thrice six thousand guns there came a sheet of smoky flame, a crash, a rush of leaden death. The line literally melted away; but there came the second, resistless still. It had been our supreme effort; on the moment we were not equal to another.

"Up to the rifle-pits, across them, over the barricades—the momentum of their charge, the mere machine-strength of their combined action, swept them on. Our thin line could fight, but it had not weight enough to oppose to this momentum. It was pushed behind the guns. Right on came the Rebels. They were upon our guns—were bayoneting the gunners—were waving their flags over our pieces.

"But they had penetrated to the fatal point. A storm of grape and canister tore its way from man to man, and marked its track with corpses straight down their line! They had exposed themselves to the enfilading fire of the guns on the western slope of Cemetery Hill; that exposure sealed their fate.

"The line reeled back—disjointed already—in an instant in fragments. Our men were just behind the guns. They leaped forward upon the disordered mass; but there was little need of fighting now. A regiment threw down its arms, and, with colors at its head, rushed over and surrendered. All along the field smaller detachments did the same. Webb's brigade brought in eight hundred: taken in as little time as it requires to write the simple sentence that tells it. Gibbon's old division took fifteen stand of colors.

"Over the fields the escaped fragments of the charging line fell back—the battle there was over. A single brigade, Harrow's (of which the Seventh Michigan is part), came out with fifty-four less officers, and seven hundred and ninety-three less men, than it took in! So the whole corps fought; so, too, they fought farther down the line.

"It was fruitless sacrifice. They gathered up their broken fragments, formed their lines, and slowly marched away. It was not a rout; it was a bitter, crushing defeat. For once the Army of the Potomac had won a clean, honest, acknowledged victory."

General Pickett's division was nearly annihilated. One of his officers recounted, that, as they were charging over the grassy plain, he threw himself down before a murderous discharge of grape and canister, which mowed the grass and men all around him, as though a scythe had been swung just above his prostrate form.

During the terrific cannonade and subsequent charges, our ammunition and other trains had been parked in rear of Round Top, which gave them splendid shelter. Partly to possess this train, but mainly to secure this commanding position, General Longstreet sent two strong divisions of infantry, with heavy artillery, to turn our flank, and to drive us from this ground. Kilpatrick, with his division, which had been strengthened by Merritt's Regular brigade, was watching this point, and waiting for an opportunity to strike the foe. It came at last. Emerging from the woods in front of him came a strong battle-line followed by others.

To the young Farnsworth was committed the task of meeting infantry with cavalry in an open field. Placing the Fifth New York in support of Elder's battery, which was exposed to a galling fire, but made reply with characteristic rapidity, precision, and slaughter, Farnsworth quickly ordered the First Virginia, First Vermont, and Eighteenth Pennsylvania in line of battle, and galloped away and charged upon the flank of the advancing columns. The attack was sharp, brief, and successful, though attended with great slaughter. But the Rebels were driven upon their main lines, and the flank movement was prevented. Thus the cavalry added another dearly-earned laurel to its chaplet of honor—dearly earned, because many of their bravest champions fell upon that bloody field.

Kilpatrick, in his official report of this sanguinary contest, says: "In this charge fell the brave Farnsworth. Short and brilliant was his career. On the twenty-ninth of June a general; on the first of July he baptized his star in blood; and on the third, for the honor of his young brigade and the glory of his corps, he yielded up his noble life."

Thus ended the battle of Gettysburg—the bloody turning-point of the Rebellion—the bloody baptism of the redeemed Republic. Nearly twenty thousand men from the Union ranks had been killed and wounded, and a larger number of the Rebels, making the enormous aggregate of at least forty thousand, whose blood was shed to fertilize the Tree of Liberty.

In the evening twilight of that eventful day General Meade penned the following interesting despatch to the Government:

Headquarters Army of the Potomac,
Near Gettysburg, July 3, 8.30 P. M.

To Major-General Halleck, General-in-Chief:

The enemy opened at one o'clock P. M., from about one hundred and fifty guns. They concentrated upon my left centre, continuing without intermission for about three hours, at the expiration of which time he assaulted my left centre twice, being, upon both occasions, handsomely repulsed with severe loss to them, leaving in our hands nearly three thousand prisoners. Among the prisoners are Major-General Armistead, and many colonels and officers of lesser note. The enemy left many dead upon the field, and a large number of wounded in our hands. The loss upon our side has been considerable. Major-General Hancock and Brigadier-General Gibbon were wounded.

After the repelling of the assault, indications leading to the belief that the enemy might be withdrawing, an armed reconnoissance was pushed forward from the left, and the enemy found to be in force. At the present hour all is quiet.

The New York cavalry have been engaged all day on both flanks of the enemy, harassing and vigorously attacking him with great success, notwithstanding they encountered superior numbers, both of cavalry and artillery. The army is in fine spirits.

George G. Meade,
Major-General Commanding.

On the morning of the Fourth of July, General Meade issued an address to the army:

Headquarters Army of the Potomac,
Near Gettysburg, July 4.

The commanding general, in behalf of the country, thanks the Army of the Potomac for the glorious result of the recent operations. Our enemy, superior in numbers and flushed with the pride of a successful invasion, attempted to overcome or destroy this army. Utterly baffled and defeated, he has now withdrawn from the contest.

The privations and fatigues the army has endured, and the heroic courage and gallantry it has displayed, will be matters of history to be ever remembered. Our task is not yet accomplished, and the commanding general looks to the army for greater efforts, to drive from our soil every vestige of the presence of the invader.

It is right and proper that we should, on suitable occasions, return our grateful thanks to the Almighty Disposer of events, that, in the goodness of His providence, He has thought fit to give victory to the cause of the just.

By command of Major-General Meade.

S.Williams, A. A.-General.

It is fitting we should close this chapter with President Lincoln's brief yet comprehensive announcement to the country:

Washington, D. C., July 4, 1863, 10 A. M.

The President of the United States announces to the country, that the news from the Army of the Potomac, up to ten o'clock P. M. of the third, is such as to cover the army with the highest honor—to promise great success to the cause of the Union—and to claim the condolence of all for the many gallant fallen; and that for this he especially desires that on this day, "He whose will, not ours, should ever be done," be everywhere remembered and reverenced with the profoundest gratitude.

Abraham Lincoln.

Chapter XIII - Retreat of the Rebels from Gettysburg.

1863.—National Rejoicing.—The Enemy Retreating.—Feebly Pursued.—Reconnoissances.—Kilpatrick Gives the Enemy a Fourth of July Entertainment at Monterey Pass.—Storm and Terror.—Immense Train Destroyed, and Hosts of Prisoners Taken.—Pitiable Condition of Stuart's Cavalry.—Battle of Hagerstown.—Captains Penfield and Dahlgren Wounded.—Wonderful Exploits of a Union Scout.—Kilpatrick and Buford at Williamsport.—Cavalry Fight at Boonsboro'.—Stuart Defeated.—Hagerstown Retaken.—Orders to Advance, One Day Too Late.—Kilpatrick Chases the Flying Foe.—Fight at Falling Waters, Last Act in the Drama.—Great Bravery of Union Troops.—Last Vestige of the Invaders Wiped Out.—Bivouac and Rest.

The victory at Gettysburg, though purchased at so dear a price, when announced to the people, produced a deep and widespread joy, which contributed to make the Fourth of July doubly memorable. The gallant behavior of our men furnished a theme for general exultation, and the removal of the threatened disaster foreshadowed in the pompous and successful invasion, made every true American breathe more freely.

But the work of the soldier was not yet done. The feet of the invaders were still upon free soil; and though his ranks had been thinned by desertions, and by unprecedented casualties in battle, and he had been thwarted in all the important minutiæ of his plan, he was still formidable, and compelled to fight with desperation, if attacked, to prevent utter destruction.

Some apprehension that the enemy was at least contemplating a speedy retreat was entertained during the night that followed the third bloody day. General Pleasonton, chief of cavalry, urged General Meade to advance in force upon the beaten foe, alleging that they were not only greatly weakened by their losses, but undoubtedly demoralized, in consequence of repulse and probable scarcity of ammunition. To ascertain positively what could be of these probabilities, Pleasonton was directed to make a reconnoissance toward the Rebel rear. Accordingly, several detachments of cavalry were thrust out on different roads, where they rode all night. General Gregg, on our right, went about twenty-two miles on the road to Chambersburg, and returning early on the morning of the fourth, reported that the road was strewn with wounded and stragglers, ambulances and caissons, and general débris, which indicated that the enemy was retreating as rapidly as possible, and was passing through a terrible season of demoralization. The testimony of the mute witnesses of disaster was corroborated by that of the many prisoners which easily fell into Gregg's hands. Other expeditions, returning later in the day, had similar reports to render of what they had seen and heard. And now came the time for energetic cavalry movements. While our infantry was resting, or engaged in burying our own and the Rebel dead within our lines, the cavalry was despatched to do all the damage it could upon the retreating Rebel columns.

KILPATRICK ON THEIR TRAIL.

Kilpatrick, having assembled his immortalized division on the plain at the foot of Round Top, on the morning of the fourth, discoursed to them eloquently for a few moments on the interests of the times. He assured his men that their noble deeds were not passing by unnoticed, nor would be unrequited, and that they were already a part of a grand history. He trusted that their future conduct would be a fair copy of the past. But his pathetic and patriotic accents had scarcely died upon the ear of his brave command, when the shrill bugle-blast brought eager men and grazing horses in line of march. Orders had been received by Kilpatrick to repair as swiftly as possible to the passes in the Catoctin Mountains, to intercept the enemy now known to be flying southward at a rapid rate.

The command had gone but a short distance when rain began to fall in torrents, as is usually the case after great battles, especially when much artillery is used. But through mud, in places to the horses' bodies; through brooks swollen enormously, and through the falling floods, the troopers pressed forward to the accomplishment of their task. About five o'clock P. M. Kilpatrick reached Emmitsburg, where he was joined by portions of General Gregg's command, including the Harris Light, which had been kept mostly in reserve during the conflicts of the past few days. Thus reënforced, this intrepid leader marched directly toward the Monterey Pass, arriving at the foot of this rocky defile in the mountains in the midst of pitchy darkness.

As was anticipated, a heavy Rebel train was then trying to make its escape through the gorge, guarded by Stuart's Cavalry, with light artillery. This artillery was planted in a position to rake the narrow road upon which Kilpatrick was advancing. But the darkness was so intense that the guns could be of little use, except to make the night terribly hideous with their bellowings, the echoes of which reverberated in the mountain gorges in a most frightful manner. To add to the horrors of the scene and position, the rain fell in floods, accompanied with groaning thunders, while lightnings flashed from cloud to cloud over our heads, and cleft the darkness only to leave friend and foe enveloped in greater darkness in the intervals of light. By these flashes, however, we gained a momentary glimpse of each other's position, and as we dashed forward in the gloom, we were further directed by the fire of the artillery and the desultory fire of the cavalry.

Surgeon Moore gives the following account of this affair: "We do not hesitate in saying, and have good reason to know, that had any want of firmness on the part of the leader, or any indecision or vacillation appeared, and a mischance occurred, this splendid command would then and there have been lost.

"But with unflinching and steady purpose, bold bearing, and a mind equal to the emergency, the general rode to the head of the column, reassured his frightened people, and, notwithstanding the intense darkness that hid friend from foe, made such skilful dispositions, and then attacked the hidden foe with such impetuosity that he fled in wild dismay, leaving his guns, a battle-flag, and four hundred prisoners in the victor's hands.

"The pass was gained, and Pennington's and Elder's guns were soon echoing and reëchoing through the mountain defiles. The artillery opened thus on the flying columns of the routed foe, who, with wagons, ambulances, caissons, and the débris of a shattered army, were rushing in chaotic confusion down the narrow mountain road, and scattering through the fields and woods on the plains below."

All night long Kilpatrick and his successful followers were gathering the spoils of their evening work. Wagon after wagon was overtaken, captured, and destroyed, while hundreds of prisoners were easily captured. This daring exploit placed Kilpatrick in advance of the Rebel army, giving him a fine opportunity to obstruct their pathway of retreat, and to destroy whatever could be of any use to them. Had he not been cumbered with so many prisoners, it is not in the power of any one to estimate the damage he would have done. In his official report he says: "On this day I captured eighteen hundred and sixty prisoners, including many officers of rank, and destroyed the Rebel General Ewell's immense wagon-train, nine miles long."

It should be stated that these wagons were mostly laden with the ripened and gathered crops of Pennsylvania and Maryland, and with the plunder of private and public stores, including dry goods and groceries of every variety and quality. None who saw it will ever forget the appearance of that mountain road the day following this night's foray.

Stuart, who was ingloriously defeated at Monterey, retired towards Emmitsburg with about fifty prisoners that he had captured during and after the fight. He then moved southward until he struck an unfrequented road which leads over the mountain viâ Wolfe's Tavern. By this turn he avoided immediate contact with our cavalry. But about five o'clock P. M., as he was about to debouch into the valley, Kilpatrick, who was watching for him as a cat does a mouse, attacked him with artillery and fought him till dark. This fight occurred near Smithburg, whence the prisoners in Kilpatrick's hands were sent to South Mountain, guarded by the Harris Light.

Darkness having put an end to the contest, Kilpatrick marched through Cavetown to Boonsboro', where he bivouacked for the night. Stuart, it was ascertained, marched till about midnight to the small town of Leitersburgh, where he rested his worn and wearied command. His condition was really pitiable. A large number of his men were mounted on shoeless horses, whose leanness showed that they had made many a long march through and from Virginia. Or, as was the case with a large proportion of them, they had fat horses, which were stolen from the fields and stalls of the invaded States, but, being entirely unused to such hard and cruel treatment as they were now receiving, were well-nigh unserviceable. Lameness and demoralization were prominent characteristics among animals and men.

July 6.—This morning, at an early hour, Kilpatrick's crowd of prisoners were turned over into the hands of General French, and then his command marched to Hagerstown, taking possession of the place in advance of Stuart, whose approach about eleven o'clock was met with determined resistance, and, at first, with great success. A heavy battle was fought, in which Kilpatrick's men showed their usual prowess and strength. Had not Rebel infantry come to the aid of his cavalry, Stuart would have suffered a stunning blow. For several hours the contest was wholly between cavalry and light artillery. Charges of great daring and skill were made. One reporter says: "Elder gave them grape and canister, and the Fifth New York sabres, while the First Vermont used their carbines."

In one of those charges, made in the face of a very superior force, Captain James A. Penfield, of the Fifth New York, at the head of his company, had his horse killed under him, and, while struggling to extricate himself from the animal, which lay upon him in part, he was struck a fearful blow of a sabre on the head, which came near severing it in twain. Thus wounded, with blood streaming down upon his long beard and clothes, he was made a prisoner. In a similar charge the gallant Captain Ulric Dahlgren lost a leg, though not his valuable life.

It appeared as though the Rebels were afforded an opportunity to avenge themselves in part for the shameful losses which they had sustained in this very place by the strategic operations of a Union scout, by the name of C. A. Phelps, during the incipient step of the invasion. We will let the scout relate his own story, which is corroborated by a signal-officer, who, from one of the lofty peaks of the mountains, witnessed the exciting denouement. The scout proceeds to say:

"I was very anxious to learn all about General Stuart's force and contemplated movements, and resolved to see the general himself or some of his staff-officers, soon after he entered Hagerstown.

"Accordingly I procured of a Union man a suit of raglings, knocked off one boot-heel to make one leg appear shorter than the other, and put a gimblet, a tow-string, and an old broken jack-knife in my pockets. My jewelry corresponded with my clothes. I adopted the name of George Fry, a harvest-hand of Dr. Farney, from Wolfetown, on the north side of the mountain, and I was a cripple from rheumatism. Having completed arrangements with Dr. Farney, Mr. Landers, and other Union men, that they might be of service to me in case the Rebels should be suspicious of my character, I hobbled away on my perilous journey, and entered the city by leaping the high stone wall which guards it on the north side near the dépôt. This occurred just as the town-clock struck one.

"It was a clear, starlight night, and the glistening sabres of the sentries could be seen as they walked their lonely beat. Scarcely had I gained the sidewalk leading to the centre of the town when the sentry nearest me cried, 'Halt! who goes there?' 'A friend,' I replied.

"'A friend to North or South?'

"'To the South, of course, and all right.'

"'Advance, then,' was the response. On reaching him, he asked me what could be my business at this hour of the night. I told him I had come in to see our brave boys, who could whip the Yankees so handsomely, as they had done especially at Bull Run and Chancellorsville. We fell at once to the discussion of the war-questions of the day. In the midst of our colloquy up came the officer of the guard on his 'grand rounds,' who, after probing me thoroughly, as he thought, with many questions, finally said, 'Had you not better go with me to see General Stuart?'

"'I should reelly like ter git a sight of the gin'ral,' I quickly replied, 'for I never seen a reel gin'ral in all my life.'

"I was soon in the presence of the general, who received me very cordially. I found him to be a man a little above the medium height, and fine looking. His features are very distinct in outline, his nose long and sharp, his eye keen and restless. His complexion is florid and his manners affable. I told him who I was and where I lived when at home. 'Wolfetown!' exclaimed the general, 'have not the Yankees a large wagon-train there?' I told him they had; and then, turning to one of his staff-officers, he said, 'I must have it; it would be a fine prize.'

"I noted his words and determined, if I possessed any Yankee wit, to make use of it on this occasion.

"'Gin'ral,' said I, 'you all don't think of capterin' them are Yankee wagons, do you?'

"'Why not? I have here five thousand cavalry and sixteen pieces of artillery, and I understand the train is lightly guarded.'

"I saw that he had been properly informed, and I told him they came there last evening with twelve big brass cannon and three regiments of foot-soldiers, and if he was to try to go through the gap of the mountain they would shoot all the cannon off right in the gap, and kill all his horses and men. The general smiled at my naïve answer, and said I had a strange idea of war if I thought so many men would be killed at once, and added that I would not be a very brave soldier. I replied that many times I had felt like going into the Confederate army, but my rheumatism kept me out.

"After a while the general concluded not to try the train, and I was heartily glad, for he would have taken at least two hundred wagons easily, as they were guarded by not more than three hundred men.

"He then gave orders to have the main body of his cavalry move towards Green Castle; and I distinctly heard him give orders to the Major to remain in town with fifty men as rearguard, and to send on the army mail, which was expected there about six the next evening. I made up my mind that it would be a small mail he would get, as I proposed to myself to be postmaster for once.

"After seeing the general and his cavalry move out of town, I went directly for my horse, which I had concealed in a safe place some distance from the city, meanwhile surveying the ground to see which way I could best come in to capture the mail, and determined to charge the place on the pike from Boonsboro', and made my arrangements to that effect. I got a Union man, by the name of Thornburgh, to go into the town and notify the Union people that, when the town-clock struck six P. M., I would charge in and capture the Rebel mail, at the risk of losing my own life and every man with me. I had now but eight men, two having been sent to General Stahel with despatches.

"I then returned to Boonsboro', and found my men waiting for me. I told them my intentions, and offered to send back to his regiment any man who feared to go with me. But every one bravely said he would not leave me, nor surrender without my order. I then ordered them to bring out their horses, and we were soon on the road. It was a moment of thrilling interest to us all, as we approached Hagerstown, and lingered to hear the signal-strokes of that monitor in the old church-tower. At the appointed time (we had already entered into the edge of the town), with a wild shout we dashed into the streets, and the Major and his fifty braves fled without firing a shot. We captured sixteen prisoners, twenty-six horses, several small-arms, and a heavy army mail, which contained three important despatches from Jeff. Davis, and two from the Rebel Secretary of War to General Lee. All this substantial booty we safely carried within our own lines, without the loss of a man or a horse.

143

"Many thanks are due to Dr. C. R. Doran and Mr. Robert Thornburgh, for their kind and timely assistance, and also to Misses Susie Carson and Addie Brenner, who did so much for the comfort of our brave men. I still have in my possession some choice flowers, preserved from a bouquet presented to me by Miss Carson the evening we captured the Rebel mail; and though the flowers have faded, the good deeds done by the giver will ever grow bright through coming time. All honor to the brave Union ladies."

In these same streets, where Captain Briggs with his telescope witnessed the successful charge of the scouting party, raged the battle hotly on the sixth of July. But, as the Rebel infantry was advancing with heavy artillery to the aid of Stuart's cavalry, Kilpatrick was sorely pressed, and, at length, compelled to retire. His ears were now saluted with the sound of artillery in the direction of Williamsport, and a messenger arrived with the intelligence that General John Buford, who had advanced through the South Mountain Pass, was now attempting to destroy Lee's immense supply train, which was packed near Williamsport, and not very heavily guarded.

Kilpatrick desired no better work than to assist his brave comrade, and he at once hastened down the main road, and soon joined Buford in the work of destruction. These combined commands were making fearful havoc in the Rebel commissary and quartermaster stores. Many wagons were burned, and the whole train would have shared the same fate had not the united infantry and cavalry of the enemy come down upon us in overwhelming force. But we were not to be driven away very suddenly nor cheaply. Long and desperately we contended with the accumulating forces, until darkness came on, when we found ourselves completely enveloped by the foe. Nothing but splendid generalship and true bravery on the part of our officers and men saved us from capture and destruction. Some of our number were made prisoners, but our losses were very small considering the amount of depredations we had committed, and the great danger to which we were exposed. As it was, the commands were successfully withdrawn from their hazardous position, and through the darkness of the night we crossed Antietam Creek, and bivouacked in safety on the opposite bank. Several prisoners were captured from the Rebels during the fights of the day. They were mostly from Alabama and Louisiana regiments; and they state that their army is all together, and well on its way to the river. They speak doubtfully of Lee's recrossing the Potomac.

The Cavalry Bivouac.

July 7.—Our cavalry is in the vicinity of Boonsboro', and is acting mostly on the defensive. The enemy in force is in our front, and an attack is momentarily expected. At six P. M. "to horse" was sounded throughout our camps; and, after waiting two hours in rain, ready for a move, orders were received to return to our quarters. Rain is now falling in torrents, accompanied with fearful thunderings and lightnings. Unpleasant as it is, we welcome its peltings, hoping that the storm will raise the Potomac above the fording mark, and thus give Meade an opportunity to attack Lee before he has time to recross the river into Virginia. We know that his pontoons at Falling Waters have been totally destroyed by our cavalry and by the high water, and that the only ford available is at Williamsport, and hence we welcome the falling floods. Many of us have to lie down in water, which, however, is not very cold. But the night is very tedious.

July 8.—The sun came out bright and warm this morning, enabling us in a few moments to dry our drenched blankets and garments. The roads, however, abound in mud, and the streams are enormously swollen. Early in the day our pickets were driven in along the Antietam, and the enemy advanced with such force that by noon the plains around Boonsboro' were the scene of a furious cavalry engagement.

CAVALRY BATTLE AT BOONSBORO'.

Dr. Moore, from whose excellent reports we have before quoted, gives the following graphic description of this cavalry duel: "Buford had the right and Kilpatrick the left. The movements of the cavalry lines in this battle were among the finest sights the author remembers ever to have seen. It was here he first saw the young general (Kilpatrick), and little thought that one day the deeds he saw him perform he would transmit to paper and to posterity. Here, all day long, the Rebel and the Union cavalry-chiefs fought, mounted and dismounted, and striving in every manner possible to defeat and rout the other. The din and roar of battle that, from ten A. M. until long after dark, had rolled over the plains and back through the mountains, told to the most anxious generals of them all, Meade and Lee, how desperate was the struggle—Stuart and his men fighting for the safety of the Rebel army, Buford and Kilpatrick for South Mountain's narrow Pass.

"Just as the setting sun sent his last rays over that muddy battle-field, Buford and Kilpatrick were seen rapidly approaching each other from opposite directions. They met; a few hasty words were exchanged, and away dashed Buford far off to the right, and Kilpatrick straight to the centre; and in less than twenty minutes, from right to centre, and from centre to left, the clear notes of the bugles rang out the welcome charging, and with one long, wild shout, those glorious squadrons of Buford and Kilpatrick, from right to left, as far as the eye could see, in one unbroken line, charged upon the foe. The shock was irresistible; the Rebel line was broken—the routed enemy confessed the superiority of our men as they fled from the well-fought field, leaving their dead and dying behind them; and our heroic chiefs led back their victorious squadrons, and, while resting on their laurels, gave their brave, wearied troops a momentary repose."

Thus far our cavalry had done much to obstruct the retreat of the Rebel army, and had inflicted incalculable losses of men and materials. But the pursuit of our main army was not correspondingly vigorous. Two pretty good reasons may be assigned for this seeming incompetency or want of energy. The first reason is found in the fact that scarcely more than a brigade of infantry had been kept in reserve during the great and destructive battle of Gettysburg, while the three days of struggle had well-nigh exhausted our entire strength. Rest was therefore greatly needed, and a general engagement was to be guarded against. It should also be remembered that nearly one fourth of our entire army was hors de combat. The second reason may be found in the heavy rains which fell, "impeding pursuers," as one writer says, "more than pursued, though they need not." But the retreating army has this advantage; it usually chooses its own route, which it can generally cover or hide by means of stratagem, so that it requires time as well as study to effectually pursue. Perhaps a third reason for our tardiness of pursuit should be presented. Does it not appear to be an overruling act of Providence? Had General Meade advanced, as it seems he might have done with the resources at his command, against the demoralized, decimated, and flying army, with its ammunition quite exhausted, and a swollen river, unfordable and bridgeless, between it and safety, Lee could not have escaped annihilation. But the public sentiment of the country, though forming and improving rapidly, was not yet prepared for such a victory. We needed to spend more treasure, spill more blood, sacrifice more precious lives, to lift us up to those heights of public and political virtue, where we could be safely entrusted with so dear a boon. We were not then prepared for peace, that sovereign balm for a nation's woes. The tardiness with which our movements were made enabled the enemy to reach a good position near Hagerstown, which he began to fortify in such a manner as to cover his crossing. Meantime we understood that successful efforts were made to rebuild the bridge at Falling Waters.

General Meade, in his official report, gives the following account of his pursuit: "The fifth and sixth of July were employed in succoring the wounded and burying the dead. Major-General Sedgwick, commanding the Sixth Corps, having pushed the pursuit of the enemy as far as the Fairfield Pass and the mountains, and reporting that the pass was very strong—one in which a small force of the enemy could hold in check and delay for a considerable time any pursuing force—I determined to follow the enemy by a flank movement, and, accordingly, leaving McIntosh's brigade of cavalry and Neil's brigade of infantry to continue harassing the enemy, I put the army in motion for Middletown, and orders were immediately sent to Major-General French, at Frederick, to reoccupy Harper's Ferry, and send a force to occupy Turner's Pass, in South Mountains. I subsequently ascertained that Major-General French had not only anticipated these orders in part, but had pushed a cavalry force to Williamsport and Falling Waters, where they destroyed the enemy's pontoon bridge, and captured its guard. Buford was at the same time sent to Williamsport and Hagerstown. The duty above assigned to the cavalry was most successfully accomplished, the enemy being greatly harassed, his trains destroyed, and many captures of guns and prisoners made."

July 10.—This morning, at five o'clock, the cavalry advanced from Boonsboro', passed through Keedysville, and crossed the Antietam about ten o'clock. At twelve o'clock we engaged the enemy at Jones' Cross Roads. The Harris Light led the advance, dismounted. The Rebels were driven three consecutive times from as many positions which they had chosen. Their resistance was by no means strong nor determined. Before night Buford moved his command to Sharpsburg, on the extreme left of our lines, and Kilpatrick advanced to a position on the extreme right, in the vicinity of Hagerstown, where he covered the road to Gettysburg. On the eleventh only picket skirmishes occupied the time. But on the twelfth Kilpatrick, supported by a brigade of infantry under the command of Brigadier-General Ames, of Howard's Corps, advanced upon the enemy near Hagerstown, drove them from their works, and then out of the streets of the city, and took permanent possession. This successful movement greatly contracted our lines, and brought our forces into a better position. At the close of this enterprise, as we are informed, General Meade called a council of war, at which was discussed earnestly and long the propriety of attacking the enemy. Notwithstanding the anxiety of the chief commander to advance and reap fully the fruit of Gettysburg, five of his corps commanders, out of eight, argued against the measure, and as Meade did not desire to assume the grave responsibility of a movement against such protests, no move was immediately attempted.

This statement may modify the condemnatory judgments which were formed against General Meade, and may prepare our minds rightly to interpret General A. P. Howe's report of the general pursuit. In narrating its spirit and progress, he says: "On the fourth of July it seemed evident enough that the enemy were retreating. How far they were gone we could not see from the front. We could see but a comparatively small force from the position where I was. On Sunday the Fifth and Sixth Corps moved in pursuit. As we moved, a small rearguard of the enemy retreated. We followed them, with this small rearguard of the enemy before us, up to Fairfield, in a gorge of the mountains. There we again waited for them to go on. There seemed to be no disposition to push this rearguard when we got up to Fairfield. A lieutenant from the enemy came into our lines and gave himself up. He was a Northern Union man, in service in one of the Georgia regiments; and, without being asked, he unhesitatingly told me, when I met him as he was being brought in, that he belonged to the artillery of the rearguard of the enemy, and that they had but two rounds of ammunition with the rearguard. But we waited there without receiving any orders to attack. It was a place where, as I informed General Sedgwick, we could easily attack the enemy with advantage. But no movement was made by us until the enemy went away. Then one brigade of my division, with some cavalry, was sent to follow after them, while the remainder of the Sixth Corps moved to the left. We moved on through Boonsboro', and passed up on the pike-road leading to Hagerstown.

"After passing Boonsboro' it became my turn to lead the Sixth Corps. That day, just before we started, General Sedgwick ordered me to move on and take up the best position I could over a little stream on the Frederick side of Funkstown. As I moved on, it was suggested to me by him to move carefully. 'Don't come into contact with the enemy; we don't want to bring on a general engagement.' It seemed to be the current impression that it was not desired to bring on a general engagement. I moved on until we came near Funkstown. General Buford was along that way with his cavalry. I had passed over the stream referred to, and found a strong position, which I concluded to take, and wait for the Sixth Corps to come up. In the meantime General Buford, who was in front, came back to me, and said, 'I am pretty hardly engaged here; I have used a great deal of my ammunition; it is a strong place in front; it is an excellent position.' It was a little farther out than I was—near Funkstown. He said, 'I have used a great deal of my ammunition, and I ought to go to the right; suppose you move up there, or send up a brigade, or even a part of one, and hold that position.' Said I, 'I will do so at once, if I can just communicate with

General Sedgwick; I am ordered to take up a position over here, and hold it, and the intimation conveyed to me was, that they did not want to get into a general engagement; I will send for General Sedgwick, and ask permission to hold that position, and relieve you.' I accordingly sent a staff-officer to General Sedgwick with a request that I might go up at once and assist General Buford, stating that he had a strong position, but his ammunition was giving out. General Buford remained with me until I should get an answer. The answer was, 'No; we do not want to bring on a general engagement.' 'Well,' said I, 'Buford, what can I do?' He said, 'They expect me to go farther to the right; my ammunition is pretty much out. That position is a strong one, and we ought not to let it go.' I sent down again to General Sedgwick, stating the condition of General Buford, and that he would have to leave unless he could get some assistance; that his position was not far in front, and that it seemed to me that we should hold it, and I should like to send some force up to picket it at least. After a time I got a reply that, if General Buford left, I might occupy the position. General Buford was still with me, and I said to him, 'If you go away from there I will have to hold it.' 'That's all right,' said he, 'I will go away.' He did so, and I moved right up. It was a pretty good position when you cover your troops. Soon after relieving Buford, we saw some Rebel infantry advancing. I do not know whether they brought them from Hagerstown, or from some other place. They made three dashes, not in heavy force, upon our line to drive us back. The troops that happened to be there on our line were what we considered, in the Army of the Potomac, unusually good ones. They quietly repulsed the Rebels twice, and the third time they came up they sent them flying into Funkstown.

"Yet there was no permission to move on and follow up the enemy. We remained there some time, until we had orders to move on and take a position a mile or more nearer Hagerstown. As we moved up we saw that the Rebels had some light field-works—hurriedly thrown up, apparently—to cover themselves while they recrossed the river. I think we remained there three days; and the third night, I think, after we got up into that position, it was said the Rebels recrossed the river."

Sunday, July 12.—I had the misfortune to be kicked off my pins last night, just before we were relieved at the front. Approaching my sorrel pony from the rear, in a careless manner, for he could not see me until I got within short range, when he raised his heels very suddenly, and, without ceremony, planted them in my breast, laying me, not in the most gentle manner, flat upon the ground. Medical aid is considered necessary to-day, as I am suffering not a little. But, as the conflict was purely caused by my own folly, I endure my pains with becoming patience.

To-day I found the following despatches in some Northern paper, and I record them to show what contradictory reports will often find their way into the public press concerning men and measures:

"**Mountain-House, near Boonsboro', July 9.**—There has been no fighting this morning. The fight of yesterday, near Boonsboro', was between Generals Buford and Kilpatrick's cavalry and Rebel infantry, principally on the bushwhacking style. Our troops fell back early in the day, but subsequently reoccupied the ground. Artillery was used on both sides.

"There is no truth in the reported death of General Kilpatrick."

(SECOND DESPATCH.)

"**Boonsboro', July 9, 8 P. M.**—There have been no active operations on our front to-day. After the cavalry fight of yesterday the enemy drew in their forces towards Hagerstown, and formed a line on elevated ground from Funkstown on the right to the bend of the river below Williamsport on the left, thus uncovering the Shepherdstown crossing. Scouts and reconnoitring parties report that Lee is entrenching his front and drawing from his train on the Virginia side, and making general preparations for another battle. It is contradicted, to-night, that we have a force on General Lee's line of retreat in Virginia."

July 13.—All has been quiet along our lines to-day. The army, being pretty well rested by this time, is waiting impatiently for the command to advance. Our position is also a good one, though not better than that of the enemy. We have every reason to believe that the Rebel army is still on the north bank of the Potomac. The recent rains have raised the river above the fording mark. However, Lee will undoubtedly fall back into Virginia if he finds a good opportunity. During the latter part of the day General Meade finally decided to assault the position of the invaders. Very much to the delight of the rank and file of the army, orders were promulgated to the effect that a strong and simultaneous advance must be made early on the morning of the fourteenth. Preparations were immediately begun.

FALLING WATERS.

Kilpatrick and his cavalry were sent out on picket, and advanced as near the enemy's lines as it was prudent. Not many hours of the night had passed away when Kilpatrick discovered certain movements which indicated that the enemy was leaving his front. Prepared as he was to attack them by the morning light, he was ready to follow up any movement which they might make. Hence, at three o'clock in the morning of the fourteenth, his advance-guard moved forward upon the retiring enemy. While information of this unexpected movement of the enemy was despatched to General Meade, Kilpatrick advanced towards Williamsport with his usual rapidity and power, driving and capturing every thing before him. Informed by citizens that the rearguard of the retreating army had but a few moments before started from the river, he followed closely in their tracks, and struck them at Falling Waters, where, after a brilliant and sharp conflict, he bagged a large number of prisoners. Many a poor fellow never reached the long-looked-for Virginia shore.

General Meade then sent the following despatch to Washington:

Headquarters Army of the Potomac,
July 14, 3 P. M.

H. W. Halleck, General-in-Chief:

My cavalry now occupy Falling Waters, having overtaken and captured a brigade of infantry, fifteen hundred strong, two guns, two caissons, two battle-flags, and a large number of small-arms. The enemy are all across the Potomac.

George G. Meade, Major-General.

Later in the day he sent the following:

Headquarters Army of the Potomac,
July 14, 3.30 P. M.

Major-General Halleck, General-in-Chief:

My cavalry have captured five hundred prisoners, in addition to those previously reported. General Pettigrew, of the Confederate army, was killed this morning in the attack on the enemy's rearguard. His body is in our hands.

G. G. Meade, Major-General.

These despatches were afterward denied by General Lee in a letter to his authorities, as follows:

Headquarters Army of Northern Virginia,
July ——, 1863.

General S. Cooper, Adjutant and Inspector-General C. S. A.:

General: I have seen in the Northern papers what purports to be an official despatch from General Meade, stating that he had captured a brigade of infantry, two pieces of artillery, two caissons, and a large number of small-arms, as this army retired to the south bank of the Potomac on the thirteenth and fourteenth instant. This despatch has been copied into the Richmond papers; and, as its official character may cause it to be believed, I desire to state that it is incorrect. The enemy did not capture any organized body of men on that occasion, but only stragglers, and such as were left asleep on the road, exhausted by the fatigue and exposure of one of the most inclement nights I have ever known at this season of the year. It rained without cessation, rendering the road by which, our troops marched toward the bridge at Falling Waters very difficult to pass, and causing so much delay that the last of the troops did not cross the river at the bridge until one A. M. on the morning of the fourteenth.

While the column was thus detained on the road a number of men, worn down with fatigue, laid down in barns and by the roadside, and though officers were sent back to arouse them as the troops moved on, the darkness and rain prevented them from finding all, and many were in this way left behind. Two guns were left on the road; the horses that drew them became exhausted, and the officers went back to procure others. When they returned, the rear of the column had passed the guns so far that it was deemed unsafe to send back for them, and they were thus lost. No arms, cannon, or prisoners were taken by the enemy in battle, but only such as were left behind, as I have described, under the circumstances. The number of stragglers thus lost I am unable to state with accuracy, but it is greatly exaggerated in the despatch referred to. I am, with great respect, your obedient servant,

R. E. Lee, General.

This was evidently an attempt, on the part of the Rebel leader, to disparage our victories and to wipe out of his record, with a sort of legerdemain, the disgraceful and disastrous denouement of his invasion. In the following important statement General Meade confirms his position by incontestable facts, and shows how the matter stood:

Headquarters Army of the Potomac,
Aug. ——, 1863.}

Major-General Halleck, General-in-Chief:

My attention has been called to what purports to be an official despatch of General R. E. Lee, commanding the Rebel army, to General S. Cooper, Adjutant and Inspector-General, denying the accuracy of my telegram to you, of July fourteenth, announcing the result of the cavalry affair at Falling Waters. I have delayed taking any notice of Lee's report until the return of Brigadier-General Kilpatrick, absent on leave, who commanded the cavalry on the occasion referred to, and on whose report from the field my telegram was based. I now enclose the official report of Brigadier-General Kilpatrick, made after his attention had been called to Lee's report. You will see that he reiterates and confirms all that my despatch averred, and proves most conclusively that General Lee has been deceived by his subordinates, or he would never, in the face of the facts now alleged, have made the assertion his report claims.

It appears that I was in error in stating that the body of General Pettigrew was left in our hands, although I did not communicate that fact until an officer from the field reported to me he had seen the body. It is now ascertained, from the Richmond papers, that General Pettigrew, though mortally wounded in the affair, was taken to Winchester, where he subsequently died. The three battle-flags captured on this occasion, and sent to Washington, belonged to the Fortieth, Forty-seventh, and Fifty-fifth Virginia regiments of infantry. General Lee will surely acknowledge these were not left in the hands of stragglers asleep in barns.

George G. Meade, Major-General Commanding.

Kilpatrick, in his letter of explanation, referred to in the above despatch, gives the following graphic account of this last scene in the great drama of the invasion:

Headquarters Third Division Cavalry Corps,
Warrenton Junction, Va., Aug. ——.

To Colonel A. J. Alexander, Chief of Staff of Cavalry Corps:

Colonel: In compliance with a letter just received from the headquarters of the Cavalry Corps of the Army of the Potomac, directing me to give the facts connected with the fight at Falling Waters, I have the honor to state that, at three A. M. of the fourteenth ultimo, I learned that the enemy's pickets were retiring in my front. Having been previously ordered to attack at seven A. M., I was ready to move at once.

At daylight I had reached the crest of hills occupied by the enemy an hour before, and, a few minutes before six, General Custer drove the rearguard of the enemy into the river at Williamsport. Learning from citizens that a portion of the enemy had retreated in the direction of Falling Waters, I at once moved rapidly for that point, and came up with this rearguard of the enemy at seven-thirty A. M., at a point two miles distant from Falling Waters. We pressed on, driving them before us, capturing many prisoners and one gun. When within a mile and a half of Falling Waters, the enemy was found in large force, drawn up in line of battle on the crest of a hill, commanding the road on which I was advancing. His left was protected by earthworks, and his right extended to the woods on our left.

The enemy was, when first seen, in two lines of battle, with arms stacked within less than one thousand yards of the large force. A second piece of artillery, with its support, consisting of infantry, was captured while attempting to get into position. The gun was taken to the rear. A portion of the Sixth Michigan Cavalry, seeing only that portion of the enemy behind the earthworks, charged. This charge was led by Major Webber, and was the most gallant ever made. At a trot he passed up the hill, received the fire from the whole line, and the next moment rode through and over the earthworks, and passed to the right, sabring the Rebels along the entire line, and returned with a loss of thirty killed, wounded, and missing, including the gallant Major Webber, killed.

I directed General Custer to send forward one regiment as skirmishers. They were repulsed before support could be sent them, and driven back, closely followed by the Rebels, until checked by the First Michigan and a squadron of the Eighth New York. The Second brigade having come up, it was quickly thrown into position, and, after a fight of two hours and thirty minutes, routed the enemy at all points and drove him toward the river.

When within a short distance of the bridge, General Buford's command came up and took the advance. We lost twenty-nine killed, thirty-six wounded, and forty missing. We found upon the field one hundred and twenty-five dead Rebels, and brought away upward of fifty wounded. A large number of the enemy's wounded were left upon the field in charge of their own surgeons. We captured two guns, three battle-flags, and upward of fifteen hundred prisoners.

To General Custer and his brigade, Lieutenant Pennington and his battery, and one squadron of the Eighth New York Cavalry, of General Buford's command, all praise is due.

Very respectfully, your obedient servant,

J. Kilpatrick, Brigadier-General.

In his official report of operations from the twenty-eighth of June, when he assumed command of the Third division, Kilpatrick says: "In this campaign my command has captured forty-five hundred prisoners, nine guns, and eleven battle-flags." Never before, in the history of warfare, has it been permitted to any man commanding a division to include, in a report of about forty-five days' operations, such magnificent results.

As the last foot of the invaders disappeared from the soil where they had never been successful, our gallant boys built their bivouac fires and rested themselves and their weary animals near the scene of their recent victory. The telegraph lines, which had so often been burdened with news of disaster, now sang with joyful intelligence from all departments of our vast armies. Gettysburg was soon followed by Vicksburg, then Port Hudson, the names being emblazoned upon many a glowing transparency, to the honor of the heroes who had planned, and the braves who had fought, so successfully and well. The news was welcomed with salutes of artillery and bonfires in most of the Northern cities and villages, while the whole mass of our people was jubilant and rejoicing.

On the fifteenth the President issued a proclamation of Thanksgiving, in which he recognized the hand of God in our victories, and called upon the people to "render the homage due to the Divine Majesty for the wonderful things He has done in the nation's behalf, and to invoke the influence of His Holy Spirit to subdue the anger which has produced, and so long sustained, a needless and cruel rebellion." In the midst of these rejoicings we end our chapter.

Chapter XIV - Kilpatrick's Gunboat Expedition

1863.—Escape of Lee into Virginia.—Reasons.—Cavalry Advance into the Valley via Harper's Ferry, and Fight.—Riot in New York and other Northern Cities.—Again Across the Potomac on "Sacred Soil." —Blackberries and Discipline.—Mails.—Battle of Manassas Gap.—Mosby Again, and His Bands.—Author's Birthday.—Kilpatrick's Gunboat Expedition on the Rappahannock.—Cavalry Captures Navy.— Complimented by Superiors.—General Advance of the Army.—Third Cavalry Battle at Brandy Station.—Stuart's Cavalry Worsted at Culpepper Court House.—Sharp Artillery Practice at Raccoon Ford, on the Rapidan.—Special Duties and Special Dangers.—Good Living Along the Hazel and Robertson Rivers.—Important Reconnoissance and Raid.—Hard Fighting and Narrow Escape.—Needed Rest Received.—The Paymaster.—Rebel Plan of Attack Foiled by a Citizen Informer.— Suspicious Activity on Our Front.

This sudden and masterly movement of the Rebels was a cutting surprise to General Meade, and a source of mortification and chagrin to all. Gloriously successful as we had been, it was evident that hesitation and indecision had greatly detracted from our laurels. We had won a world-renowned victory, but we had failed to reap all the legitimate fruits which our situation placed within our reach.

General Lee had been terribly punished, but his escape was quite marvellous. One writer says: "When his shattered columns commenced their retreat from Gettysburg, few of his officers can have imagined that they would ever reach Virginia with their artillery and most of their trains." And though their trains were severely handled and greatly injured, yet the old Rebel army of Northern Virginia, with nearly all its artillery, made its exit from soil too sacred to freedom for a Rebel victory. Their losses, however, had been immense, and they were only too glad to escape in a manner very unlike the audacious way in which they had advanced but a few weeks previous into the Northern States.

It now became the policy of our leader to follow the fugitives as closely as the changed circumstances of affairs would permit, and to give the Rebels no rest, while he endeavored to press them determinedly, and watched them by means of scouts and signal-stations with a jealous eye. "There is, however, a limit to the endurance which men and horses are capable of, and, beyond this, the overtaxed powers give way, and exhausted nature claims her rights. Few there are, except those who have had experience, who know how much privation the brave soldier and his general suffer in the toils of the field, on the rapid march, the hasty bivouac, the broken slumbers, the wakeful watchings, and the scanty fare." It must be remembered, also, that our army had made many forced marches, describing in its route a line somewhat resembling the circumference of a great circle, as a careful survey of the map of movements will show; while the route of the enemy, who had several days the start of us, was more like the diameter of that circle. Our cavalry had not only fought and defeated the Rebel cavalry on many sanguinary fields, but it had met the serried lines of their infantry also, as at Gettysburg, where the brave Farnsworth fell. Owing to this fatigue of our forces, our pursuit of the enemy was not as vigorous, it would seem in a cursory glance, as it should have been.

As soon as it was ascertained that the Rebel army was in full retreat, a force of our cavalry was sent across the Potomac at Harper's Ferry, bivouacking, the night of the fourteenth of July, on Bolivar Heights. Early the next morning we advanced on the Winchester Turnpike as far as Halltown, where we deflected to the right on the road to Shepherdstown. We had not proceeded far before we encountered the enemy's cavalry under Fitzhugh Lee, with which we were soon involved in a spirited contest. At first our troopers were worsted and driven back a short distance. But, having found a good position, we rallied, and repulsed several desperate charges, inflicting heavy losses, until the Rebels were glad to give up the game, and consequently retired. Colonel Drake (First Virginia) and Colonel Gregg were among the Rebel slain, while on our side the highest officer killed was Captain Fisher, of the Sixteenth Pennsylvania. The fighting was done principally on foot.

While these things were transpiring, Kilpatrick moved his division from Falling Waters to Boonsboro' by way of Williamsport and Hagerstown. Sad evidences of the recent battles and marches, in dead animals and general débris, were seen all along the way. Having reached our bivouac near Boonsboro', our men and horses came to their rations and rest with a wonderful relish.

During the day we have been reading of the murderous riots made in Northern cities, especially in New York, where men in mobs have ostensibly leagued against the authority of the Government. The bloody accounts are stirring the rank and file of our army terribly. A feeling of intense indignation exists against traitorous demagogues, who are undoubtedly at the bottom of all this anarchy. Detachments from many of the old regiments are now being sent North to look after Northern traitors. This depletion of our ranks we cannot well afford, for every available man is needed in the field. Many of our regiments are much reduced. The Harris Light now musters but one hundred men fit for duty, scarcely one tenth the number with which we entered upon the campaign. Our horses are also much used up. Hundreds of them have been killed and wounded in battle, and not a few have "played out," so that they are utterly unserviceable. The author of these records has worn out completely two horses since he had a second horse shot under him in the cavalry fight near Upperville.

July 16.—"Boots and Saddles" sounded at four o'clock, and before daylight we were on our way toward Harper's Ferry. We revisited Rhorersville, crossed Crampton's Gap, and at last reached the Potomac at Berlin, where the division was separated, a portion of it moving to Harper's Ferry, where they bivouacked at night in the yard of the destroyed United States arsenal. Pontoons at Harper's Ferry and Berlin were used for crossing the army into Virginia. The crossing was being effected as rapidly as possible, yet for so vast an army it is always slow and tedious.

Our troops are daily crossing and advancing, but all is otherwise quiet. We are now receiving an issue of clothing, which we greatly need. Our ranks are putting on a new-revived appearance. The first sergeants of the Harris Light have received orders to finish their pay-rolls. General Lee is reported to be falling back to the Rappahannock.

Sunday, July 19.—Our cavalry left Harper's Ferry at two o'clock P. M., crossed the river on pontoons at Sandy Hook, and advanced into Virginia. Monthly returns for June were made before our march commenced. The weather is very warm and sultry. On the twentieth we resumed our march at ten A. M., and advanced to Leesburg, where we fed our horses and rested. In the decline of the day we marched to Goose Creek, on whose grassy banks we bivouacked for the night.

The whole cavalry force is moving towards the Rappahannock. On the twenty-first we advanced viâ Gum Spring and Centreville to Manassas Junction. The boys have had some gay times to-day after blackberries, which we found in great abundance all along our line of march. General Gregg was compelled to dismount several men in the forenoon, and ordered them to march on foot, for the offence of leaving the ranks for berries, without permission. A command would soon be totally demoralized, if such tendencies to unsoldierly conduct were not checked. And though at times discipline seems severe, yet, especially with us, it is absolutely necessary.

July 22.—To-day we marched to the vicinity of Gainesville. We fell in with Scott's Nine Hundred as we were marching across the old field of Bull Run, among whom we found several old acquaintances. We spent a few very interesting moments together.

July 23.—Our command was cheered to-day by the arrival of a large mail, which brought a message to nearly every man. During active campaigning, as in the invasion of Pennsylvania and Maryland, it is difficult to keep up postal connections with the civil world, and, with the very best efforts which can be made, our mails are greatly delayed, sometimes even for weeks together. But when they do come, they are hailed with a delight which is almost frantic. The post-boys are cheered as far as they can be seen, as they wend their way from camp to camp, with their horses loaded down with the enormously swollen mail-bags. Several bushels of letters are sometimes brought by one carrier, as was the case to-day.

FIGHTING AT MANASSAS GAP.

During the day we have heard very heavy cannonading in the direction of White Plains. It appears that General Meade, misled by the information brought by some of his scouts, expected to engage the Rebel army in Manassas Gap, or west of that, where General Buford found the enemy in force. Our army was accordingly concentrated upon this point. The Third Corps, under General French, which occupied Ashby's Gap, was sent forward rapidly to Buford's support, where its First Division, commanded by General Hobart Ward, pushed through the Gap, driving the enemy before it, but with mutual loss. Here the New York Excelsior Brigade, General F. B. Spinola commanding, greatly distinguished itself, by making three heroic charges up the frowning steeps, where the Rebels were strongly posted. Their general was twice wounded. But the effort was a success.

On the morning of the twenty-fourth our soldiers pushed forward as far as Front Royal, but found no enemy. They then learned that they had been fighting only a portion of Lee's rearguard, which in the night had slipped away in the trail of their main army southward. By this move General Meade's army lost about two days' march; and when again we reached the bank of the Rappahannock, the old foe was facing us in threatening attitude from the opposite shore.

This afternoon the Harris Light was sent on a scout to Thoroughfare Gap. From the heights beyond the Gap we saw the wagon-train of the Eleventh Corps moving toward Warrenton. This was a portion of the force which had expected a fight at Manassas Gap.

July 25.—Our cavalry force reached the vicinity of Warrenton Junction, when we went into bivouac. The second squadron of our regiment, under Captain O. J. Downing, moved to Thoroughfare Gap and returned to Gainesville, where it joined the regiment, and then marched with us to the Junction viâ Bristoe and Catlett's. Before night we were sent out on picket in the vicinity of Catlett's Station, where we relieved the First Virginia Cavalry. We continued on picket through the twenty-sixth, but all was quiet along the lines.

An inspection of horses was made this morning, when a large number were condemned as utterly unserviceable; and they were started off toward Washington, to be exchanged for better ones.

July 27.—I have the responsibility and honor of being in command of a company. This afternoon a detachment of our forces was sent out on a sort of bushwhacking expedition. A portion of Company F was captured by the Fourth Virginia Cavalry, while patrolling the road near Bristersburg.

We are not doing much these days, except picketing, scouting, recruiting, resting. On the twenty-ninth our entire brigade was marched to within three miles of Warrenton, and then countermarched to the old camp; and on the last day of the month we advanced to Warrenton in heavy force, where General Meade has had his headquarters for several days.

August 1.—To-day General Meade moved his headquarters to Rappahannock Station. The heat is excessive. Two men of the Harris Light were sunstruck during the day. We left Warrenton at seven o'clock A. M., and moved very slowly. At night we bivouacked not far from New Baltimore. On the following day we were sent out on picket, which here is neither difficult nor dangerous. Our Colonel, Otto Harhaus, is ill, and is awaiting his documents for a leave of absence from the regiment.

August 3.—The colonel received his papers to-day, and started forthwith for New York. Captain L. H. Southard, the senior officer, is in command. The regiment was sent to Thoroughfare Gap, where we encamped in an apple-orchard.

Our infantry lines now extend down the Rappahannock as far as Fredericksburg, which we hold. The cavalry is picketing and patrolling all this territory. However, as there are so many regiments to engage in this work, the duty is comparatively light. "Many hands make light work."

Sunday, August 9.—We still continue near Thoroughfare Gap. Occasionally, as our turn comes, we picket along the Manassas Gap Railroad. Major E. F. Cooke, who has been absent for some time, returned to us to-day and took command. My old company, E, shows the following report: Present, thirty-two; fit for duty, twenty-two.

On Monday the regiment left camp at nine A. M., and, separating into several detachments, moved upon White Plains and Middleburg from different directions. These places have been occupied for some time past by Mosby's guerilla bands. We did not succeed, however, in bringing them into an engagement, as they were sharply on the lookout, and studiously kept beyond the reach of our carbines. Occasionally our pickets are attacked by them, and some lively times are experienced.

August 13.—I was detailed by the adjutant this morning to act as sergeant-major in place of Sergeant Temple, who is assigned to the command of a company. Very few commissioned officers are with the regiment at present. This leaves the command of several companies to enlisted men. Some of our officers are out on detached service, while not a few, during the lull of army operations, have asked and received leaves of absence, and are visiting their friends in the North. It might indeed be said that we are all rusticating; and, were it not for the guerilla bands that infest the country, attacking our outposts, and frequently disturbing our lines of communication with our bases of supply as well as the outer world, our condition would be one of pleasing rest.

On the fourteenth a little excitement was afforded us, to relieve us from the monotonous life which we are spending. A detachment of the regiment, commanded by Captain Griggs, made a bold dash upon an ill-starred portion of Mosby's band, near Aldie, where we captured three men and twenty horses and equipments, most of which had formerly belonged to our service, having been taken by these wily guerillas. Nearly every horse had the familiar "U. S." upon his shoulder; and the saddles, with very few exceptions, were of Northern manufacture.

August 15.—The Harris Light moved from Thoroughfare Gap at ten A. M. We reached Hartwood Church at eight in the evening, viâ New Baltimore and Greenwich. A considerable halt was made at Warrenton Junction, where we drew rations and forage.

Henry E. Davies, Jr., just promoted to the colonelcy of the regiment, joined us at the Junction, and took command. He is immensely popular with the men, especially with those who admire bravery and heroism, and who covet to be thoroughly drilled and disciplined.

August 17.—We continue at Hartwood Church, with our camp located very near General Kilpatrick's headquarters. During the day Colonel Davies appointed me second lieutenant, and assigned me to the command of Company M, as both the captain and first lieutenant of the company are absent on detached service.

Late in the evening I received orders to report, with my company, at an early hour next day, to Captain Meade, division quartermaster. At five o'clock on the morning of the eighteenth we made our bow to the captain, who despatched us as an escort or guard to a train from Hartwood to Warrenton Junction. During the march we made an exciting dash upon a band of guerillas, who were watching for us, expecting to make some captures. But they were disappointed, for we were not only prepared to resist them, but would have captured them but for the superior fleetness of their horses. After accomplishing the work we were sent out to do, and resting one night, we returned to the regiment.

August 22.—This is my natal day. I find myself twenty-two years of age. I am not surrounded on this anniversary, as in former years, by the friends of my childhood. But memories of the past come trooping up in such vivid lines, as to make the day one of deep interest.

August 28.—My company, which forms a part of Captain Mitchell's battalion, is doing picket-duty at present with the battalion on the Rappahannock between Banks and United States Fords. My company is at the captain's headquarters, and acts as grand guard.

Sunday, August 30.—To-day I accompanied the division and brigade officers of the day in their visit to and inspection of the pickets along the Rappahannock. Our ride was very pleasant. Captain Barker, of the Fifth New York Cavalry, dined with Captain Mitchell and myself. He is a lively companion; was in the hands of Mosby last Spring; and has a fund of amusing and interesting incidents of army-life with which to enliven his conversation.

On the last day of August, Captain Mitchell was ordered to report to the regiment at Hartwood Church, with his reserves. The pickets are to remain on the river until attacked by the enemy or recalled by orders from division headquarters.

CAVALRY GUNBOAT EXPEDITION.

September 4.—To break the monotony of picketing and to subserve the cause of freedom, a most novel scheme was lately undertaken, known as Kilpatrick's Gunboat Expedition. The object was to destroy a portion of the Rebel navy anchored in the Rappahannock, near Port Conway, opposite Port Royal. This peculiar kind of warfare, which required genius and dash, was waged by the troopers with complete success, and they returned to their bivouac fires to enliven the weary hours with stories of their long march down the river, and their destructive charge upon the gunboats of the enemy. The expedition set out about two o'clock on the morning of September first.

Doctor Lucius P. Woods, Surgeon-in-Chief of the First Brigade, Third Division, gives the following interesting description of the above raid in a letter to Mrs. Woods:

"I returned yesterday after a three days' expedition after gunboats! We all laughed at the order sending cavalry after such craft, but I am happy to say that the object of the expedition was accomplished. We left camp at two o'clock A. M., marched all day and all the following night, till three o'clock next morning, when we made a furious charge upon Rebel infantry. They ran so fast as to disarrange the general's plan of attack. The morning was so dark that we could not see one rod in advance.

"We captured twelve or fifteen prisoners, and General Kilpatrick gave orders in their hearing to have the whole command fall back, stating that the gunboats would be alarmed and the expedition be a failure. The general took particular pains to allow half the prisoners to escape and to get across the Rappahannock. After falling back two miles, we were countermarched toward the river, near which we were formed in line of battle. We sat there on our horses waiting for daylight. Then the flying artillery of ten guns, supported by the old Fifth New York and First Michigan, dashed at a full run down to the river-bank, wheeled into position, and gave the Rebels a small cargo of hissing cast-iron, which waked them up more effectually than their ordinary morning-call. They soon came to their senses, and for half an hour sent over to us what I should think to be, by the noise they made, tea-kettles, cooking-stoves, large cast-iron hats, etc. But our smaller and more active guns soon silenced theirs, and drove the gunners away, when we turned our attention to the boring of holes in their boats with conical pieces of iron, vulgarly called solid shot. I am sure I can recommend them as first-class augers, for they sank the boats in time for all hands to sit down to breakfast at half-past nine o'clock. The repast consisted of muddy water, rusty salt-pork, and half a hard cracker, termed by us "an iron-clad breakfast." We were absent from camp three days, and had only nine hours' sleep."

Further interesting particulars were given in a New York daily, as follows:

"The expedition under General Kilpatrick, sent out a few days since to recapture, in conjunction with the navy, the gunboats Satellite and Reliance, which recently fell into the hands of the Rebels, was, so far as the cavalry is concerned, successful.

"On Tuesday evening General Kilpatrick arrived on this side the river, at Port Conway, and brilliantly dashed upon the enemy's pickets under Colonel Low. The Rebels did not even make a show of resistance, but rushed into a number of flat-boats in the wildest confusion, and landed safely on the opposite bank. If they had made a show of fight, they would have most likely been captured. "After the escape of the enemy, General Kilpatrick waited two hours for the coöperation of the navy, which is understood to have been agreed upon. The vessels did not arrive, and General Kilpatrick ordered a battery to open fire upon the gunboats Reliance and Satellite. This was done at the distance of six hundred and fifty yards. The enemy immediately abandoned the gunboats—very fortunately for themselves, for only a few moments elapsed before the Satellite was in a sinking condition, and the Reliance rendered useless. Both boats were completely riddled by shot and shell. The force under Kilpatrick consisted of cavalry and two batteries of artillery. The Satellite is sunk, and the Reliance so completely disabled as to be beyond hope of being repaired by the Rebels."

On our return from Port Conway we passed through Falmouth, where we halted a short time. It was pleasant to survey the scenes of former labors and conflicts. Much alarm appears to have been created among the Rebels by our gunboat disturbance. A large force of Rebel cavalry can be distinctly seen approaching Fredericksburg on the Telegraph Road, and more or less commotion prevails across the river. From Falmouth we marched directly to Hartwood Church. On arriving here, Captain Mitchell's battalion was ordered back to its old position on picket, to relieve the infantry which took our places before the expedition to Port Conway.

September 5.—We continue on picket near United States Ford. This morning the regiment was mustered in for pay by Major McIrvin, who is temporarily in command, Colonel Davies having been placed in command of a brigade.

At ten o'clock A. M. I received my commission of second lieutenant. It was brought from the headquarters of the regiment by the bugler of Company H. It dates back to the cavalry fight at Aldie, which occurred on the seventeenth of June.

On this line of pickets we have continued uninterruptedly for a week. On the seventh, Colonel Davies, with his assistant adjutant-general, visited our post. It was very gratifying to Captain Mitchell and myself to receive the colonel's compliments for promptness and vigilance in our work, especially as he has the reputation of never bestowing praise where it is not deserved.

I rode down to Lieutenant Temple's picket-reserve, at Richard's Ferry, on the eighth. I found the lieutenant in excellent humor, but decidedly opposed to picketing as a permanent occupation. We were, however, consoled with the hope of relief ere long.

In the afternoon the brigade officer of the day called at the bivouac of the "grand guard," and expressed himself as being highly pleased with the disposition and management of the pickets. The enemy's pickets confront ours at all the fords of the river, and appear in heavy force.

For some time past we have understood that General Lee's headquarters are at Orange Court House, while his infantry occupies the south banks and bluffs of the Rapidan. Stuart occupies Culpepper Court House, and pickets and patrols the territory between the Rapidan and the Rappahannock, a region shaped much like an old-fashioned harrow.

September 13.—An advance of the Union army was ordered yesterday by its Chief, in which the cavalry was to take a prominent part. Orders were issued accordingly last evening, and every needed preparation made for our work. At an early hour this morning the entire cavalry corps was on the march. In order that the enemy might not be prematurely warned of our design, the several commands were ordered to make as little noise as possible. Consequently the bugle-calls were dispensed with, and commanders made use of their voices, and in some instances the orders were conveyed from rank to rank in a whisper. The three great divisions of the corps were to cross the river as follows: Gregg's, at Sulphur Springs; Buford's, at Rappahannock Bridge; and Kilpatrick's, at Kelly's Ford.

BRANDY STATION NO. 3.

At six o'clock the Harris Light plunged into the river at Kelly's Ford, leading the advance. A strong detachment of Stuart's cavalry, consisting of pickets and reserves, opposed our crossing with dogged pertinacity, but finally, yielding to our superior numbers and to the deadly accuracy of our carbines, gave way. He then advanced in the direction of Brandy Station. The farther we advanced the stronger grew the ever-accumulating force of the enemy, who disputed every inch of ground with great stubbornness. On arriving near the Station we found the enemy in strong force, with artillery posted on the surrounding hills. We saw clearly that a third cavalry fight was destined to be fought on this historic field, and we began to make preparations for the onset. It was my fortune to lead the advance company in the first charge. Three men and four horses were killed and wounded in this company by the first discharge of the enemy's artillery, whose fire was terribly accurate.

But we had not been fighting long before the other divisions joined us. At their approach great enthusiasm among our boys prevailed. Before our combined force the enemy was swept from those plains like chaff before the whirlwind. They fled in the direction of Culpepper, a naturally strong and now fortified position, where we knew we must soon encounter the Rebel chivalry en masse upon their chosen field.

FIGHT AT CULPEPPER COURT HOUSE.

From Brandy Station General Pleasonton directed Kilpatrick to make a détour viâ Stevensburg, in order to operate as a flanking column upon the enemy at the proper time. With the First and Second divisions Pleasonton pushed straight on to Culpepper, driving the enemy before him without much resistance until within about a mile of the town. Here our advance was effectually checked. A fearful duel now took place with varying fortunes. For some time the enemy baffled all our efforts to dislodge him from his strong position, and our men began to look wishfully for the flankers, when lo! Kilpatrick's flags were seen advancing from the direction of Stevensburg, and his artillery was soon thundering in the enemy's flank and rear. Under this unexpected and well-directed fire, that portion of the enemy which had kept our main column at bay fell back in confusion into the town; and, before they had time to re-form their broken lines, the Harris Light, Fifth New York, First Vermont, and First Michigan, led by General Custer, dashed upon the "Johnnies" in the streets, throwing the boast of the chivalry into a perfect rout. Many prisoners were captured, more or less material of war, and three Blakely guns. The Rebels retreated hastily in the direction of Pony Mountain and Rapidan Bridge, whither they were closely pursued by our victorious squadrons. The day following this brilliant advance Pleasonton occupied all the fords of the Rapidan, extending his pickets on our right as far forward as the Robertson and Hazel Rivers.

The way having been thus prepared by his heroic avant-couriers, General Meade advanced the Army of the Potomac across the Rappahannock, and took his temporary residence in Culpepper.

September 15.—Kilpatrick's division advanced from Culpepper to Raccoon Ford on the Rapidan. Colonel Davies' brigade supported a battery of artillery a short distance from the ford from one till four P. M. The shelling from the enemy's batteries was terrific. Their position was admirable on the high bluff south of the ford, and the range was just right for execution. Their artillery was of a heavy calibre, and supported by infantry. They were finely screened by earthworks, while our forces were almost entirely exposed, and protected only here and there by a little knoll. In the unequal duel which took place, two of our guns were dismounted and disabled, while several artillerymen and horses were killed. It was not at all practicable for us to attempt a crossing. Before night we retired from the ford, and the divisions took up their headquarters, Gregg's, at Rappahannock Bridge; Buford's, at Stevensburg; and Kilpatrick's, on the extreme right, at James City.

September 16.—To-day we are picketing the fords of the Robertson River, a branch of the Rapidan. At five o'clock P. M. the Fifth New York pickets were attacked and driven to within a few rods of their reserve; but being reënforced by ourselves, who were ordered to relieve them, the enemy was compelled to retire hastily, and we reoccupied the line which was taken up by the Fifth in the morning.

At ten o'clock in the night I received orders to take four men and communicate with Major McIrvin at Newman's Ford, two miles above our post on the Robertson. This was by no means an easy task, as the wilderness country was almost wholly unknown to us, and the Rebel pickets in this quarter had not been sounded. Through the darkness, however, I advanced with my men as cautiously as possible, and yet at several points along our line of march we drew the fire of the Rebel pickets. At length we espied a force of cavalry approaching us, which proved to be a detachment under Major McIrvin on their way to the ford. We challenged one another simultaneously, each supposing the other to be an enemy. The major was on the point of ordering his command to fire upon me, when I recognized his voice and quickly gave him my name. The discovery was timely, and mutually enjoyable.

September 17.—The enemy advanced his picket lines this morning across the river, pushed ours back with considerable precipitancy, when a general skirmish occurred along the lines for a distance of about two miles. Captain Hasty was chief in command of our skirmishers. I assisted him, riding my sorrel pony, the only horse on the skirmish line, as all the men fought dismounted. At nine o'clock Colonel Davies arrived with his brigade and took command. The Rebels were not able to withstand our accumulated power, and rapidly retreated across the river, enabling us to reëstablish our lines where they were before the onset.

Picket-firing is very common. "Give and take" is the game we play, and sometimes the blows are as severe as they are unexpected. The cavalry is almost constantly on duty, scouting, patrolling, and very often fighting. Thus we are kept ever in motion.

The only relief for our excessive labors is our good living. Seldom are soldiers permitted to live in a country of which it may be said as emphatically as of this, that it "flows with milk and honey." The numerous flocks of sheep and herds of cattle in the neighborhood are made to contribute the basis of our rations, while the poultry-yards, larders, and orchards are made to yield the delicacies of the season. The country abounds with sorghum, apple-butter, milk, honey, sweet potatoes, peaches, apples, etc.; so that kings are not much better fed than are the cavaliers of this command.

September 19.—The weather is becoming cold and wet. Yesterday this brigade retired from the Robertson to the vicinity of Stevensburg, where we bivouacked in the pine woods.

Henry E. Davies, Jr., formerly Colonel of the Harris Light, and for some time past in command of the First brigade of Kilpatrick's division, was congratulated to-day by his friends upon his promotion to brigadier-general.

No promotion was ever more fitly made, and the "star" never graced a more perfect gentleman or more gallant soldier. The general feeling in the command is, long may he live in the service of his country and for the honor of her flag.

Sunday, September 20.—This morning very appropriate and solemn funeral services were held, conducted by Chaplain Edward P. Roe, in honor of the officers and soldiers of the Harris Light, who were killed in our recent advance to, and skirmishes along, the Rapidan and Robertson Rivers.

IMPORTANT RECONNOISSANCE AND RAID.

On the morning of the twenty-first, at day-break, an important movement was commenced by Generals Kilpatrick and Buford, while General Gregg remained on the picket lines. The object of the advance was mainly to reconnoitre the position and strength of the enemy, and at the same time to do all the mischief we could. We made a forced march directly upon Madison Court House, meeting but little opposition. The tired troopers rested themselves and their animals at night, preparatory to another early advance.

September 22.—We were early in the saddle, with our steps turned southward in the direction of Orange Court House. The two divisions advanced upon different but nearly parallel roads. We had not proceeded far before messengers from General Buford informed us that, by a rapid movement across the country between the two roads, Kilpatrick might intercept a brigade of the enemy's cavalry, which Buford was engaging and pursuing. The Harris Light had the advance of the division, and we soon came in contact with the retreating Rebel force in a dense oak forest, through which we were compelled to approach the pike by a wood road, which was so narrow as to necessitate our moving in columns of twos. Upon gaining the main road we found the entire force of the enemy advancing with skirmishers deployed, and a battery of light artillery in position, which instantaneously opened upon us with grape and canister. The situation of our regiment was extremely critical and embarrassing.

ENGAGEMENT AT LIBERTY MILLS.

Generals Kilpatrick and Davies were at the head of the column, and by them we were ordered and encouraged to present a bold front and make a desperate resistance, in order to give the division time to file out of the forest and to get into a fighting position along the road. At this juncture I was in command of the first company of the first squadron, and consequently was ordered to cross the pike, and to check the advance of the enemy in that quarter, while the balance of the regiment was to hold the pike and a small opening to the left. We had barely time to deploy as skirmishers, when the

Rebel commander, seeing that his only hope of escape from the trap we were laying for him lay in a quick and decisive charge, came down upon us like an avalanche, crushing through the force that was on the road, and sweeping a clean path for his escape. The resistance of the regiment, however, was so desperate that the killed and wounded from both sides strewed the hotly-contested ground in every direction. Not more than twenty minutes elapsed from the time we first saw the enemy before the contest was decided; and yet, in this brief period of time, the Harris Light lost several of its most gallant officers and many of its bravest men. Our loss was principally in wounded and prisoners, while that of the enemy was in killed and wounded.

By this sudden and unexpected charge of the enemy upon the force on the pike, myself and company were completely cut off from our main column. For one whole hour we were entirely enclosed within the lines of the Rebel cavalry. It is true that they had about all they could do to take care of themselves, and yet they might have bagged and gobbled our small force. But by swift and careful movements we succeeded in eluding the vigilance of the Rebels, and finally we made our exit from their lines unhurt, and with much valuable information which we had obtained. As soon as possible I reported to General Kilpatrick, who was much surprised at seeing me, having come to the conclusion that myself and men were already on our way to "Richmond!" The forces of Stuart were ultimately routed and fell back from Liberty Ford, near which the fight occurred, upon their infantry reserves at Gordonsville. My escape from the toils of the enemy was regarded as almost miraculous. General Davies sent an aid to me with his compliments, inviting me to his headquarters, where he expressed his surprise at my safe return, and complimented me for the dexterity, wisdom, and success of my movements. The day following this engagement and adventure our forces returned to the vicinity of Culpepper, where we spent a few days in comparative rest—rest which we all needed and greatly enjoyed.

September 25.—I received an order this afternoon from Major McIrvin, commanding the regiment, directing me to take command of Company H, which is without a commander.

On the twenty-sixth the paymaster made his appearance among us, much to the satisfaction of the command. Owing to the continuous movements of the Cavalry Corps, and its generally exposed condition, no opportunity has been afforded the Government to pay us for the last six months. Very little money was in the regiment, even officers as well as men being pretty well reduced. The paymaster's "stamps" were more than usually acceptable.

September 28.—Four companies, namely, B, F, H, and M, commanded by Captain Grinton, were ordered on picket to-day along the Hazel River. One half of this force occupies the picket line, the other half patrols the country. The captain commands the post, and I have the special charge of the pickets. We do not want, at present, for fresh meat and vegetables. We live almost entirely from the country, and we live well. Our bill of fare is varied and rich. Forage for our horses is also abundant in all the neighboring plantations. Picketing under these circumstances is more like a picnic than any thing else which we can remember.

October 8.—We are still in statu quo, picketing on the Hazel River. However, yesterday Captain Mitchell relieved Captain Grinton in command of the post. The reserve companies fell in line to hear the orders of the War Department, concerning veteran volunteers. They produced quite an excitement among us. The three years' enlistment of a large portion of the army is nearly expired, and the Government, in its anxiety to avail itself of the experience of the veteran troops to the end of the conflict, is now offering extra inducements, in the way of furloughs and bounties, to secure the reënlistment of these men to the end of the war. The orders propounded to us meet with universal favor, and the cry runs like wild-fire from rank to rank, "let us go in, boys!" This will be an element of great power.

A citizen-youth, of manly bearing, who professes loyalty to our cause, came to our pickets to-day, and from thence to headquarters, bringing information of a Rebel plan to surprise our picket lines to-night. We will give them a warm reception if they undertake the execution of their scheme. A regiment of infantry, and one squadron of cavalry arrived before dark, and are in readiness for the night's entertainment. The pickets are doubly strong, and are under special orders to be vigilant.

October 9.—The enemy did not venture an attack last night, but doubtless contented themselves with the maxim that "discretion is the better part of valor." Possibly they were informed of our preparation for them. Spies and informants are numerous and active on both sides.

Lieutenant Houston and privates Donahue and Pugh were captured this morning while scouting just beyond the pickets. Much activity is manifested on our front. Indeed, it is quite generally understood among us that General Lee is taking the initiatory steps of a flank movement upon us. Our scouts so report, and the suspicious movements of the pickets and forces before us corroborate the information.

The Capture—Cavalry Fight at Buckland Mills.

Chapter XV - Capture of the Author.

1863.—Fight at James City.—Music of Retreat.—Fourth Cavalry Fight at Brandy Station.—Critical Situation.—Kilpatrick Undaunted.—Davies and Custer.—The Grand Charge.—The Escape.—The Scene.—Subsequent Charges and Counter-charges.—The Cavalry Routed.—The Rappahannock Recrossed in Safety.—Infantry Reconnoissance to Brandy Station.—Comical Affair at Bealeton Station.—Thrilling Adventure of Stuart.—His Escape.—Battle of Bristoe.—Casualties.—Retreat Continued.—Destruction of Railroad by the Rebels.—Kilpatrick at Buckland Mills.—Unpleasant Surroundings.—Sagacity and Daring.—The Author's Capture.—Fall, Insensibility, Change of Scene.—The End.—Introduced to Prison Life.

Early in the morning of October tenth the enemy, in heavy force, came down upon our pickets along the Robertson River, driving us back in haste and occupying the fords. The flank movement of General Lee was fully understood. He had crossed the Rapidan, advanced to Madison Court House, and was lapping around our right wing, threatening it with destruction. Quick work on our part was now necessary. Swift messengers from officers high in command brought orders to retire with promptness, but in good order, if possible. Our boys, in many instances, were compelled to leave uneaten and even untasted their palatable preparations for breakfast of roast lamb, sweet potatoes, fine wheat bread, milk and honey, &c., to attend to the stern and always unpleasant duties of a retreat, with the enemy pressing very closely upon us.

Sharp skirmishing took place at the river, and the successive crack of carbines afforded the music of our march to James City, where the conflict deepened into a battle, which raged with fury and slaughter. The enemy, conscious of having outgeneraled us in this instance, and having at least a temporary advantage, was bold and defiant. He was met, however, with corresponding vigor. Those contesting legions, which had so often measured sabres in the fearful charge, and hand-to-hand encounter, again appealed to the God of battle, and wrested with Herculean strength for the mastery. Night came on at length to hush the strife, and the weary men and horses sought repose from the bloody fray.

October 11.—With the first pencilings of the morning light we took up our line of march toward the Rappahannock. Skirmishing continued nearly every step of the way. On the Sperryville pike to Culpepper we were closely pursued and heavily pressed. At Culpepper the corps separated. Gregg, who had come by way of Cedar Mountain, passed out on the road to Sulphur Springs. Buford moved in the direction of Stevensburg, leaving Kilpatrick alone on the main thoroughfare along the railroad line.

Kilpatrick, accompanied by Pleasonton, had scarcely left Culpepper, when Hampton's Legions made a furious attack upon his rearguard, with the hope of breaking through upon the main column to scatter it, or of so retarding its progress that a flanking column might fall upon him ere he could reach the safe shore of the Rappahannock. Our infantry, which yesterday occupied this ground, had retired, leaving the cavalry to struggle out of the toils of the enemy as best it could.

Gallantly repelling every attack of the enemy, our command moved on, without expending much of its time and material, until opposite the residence of Hon. John Minor Botts, where a few regiments suddenly wheeled about, and, facing the pursuing foe, charged upon them with pistols and sabres, giving them a severe check and an unexpected repulse. On arriving at Brandy Station Kilpatrick found himself in a most critical situation, with an accumulation of formidable difficulties on every hand, which threatened his annihilation. Buford, who had been sharply pursued by Fitzhugh Lee's division over the plains of Stevensburg, had retired more rapidly than Kilpatrick, and, unaware of his comrade's danger, had suffered Lee to plant his batteries on the high hills which commanded Kilpatrick's right, while the Rebel troopers, in three heavy lines of battle, held the only route by which Kilpatrick could retreat. Lee's sharpshooters also occupied the woods in the immediate vicinity of Kilpatrick's columns, where they were making themselves a source of damage and great annoyance. To increase the danger of the situation, Stuart, by hard marching, had swung around to Kilpatrick's left, and had taken possession of a range of hills, planted batteries, and was preparing to charge down upon the surrounded division below.

This was a situation to try the stoutest hearts. Nothing daunted, however, by this terrific array of the enemy, Kilpatrick displayed that decision and daring which have ever characterized him as a great cavalry leader, and he proved himself worthy of the brave men who compose his command. His preparation for the grand charge was soon completed. Forming his division into three lines of battle, he assigned the right to Davies, the left to Custer, and, placing himself with Pleasonton in the centre, he advanced with unwavering determination to the contest. Having approached to within a few yards of the enemy's lines on his front, he ordered his band to strike up a national air, to whose spirit-stirring strains was joined the blast of scores of bugles ringing forth the charge.

With his usual daring Davies was foremost in the fray, leading his command for the fourth time on this memorable field. To his men he had addressed these stirring words: "Soldiers of the First Brigade! I know you have not forgotten the example of your brave comrades, who, in past engagements here, were not afraid to die in defence of the old flag."

Custer, the daring, terrible demon that he is in battle, pulled off his cap and handed it to his orderly, then dashed madly forward in the charge, while his yellow locks floated like pennants on the breeze. Pennington and Elder handled their batteries with great agility and success, at times opening huge gaps in the serried lines of the enemy.

Fired to an almost divine potency, and with a majestic madness, this band of heroic troopers shook the air with their battle-cry, and dashed forward to meet the hitherto exultant foe. Ambulances, forges, and cannon, with pack-horses and mules, non-combatants and others, all joined to swell the mighty tide. Brave hearts grew braver, and faltering ones waxed warmer and stronger, until pride of country had touched this raging sea of thought and emotion, kindling an unconquerable principle, which emphatically affirmed every man a hero unto death. So swiftly swept forward this tide of animated power, that the Rebel lines broke in wild dismay before the uplifted and firmly-grasped sabres of these unflinching veterans, who, feeling that life and country were at stake, risked them both upon the fearful issue.

Kilpatrick thus escaped disaster, defeated his pursuers, captured several pieces of the enemy's artillery, and presented to the beholders one of the grandest scenes ever witnessed in the New World.

"By Heaven! it was a splendid sight to see,
For one who had no friend or brother there."

No one who looked upon that wonderful panorama can ever forget it. On the great field were riderless horses and dying men; clouds of dust from solid shot and bursting shell occasionally obscured the sky; broken caissons and upturned ambulances obstructed the way, while long lines of cavalry were pressing forward in the charge, with their drawn sabres, glistening in the bright sunlight. Far beyond the scene of tumult were the quiet, dark green forests which skirt the banks of the Rappahannock. The poet Havard, in his "Scauderberg," has well described the scene:

"Hark! the death-denouncing trumpet sounds.
The fatal charge, and shouts proclaim the onset.
Destruction rushes dreadful to the field
And bathes itself in blood: havoc let loose,
Now undistinguish'd, rages all around;
While Ruin, seated on her dreary throne,
Sees the plain strewed with subjects, truly hers,
Breathless and cold."

The Rebel cavalry, undoubtedly ashamed of their own conduct and defeat, reorganized their broken ranks, and again advanced upon Kilpatrick and Buford, whose divisions had united to repel the attack. For at least two long hours of slaughter these opposing squadrons dashed upon one another over these historic fields. Charges and counter-charges followed in quick succession, and at times the "gray" and the "blue" were so confusedly commingled together, that it was difficult to conjecture how they could regain their appropriate places. Quite a number of prisoners were made on both sides. It was a scene of wild commotion and blood. This carnival continued until late at night, when the exhausted and beaten foe sank back upon safer grounds to rest, while our victorious braves, crowned with undying laurels, gathered up their wounded and dead companions, and, unmolested, recrossed the Rappahannock.

October 12.—To-day a portion of our infantry was thrown across the Rappahannock. They advanced by a forced march to reconnoitre as far as Brandy Station, where they met the enemy in force and engaged him in a sharp contest. They returned, however, without serious loss. Our main army is retreating toward Washington.

On the evening of the thirteenth, while bivouacking near Bealeton Station, a serio-comical scene diverted for a time the attention of our officers and men. By a strange accident an ammunition wagon took fire, which caused the rapid explosion of its contents. Shells flew and burst in every direction, and the apparent musketry was terrible. The consequence was a widespread alarm, which brought every trooper to his horse ready to engage the foe, who was supposed to have made a furious onset. Great merriment and relished rest followed the discovery of the cause of disturbance, especially as no one was seriously hurt.

Since our last reconnoissance to Brandy Station, Stuart has been very active, following our rear very closely, and committing all the depredations possible. In his hands have fallen many stragglers, who, it is true, were of very little use to us, but who would count as well as true men in the Rebel lists of exchanges of prisoners. Some of Stuart's performances were exceedingly hazardous, as the following well-described narrative from a well-known pen will clearly show:

"Stuart, with two thousand of his cavalry, pressed our rear so eagerly that, when near Catlett's Station, he had inadvertently got ahead, by a flank movement of our Second Corps, General Warren acting as rearguard, and was hemmed in, where his whole command must have been destroyed or captured had he not succeeded in hiding it in a thicket of old field-pines, close by the road whereon our men marched by: the rear of the corps encamping close beside the enemy, utterly unsuspicious of their neighborhood, though every word uttered in our lines, as they passed, was distinctly heard by the lurking foe. Stuart at first resolved to abandon his guns and attempt to escape with moderate loss, but finally picked three of his men, gave them muskets, made them up so as to look as much as possible like our soldiers, and thus drop silently into our ranks as they passed, march awhile, then slip out on the other side of the column, and make all haste to General Lee, at Warrenton, in quest of help. During the night two of our officers, who stepped into the thicket, were quietly captured.

"At daylight the crack of skirmishers' muskets in the distance gave token that Lee had received and responded to the prayer for help, when Stuart promptly opened with grape and canister on the rear of our astounded column, which had bivouacked just in his front, throwing it into such confusion that he easily dashed by and rejoined his chief, having inflicted some loss and suffered little or none."

BATTLE OF BRISTOE.

The above manœuvre was a great and unexpected or unsought risk, which, however, did not prove disastrous to the authors, but which might not again be ventured with similar results. A performance resembling it somewhat was enacted by the Rebels, but with very different issue. Early in the morning of the fourteenth A. P. Hill's corps left Warrenton, with orders to strike our rear at Bristoe Station. They moved up the Alexandria Turnpike to Broad Run Church, where they deflected on the road to Greenwich, and soon after struck our trail just behind the Third Corps, and eagerly pursued it. They were busy picking up stragglers and making some preparation for an attack upon our unsuspecting corps, when about noon General Warren's Second Corps, which was still behind, and bringing up the rear, made its appearance on the tapis, and materially changed the programme of the scene. Hill, finding himself nicely sandwiched or trapped by his own indiscretion, turned away from the retreating Third Corps, to fight, and, if possible, drive back the advancing

Second. Warren's surprise in finding an enemy in force before him was not less than Hill's in finding one behind him; but it took Warren only about ten minutes to adjust himself to this unexpected position of affairs, when his batteries opened with such precision and effect, aided by the musketry of his infantry, that the Rebels fell back in much greater haste than they had advanced, leaving six of their guns in our hands and multitudes of dead, wounded, and prisoners. Five of the captured guns, still serviceable, were at once seized and used against the disappointed foe with telling power. One historian says, "Our loss in killed and wounded was about two hundred, including Colonel James E. Mallon, Forty-second New York, killed, and General Tile, of Pennsylvania, wounded; that of the enemy was probably four hundred (besides prisoners), including Generals Posey (mortally), Kirkland, and Cooke, wounded, and Colonels Ruffin, First North Carolina, and Thompson, Fifth North Carolina Cavalry, killed."

This Bristoe fiasco was a stunning blow to the Rebel pursuit, and greatly checked their incursions. But our soldiers held the field so lately won only until dark, and "then followed the rest of the army, whose retreat they had so effectually covered."

General Meade continued his retreat to Centreville, and then, seemingly ashamed—as well he might be—of his flight, would have retraced his steps and pushed back the insolent foe, but he was prevented from executing his plans by a heavy rain-storm, which began on the sixteenth. While he was awaiting the arrival of pontoons to enable him to recross Bull Run, which was enormously swollen, the enemy, after some daring skirmishes along his front, and some feints of attack, retreated quite rapidly, completely destroying the Orange and Alexandria Railroad from Manassas Junction to the Rappahannock. A more thorough work of destruction was never witnessed. Scarcely a tie even remained. The ties were generally heaped together, and set on fire, and the rails were laid upon the heaps cross-wise. As the middle of the rails became heated, the ends lopped down, forming a graceful bow. They were thus effectually ruined. In many instances the rails thus heated were twisted around the trees. The road and the telegraph lines and posts were utterly demolished.

For a few days the Harris Light was bivouacking near Sudley Church, and the cavalry was picketing, scouting, and patrolling on either side of Bull Run; and, on one occasion, while endeavoring to ford the swollen stream, several men and horses were drowned.

October 18.—To-day Kilpatrick advanced with his division, which consists of Custer's and Davies' brigades, to within a half-mile of Gainesville, where we bivouacked for the night. A terrific rain-storm raged nearly all night, making our condition very uncomfortable, and rendering the going impracticable, except upon the turnpikes. At this time of the year these night-storms in

Virginia are very cold, and the sufferings of men mostly unsheltered, as we were, are beyond description. On such a night one will naturally recall such passages as the following, from Byron's "Childe Harold:"

"The sky is changed, and such a change! oh, night,
And storm, and darkness, ye are wondrous strong,
Yet lovely in your strength, as is the light
Of a dark eye in woman! far along
From peak to peak, the rattling crags among,
Leaps the live thunder! not from one lone cloud,
But every mountain now hath found a tongue,
And Jura answers through her misty shroud,
Back to the joyous Alps, who call to her aloud!
And this is in the night: most glorious night!
Thou wert not sent for slumber! let me be
A sharer in thy fierce and far delight,—
A portion of the tempest and of thee!"

It is true that the poet, looking out upon the storm and listening to its mutterings from his comfortable studio, may call such a night "glorious," and may find in it depths of inspiration and delight; but to us poor soldiers it seemed more appropriate to take up Shakespeare's lines:

"The tyranny of th' open night's too rough
For nature to endure,"
while every one felt to say,

"The gathering clouds, like meeting armies,
Come on apace."—Lee's "Mithridates."

All night long our pickets along Cedar Run were confronted by Stuart's pickets, though no disposition to fight us was manifest in the morning. Dripping with wet and somewhat stiffened with cold, we were ordered in battle array early in the morning, and the command, about two thousand strong, advanced toward Buckland Mills. The Rebel pickets were quickly withdrawn, and their whole force slowly and without resistance retired before us. With some degree of hesitation, yet unconscious of imminent danger, we advanced on the main turnpike toward Warrenton. Our advance-brigade had just passed New Baltimore, when Fitz-Hugh Lee, who had surprised and cut his way through a small detachment of our infantry at Thoroughfare Gap, then had swiftly swung around our right by an unpicketed road, fell upon our rearguard at Buckland Mills, and opened upon our unsuspecting column with a battery of flying artillery. At this signal Stuart, who had hitherto retired before us quietly, now turned about and advanced upon us in front with terrible determination. Thus unexpected troubles were multiplying around us. Scarcely had we time to recover our senses from the first shock of attack upon our rear and front, when General Gordon, with a division of infantry, until now concealed behind a low range of hills and woods on our left, appeared upon the scene, and advanced upon our flank with a furious attack, which threatened to sever our two small brigades and to annihilate the entire command. We were now completely surrounded by a force which outnumbered us at least four to one. This was a critical situation; but "Kil" (as the general is familiarly styled among us) seemed to comprehend it in a moment. All thought and effort now centralized into a plan of escape from the snares which the enemy had laid for us, and into which we had too easily thrown ourselves. Kilpatrick is supposed by some to have unnecessarily exposed himself, in which he suffered his first defeat, though escaping with a remarkably small loss.

Quickly ordering his force to wheel about, he led them back in a determined charge upon Lee's columns and artillery, now planted on the banks along Cedar Run. This timely order, executed with masterly skill, saved his command from utter disaster, and justified his course. As it was, however, he lost nearly three hundred men, including quite a number who were drowned in the creek while endeavoring to escape. The scene was one of great confusion and distress.

THE AUTHOR'S CAPTURE.

By the sudden evolution of the command, when the order was first executed, the Harris Light, which was in front, while advancing, was thrown in the rear, and was thus compelled to meet the desperate charges of the enemy in pursuit, and to defend itself as best it could from fire on the flank. Having reached a slight elevation of ground in the road, we made a stand, and for some time checked the advancing columns of the Rebels by pouring into their ranks rapid and deadly volleys from our carbines and revolvers. Stuart, who commanded in person, saw clearly that the quickest and almost only way to dislodge us was by charging upon us, and, consequently ordering the charge, he came with a whole brigade amid deafening yells. Our men stood firmly, almost like rocks before the surging sea. We were soon engaged in a fierce hand-to-hand conflict with the advancing columns.

In Byron's "Corsair" we find a description of the scene:

"Within a narrow ring compressed, beset,
Hopeless, not heartless, strive and struggle yet,—
Ah! now they fight in firmest file no more,

Hemmed in—cut off—cleft down—and trampled o'er,
But each strikes singly, silently, and home,
And sinks outwearied rather than o'ercome,
His last faint quittance rendering with his breath,
Till the blade glimmers in the grasp of death."

At this important juncture my faithful horse was shot under me, and we both fell to the ground. Meanwhile our little party, outnumbered ten to one, was hurled back by the overpowering shock of the Rebels, who rode directly over me. Injured somewhat by the falling of my horse, and nearly killed by the charging squadrons, which one after the other trod upon me, I lay in the mud for some time quite insensible. How long I lay there I cannot tell; but when I returned to consciousness the scene had changed. I was in the hands of a Rebel guard, who were carrying me hastily from the hard-fought field. My arms had been taken from me, and my pockets rifled of all their valuables, including my watch. I was unceremoniously borne to the vicinity of an old building, where I met a number of my comrades, who with me had shared the misfortunes of the day. And thus ended three years and more of camping and campaigning with the Harris Light.

What I saw and endured, thought and experienced, during a little more than a year among the Rebels, in several of their loathsome prisons, may be found recorded in a volume I published in 1865, entitled "The Capture, Prison-Pen, and Escape."

Made in the USA
Middletown, DE
17 June 2019